By this time, they w getting ready to pass our position. Deshazo stood up and aimed his M-16 rifle at the enemy and squeezed the trigger. . . . *Click!* His weapon misfired! He pulled the bolt back and rechambered another round and fired off a double burst on full automatic. That was my cue to spring into action. I jumped up and leaped across the hedges onto the trail and caught the two soldiers sprinting away side by side. I fired my weapon from the hip, unleashing a burst of about a hundred rounds with the M-60 machine gun. Under the heavy automatic firepower, the enemy soldier on the right went down, hitting the ground hard without breaking his fall. The other soldier helped him up and pulled him into the bushes. They vanished into the foliage.

"Get your ass down before you get your fuckin' head blown off!" Deshazo yelled to me.

But I knew that as long as I kept firing the M-60, Charlie would have to keep his head down. That was one of the beauties and advantages of having the Big Gun on a mission.

SOUL
Patrol

Ed Emanuel

BALLANTINE BOOKS • NEW YORK

A Presidio Press Book
Published by The Random House Publishing Group
Copyright © 2003 by Edwin L. Emanuel
Foreword copyright © 2003 by Gary A. Linderer

Presidio Press and colophon are trademarks of Random House, Inc.

www.ballantinebooks.com

ISBN 0-89141-817-2

Manufactured in the United States of America

First Edition: August 2003

OPM   10   9   8   7   6   5   4   3   2   1

This book is dedicated to

My cousin—Ricky Vaughn Riley
My mother—Willie Mae (Shelton) Emanuel

War is an ugly thing, but not the ugliest of things. The decayed and degraded state of moral and patriotic feeling which thinks that nothing is worth war is much worse. A man who has nothing for which he is willing to fight, nothing he cares about more than his own personal safety, is a miserable creature who has no chance of being free, unless made and kept so by the exertions of better men than himself.

The Professional Soldier

Contents

Acknowledgments

Yolanda Maria Palomo—(Sergeant) County of Los Angeles Sheriff's Department. Without her unwavering support, finishing this book would not have been possible. John Valdertcro and his wife, Jackie—for being by my side every step of the way.

My editors—Gary Linderer, Kenn Miller, Chris Evans, for their encouraging words, and Carlorline Acklen Bender for her friendship, film, and prayers.

Maj. Ben Frazier—U.S. Army (Public Affairs Officer)—Always the friend. Sefefanie Spruill—Who encouraged me to write this book.

Larry McCormick—KTLA Channel 5 News—A friend who has always been there for me.

Dave Peace—Designer of the Company F 51st LRP challenge coin.

Mark Allen Miller

George Bennett

Verline "Cricket" Mallory—(photo)

Mara and Steve Mallory—(photo shoot)

Diane English—Executive producer of the TV series *Murphy Brown* and *Love & War*, for helping me to understand that "Writing is re-writing!"

I would also like to take this opportunity to thank everyone who was interviewed, or sent their films and photographs in for the *Silent Heroes* documentary. Without your help, we wouldn't have had a complete package to tell the true story of Lurps in Vietnam. Thank you *all* for your support!

Foreword
by Gary A. Linderer

The Vietnam War was often a war of small-unit actions, not the large, pitched epic battles that Hollywood is so fond of producing. The U.S. Army's Long Range Patrols bore the brunt of these actions in a lopsided war of attrition that for years after the fighting had ended had gone virtually untold. In the late 1980s the Lurps began to tell their stories in an expanding series of individual accounts that have preserved their history and immortalized them for posterity. Never has our country produced a finer group of courageous young men who volunteered to take on such impossible odds to accomplish their mission. The LRPs, LRRPs, and Ranger teams of the Vietnam War performed so well during their six-year sojourn in Southeast Asia that the Department of the Army established the 75th Ranger Regiment and several long range surveillance detachments to carry on their rich and illustrious heritage.

Ed Emanuel's *Soul Patrol* is the latest addition to this growing list of outstanding long range patrol autobiographies that have immortalized the exploits of these courageous young warriors. *Soul Patrol* is perhaps the most unique of these works because it is the first written by an African American member of a long range patrol company. Other African-American Vietnam vets have told their stories, but this book is different, not only in content but in character. In units where the only color was "tiger stripe"; where men would readily die for each other without a moment's hesitation; where "teammate" meant far more than "brother"; the racial troubles of the sixties and seventies would never once manifest themselves. Author Ed Emanuel's *Soul Patrol* is a reaffirmation of the love and respect we Lurps still have for each other. Neither time, nor distance, nor circumstance has eroded the loyalties of fellow teammates.

I am privileged to be able to write the foreword to my friend's outstanding book. It is a work of love, respect, pain, fear, courage, hate, resolve, and devotion. It is the story of a young African-American from Los Angeles who, along with his high school buddies, answers his country's call to arms by enlisting in the U.S. Army, volunteering for the paratroops and later the LRPs. His buddies do the same, choosing the Marines and Army Airborne, both elite combat units. Three weeks after the author arrives in Vietnam and joins the LRPs, he is heading back to Los Angeles, escorting the body of his best friend and cousin, a Marine killed in I Corp. It is at this point in his life that Ed Emanuel becomes a warrior. This is all I will comment on in this brief foreword to this wonderful book. The rest of his story is for you to read and enjoy without my preemptive commentary.

Ed and I attended Airborne Infantry training and Jump School together without ever knowing each other. We flew to Vietnam and returned to the USA a year later on the same commercial flights but never actually met. We both volunteered to serve in separate long range patrol units on the very same day. But it would be twenty-five years later that we would actually meet and realize how our military careers had paralleled each other, even converging at certain points in time. Today, I count him among my very good friends, a man I respect, a brother I love.

Soul Patrol is a well-written, detailed, often emotional account of a young soldier's journey into manhood. It will take you through a gamut of emotions that will leave you emotionally drained but ultimately glad that you're an American.

SOUL
Patrol

The History and Organization of Company F, 51st Infantry

The unit 51st Infantry was organized long ago and has served with distinction. Company "F" has been a part of the unit from its initiation in 1917. Yet, units as Long Range Patrol are relatively new and rare. This type of work being ideally suited to Vietnam and this warfare, LRRP and LRP units of various sizes were formed throughout the country, and Company "F" was given such a designation.

Vietnam has many LRRP and LRP units, but there were only two LRP companies at Field Force level. We were one of them.

Company "F" reactivated for the Vietnam War, received the parenthetic notion (LRP) and the best of all (ABN). Formed at Bien Hoa Army and situated in the old Brigade area, as a company sized unit its TO&E (Table of Organization and Equipment) required command by a field grade officer. Its ranks were filled almost exclusively by veteran troops from the 173rd Airborne Brigade, and the balance came from units also stationed in Vietnam: The Big Red One, the 25th Div., the 101 Airborne Div. cavalry units, and some units from the States, Alaska, and Panama.

Everyone was Airborne, a powerful bond, and a main prerequisite.

From the outset questions were traded about what the mission of such a "special" company could be, where they would be working, etc. . . . They weren't long in being answered. As time measured, the company was almost

immediately picked up and moved down the berm to an
isolated section where it had the room and security it
needed and privacy it would learn to appreciate.

On October 10, 1967, the training began. When the
company was formed for Vietnam service, it was physically very much like any other line company. One difference was that it had four line platoons instead of three; in
addition each of these platoons had seven 6-man patrols.
Another difference was that we were given our own TOC
and motor pool. In the command structure the company
was placed under G-3 II Field Force V. Through this
command level we were to be assigned under the operational control, (OPCon), of specific Brigade or Divisions,
and mostly to II FFV.

Since our work required constant helicopter support,
the slicks, gunships, and Command and Control ship
were attached to the company and lived with us, as did
the artillery LnO.

The four line platoons were identical in structure but
operated at all times independent from one another. For
this reason the company was considered, structurally as a
battalion.

(As written in the published yearbook issued by Company F, 51st Infantry, LRP [ABN].)

Vietnam 1968: *Stars and Stripes* printed this article in
the weekly newspaper. The author is unknown. . . .

The men I am writing about could well have been the
boy next door or the gentle blond-haired kid from the corner supermarket of not so long ago.

The "boys" are bound together by their trade. They are
all volunteers. They are in the spine-tingling, brain-
twisting, nerve-wracking business of long range patrolling. They vary in age from 18 to 30.

These men operate in precision movements—like
walking through a jungle quietly and being able to tell
whether a man or an animal is moving through the brush

without seeing the cause of movement. They can sit in an ambush for hours without moving a muscle except to ease the safety off the automatic weapons in their hands at the first sign of trouble.

These men are good because they have to be to survive.

Called LRPs for short, they are despised, respected, admired—and sometimes thought to be a little short on brains by those who watch from the sidelines as a team starts out on another mission to seek out the enemy.

They are men who can take a baby or a small child in their arms and stop his crying. They share their last smoke, last ration of food, last canteen of water—kind in some ways, deadly in others.

They are men who believe in their country, freedom, and fellow men. They are a new kind of soldier in a new type of warfare. They may look the same as anyone you may have seen in a peace march, draft card burning or any other demonstration, but they are different. Just look in their eyes. Better yet, ask them; for they are men.

These men stand out in a crowd of soldiers. It is not just their tiger fatigues, but the way they walk, talk, or stand. You know they are proud because they are members of the long range patrol.

CHAPTER ONE

"What the Hell Am I Doing Here?"

The date was June 6, 1968. These were turbulent times in America. Splattered across the front page of every major newspaper were the ominous signs of social discontent. The mass anarchy and student unrest on college campuses around the country were at an all-time high. The chaos and disorder were largely due to the Vietnam War. As a nation, we were in mourning. The day before we'd lost another great leader, as Sen. Robert F. Kennedy was gunned down in the hotel kitchen of the old Coconut Grove in downtown Los Angeles.

Somehow I knew he would never become president, even though he was the front-runner during most of the presidential primaries. It was the "one" time I hated being right about a premonition. Still fresh in my mind was the death of Dr. Martin Luther King, Jr., who had been assassinated on his motel balcony in Memphis, Tennessee, just a few weeks before. These assassinations were a clear indication that a network of social demons was staunchly in place and working at full force.

I was en route to Southeast Asia. Destination, the Republic of South Vietnam! My eight months of infantry training resulted in my being flown across the Pacific Ocean to a place that would change my life forever.

Around 1100 hours, and after almost twenty hours of flying time with a few stops along the way, the Pam Am 727 jetliner made an effortless landing at Bien Hoa Airport, Vietnam. There was no turning back now. We were already here.

In 1968, I was just out of high school, a confused black male living in a world that was coming apart at the seams. Many bizarre historical events happened in my young lifetime, such as my witnessing firsthand the Watts riot, surviving the fears of the Cuban missile crisis, the constant threat of nuclear war, and the assassination of President John F. Kennedy.

I began to embrace the conclusion that Western civilization was doomed to collapse or revert to barbarism, and we had no genuine chance of a reasonable future. Life had lost its value.

Now, I had put myself in a position to engage in the most extreme episode of my life, three years of duty in the military. I had little wisdom regarding the military, or what I was doing by enlisting in the army. But I'd made up my mind, and whatever field I chose, I was going all the way no matter the outcome. I put myself into this mess, now it was up to me to make the best of it.

The 250 GIs aboard the jetliner sat quietly, waiting for the aircraft to taxi to a halt. I peered nervously outside the port window. At that moment, home seemed so far away. Vietnam is about as far from home as an American can be while still on earth. Before I had enlisted in the army, I had never taken a trip outside the state of California. Now I was on the other side of the world, landing in a country where I might be asked to forfeit my life. I felt totally intimidated.

As I sat gazing beyond the window at the new and unfamiliar surroundings, I realized that, once outside the cabin of that airplane, whatever clumsy misconceptions I had about the country of Vietnam and the war in general would soon change. I began to silently question my basic training instructors' knowledge on the subject of Vietnam. Most of my infantry training on Vietnam had been followed by conflicting stories and rumors that were hard to swallow. I was never sure if some of the instructors in basic training, advanced airborne infantry training, and airborne jump school had ever fired a bullet in anger.

Or if any of them had ever made the trip to the land

tagged as "hell on earth." The instructors who wore the CIB (Combat Infantry Badge) with a star over the top, well, you just knew to listen to them. For those with none at all, I had a raised eyebrow.

One story that continued to persist, and at the same time that I continued to reject, was the rumor that the enemy didn't go down after getting hit by bullets. The reports claimed that the enemy were so doped up on drugs that they didn't respond to getting shot. Yeah, right . . . How could I tell who was telling the truth and who wasn't?

I couldn't help but question whether or not I was ready to endure and survive the coming year. Would I be able to find the inner strength and fortitude?

Like most other kids growing up as a "baby boomer" during the John Wayne World War II movie era, I would romanticize what it would be like to fight and survive a war. It was my childish thirst for adventure and unyielding lust for knowledge that steered me this way in the first place.

Today a person might ask, what series of events could actually lead a person to volunteer to go fight a war? Well, for me that answer would be unequivocally, "Peer pressure and pride," plain and simple!

I remember a bright, sunny California Sunday afternoon. The song "Groovin' " by the Rascals played repeatedly on the old record player. My cousin Ricky Riley and I, with four of my closest friends, Gerald Burton, George Wallace, Jr., Owen Hampton (Le Le), and Lester Young, all got together to decide our future after high school. The general consensus leaned toward a three-year hitch with Uncle Sam. Ricky and Gerald wanted to serve with the U.S. Marines because of their family ties with the Corps. Le Le and Lester opted to go into the air force for their aeronautical training programs. I was wrangled into choosing a service because I had no intentions whatsoever of going into the military. But making my decision was easy. The army, airborne training, and the Special Forces schools had always piqued my interest. It really wasn't a bad deal considering I would be able to attend college on the GI Bill after completing my duty.

On occasion the military would show up at our high schools on career day. They offered an appealing assortment of training programs. On the other hand, I wanted to make a run at junior college football. As fate would have it, while training to make the football team at Harbor City College that summer, I broke my leg in a scrimmage. So during the frosty winter month of November 1967, just after my leg had healed, I joined the U.S. Army under the "buddy plan" with my high school best friend, George Wallace, Jr.

For obvious reasons we made quite a pair. We stuck together at a time when it wasn't easy for a black man in the Deep South to answer to a name like George Wallace, Jr.

It certainly was a challenge for poor George, and for me, too. With my "tough guy" attitude, I believed I could do just about anything, and George and I really got our fill of things. We were often the subject of sometimes funny and harmless ridicule administered by the drill instructors. It made life in the military just a little more interesting.

Now I would be the first to admit that it would not have gone over very well if most of my friends went off to war and I was the only one left behind. In our eclectic little circle you were either for the Vietnam War or you did something about it, like join a protest group or actively dodge the draft. I was never one who could stand on the sidelines and watch a good fight, so inevitably I joined the military to try and satisfy my passion for adventure.

While the rest of the world made deep, socially conscious decisions concerning their future and the state of the nation, I traveled the paths resolved by peer pressure and superficial football injuries. Obviously, I wasn't alone in my quest.

I tried to understand or even come to grips with the gravity of my decision, but I really had no idea what I was getting myself into by fighting a war. War wasn't at all what I'd expected it to be. War breeds an environment where every level of fear known to man will eventually surface.

First of all, I had to dig deep and draw out the courage it would take to leave home for the first time in my life.

The other part of my self-imposed journey was joining the frightening and complex world of the U.S. military. Perhaps my journey was a cry for help, an effort to prove to myself and others, like my father, my self-worth. At the tender age of eighteen and nineteen years old, a teenager's hormones are overactive. My making a potentially suicidal statement like volunteering to fight in a war was in reality my reaching out and pleading, "Please stop me before I kill myself!"

It was too late now. My test of courage had me and the jetliner full of troops steadfastly on the runway awaiting instructions. The cabin inside the jetliner started to heat up. The overhead fans began blowing recirculated warm air. The now anxious and irritated cargo of GIs commenced to voice their collected opinions. Finally the door swung open, sucking out what was left of the precious "American" oxygen. The 250 passengers expressed a big sigh of relief from the stale air and heat. Soon after, the stewardess hustled us off the airplane with a courteous but repetitious "Bye bye" and "Good luck."

A line of buses waited to transport the troops to the 90th Replacement Center in Long Binh. When we boarded the bus, the interior was as warm as an oven. What a contrast to eighteen hours of pure comfort in a climate controlled jetliner.

The windows inside the bus were half down and protected by a thick-gauge wire mesh screen to prevent the enemy from throwing hand grenades into the cargo area. Me being one of the cargo, I thought it was a good idea to have such protection.

The procession of buses weaved into the heavy traffic on a two-lane asphalt highway. The roads seemed well kept. Vietnam had a stench all its own, both politically and physically. The smell inside the city of Bien Hoa was like nothing I had ever experienced. The exposed sewer system that ran through the city streets gave off a damp, musty odor that made me want to puke.

Bien Hoa was a small, bustling rural town with a collection of U.S. and Vietnamese military personnel serving to protect its inhabitants. The motorbikes, taxis, Lambrettas, street vendors, and military vehicles made up a hefty portion of the traffic.

The "ladies of the night" had an American flair in their dress style, probably an enemy attempt to make us feel homesick. And it worked! There was no indication of a war inside the city except for the crush of military personnel roaming the streets. The city's merchants and civilians throughout the energetic marketplace seemed to go about their daily routine as if no war existed.

The caravan of brown army buses came to a stop in front of the personnel processing station. The hydraulic doors swung open revealing a short, burly "leg" (nonairborne) staff sergeant who started out by announcing his name and his height, so I thought.

"I am Staff Sergeant Robinson, and I am 'short'!"

"No kidding," I thought, snickering to myself at his five-foot-six squatty frame.

"I have only forty days left in this hellhole. Because I am so 'short,' I am in charge of you and this detail. I want you to think of me as God. Until I get on one of those big beautiful birds going home, you will obey and follow my every command!"

He ordered us off the bus to stand formation. When I stepped out into the intense heat, it was truly a rude awakening from hell. The scorching sun overcame me. It must've been every bit of 120 degrees. A thick wave of heat blanketed the long road leading to the rest of the base area. I was almost certain I was in purgatory. The sweat from my body consumed my fatigues. "Oh shit!" I thought. "This fuckin' place is hot as hell and humid, too! Boy, Ed, you really screwed up this time. You and your big ideas about facing your fears and showing the world you could handle whatever life dished out. . . ."

Staff Sergeant Robinson instructed us to stand at ease.

"Smoke 'em if you got 'em."

"What? Is he joking?" I said, complaining to the person next to me. Who in their right mind would smoke a cigarette in this heat? To light a cigarette, all you had to do was hold it up to the sun and poof, instant fire!

"When you finish your smoke break," the staff sergeant continued, "field strip the cigarettes and stuff the butts into your pockets, because you are the ones who will be policing this area."

It was a struggle to get adjusted to the new weather conditions. It took two full sweaty days just to learn how to breathe the thick heavy air.

During my first few days at the holding center, I had to pull the unpopular details like KP and perimeter guard duty. We also had to attend mandatory formations and orientations. On the third day we were paid our military salary and issued our much valued ration cards. A large air force PX was nearby on base, and believe me when I say this, getting the ration cards was like receiving the key to the city. We were given time off and dismissed from formation to go raise hell. I joined a group of guys with a jeep headed to the PX. I bought enough goodies and supplies to keep me "in pocket" for a long while. We had no idea when we would be able to visit a military store again.

For the sake of keeping track of time while pulling guard duty on the perimeter berm, I purchased a durable Casio watch with an illuminated dial. There were times when disputes surfaced in the middle of the night or early morning because the common watch that was supposed to be passed every two hours didn't make it. Some of the troops couldn't stay awake for two and four hours at a time and frequently fell asleep during their guard shift. They would then try to pass the blame and the remaining time on to you or to whomever was next in line. It was smart to have your own watch at all times.

I realized how far down the bottom of the food chain I was when I had to perform the "shit-burning detail," especially when I had to do it three days in a row. The only way the military installations were able to get rid of the human waste and feces around the camp areas was to burn it. A fifty-five gallon oil drum was cut in half and shoved under the latrine housing. When the half drum cans became full, they were pulled away from the latrine structures, doused with diesel fuel, and set ablaze for hours. Every hour or so we would have to stir it to make sure the shit burned thoroughly. I kept thinking, "I gave up going to college to do this?"

After a few days of trying to dodge KP and the annoying shit-burning detail, a group of twelve paratroopers including myself was called out of formation and dispatched to a remote part of Bien Hoa Air Base for sandbag duty. We were told we would be shipping out to our new units directly from the detail site.

I took the moment to peruse the eleven faces I'd been traveling with for the past few days. I don't remember seeing any smiles on the scared, long faces. I watched Thad Givins who sat across from me. He was from the Bronx, New York. Thad and I boxed on the airborne boxing team and became buddies while training. At the time we had no idea we would later become best friends. PFC Thaddeus Givins was a well-adjusted black soldier and the proverbial all-around tough guy. He was a well built macho man with an attitude and ego to match. Thad Givins was the kind of person who projected strength and self-confidence with his cool demeanor. He was the pride of the U.S. Army. I was glad he was on our side.

While sitting in the extremely upright uncomfortable seats on the transport bus, I began asking myself, "What the hell am I doing here?" I actually gave up the opportunity to go to college and dodge the draft like everyone else. I chose to throw myself and my future directly into the hands of fate. Every reason I had to get myself into this mess now had no meaning at all. I began to wonder if I had taken complete leave of my senses. The gruesome doubts and second thoughts hammered away at me and my inner spirit.

The army made a concerted effort to keep us new troops busy while we were in limbo. The formation of our little group turned out to be sandbag duty at the dreaded X-marks-the-spot area. We were warned in advance, "The work area where you are being shipped has been marked for mortar attacks by Charlie." No sooner had we started to fill sandbags than the Viet Cong greeted us with their morning ritual by launching a mortar attack. We could hear the *cruummps* and see the impacting mortar rounds kicking up smoke along the perimeter of the airport. But then the U.S. Army artillery came alive with their return fire. Jolting booms of outgoing artillery rounds shook the ground underneath our feet. It made for a pretty noisy confrontation. The enemy missed their targets by great distances. Charlie's efforts seemed to be intended more for show and harassment rather than actual destruction.

Not long after the show of firepower came to a close, we watched a deuce-and-a-half (two and a half ton) truck barrel straight toward us and slide to a stop in an all-wheel drift. The breakneck stop jolted the truckload of 82d Airborne riflemen who were sitting in the back. Obviously just out of the boonies, their uniforms were completely covered with muddy red clay. There was one element too unambiguous to overlook; they were all African-Americans, or as we were often referred to in Vietnam, "soul brothers." As quickly as they drove up, they started taunting us.

"Hey look, we got some fuckin' new guys over here! What are you guys, a bunch of tough motherfuckas coming over here to save the war? You cherry motherfuckas!" They were having a big laugh.

I suppose they had a great need to get their pent-up rage off their chests, because soon after they ran out of shit to call us, their tone changed, and they became more serious. One scrawny, boisterous "brother" with a sparkling gold front tooth wouldn't stop running his mouth. He made sure we heard his message.

"No shit, man. You motherfuckas got yourselves into some real bullshit coming over here, man! These white motherfuckas over here are the same devils killing your families back home. The real war is on the home front, fool!

You Brothers really fucked up bringing yo' dumb asses over here! You'd better be trying to get yo' asses out of this motherfuckin' Vietnam shit, man! This shit over here ain't no game. Brothers are dying over here like flies, and for what? The Pig? These white motherfuckas over here hate yo' asses as much as the gooks hate you."

I couldn't pass up the chance to ask, "So why are you here?"

The paratrooper made a slow deliberate head turn in my direction and replied, "None of yo' motherfuckin' business! The point is, I'm trying to help yo' sorry asses. Hey man, this shit over here ain't no joke. I ain't bullshittin' you motherfuckas."

He pointed to a hill where there was a small-arms firefight going on.

"We just lost five of our homeboys out there in that motherfuckin' shit, man!"

I couldn't help but notice the soldiers aboard the truck that day. I watched them react to a firefight taking place on the nearby hill. I was suddenly overwhelmed by their sense of fear and uncertainty. I looked into their eyes as they tried to turn away unnoticed. It was no mistake, there were tears, tears of frustration and fear. They were scared as hell, and that scared the hell out of me. Something was seriously wrong with this picture.

Moments later the verbal jousting flared up again. Thad Givins gave one of his usual classic retorts by blurting out, "You better worry about your own dusty asses! All you mudderfuckers over here have me to deal with now!"

Everyone in our formation, including the white soldiers, emphatically yelled "Airborne!"

After a few more wisecracks, we watched another truck approach us down the middle of the tarmac. The Spec Four driver got out of the truck, dressed in freshly pressed camouflage fatigues and spit-shined jungle boots. One of the 82d soldiers aboard the truck shouted to the driver, "Hey man, are you a Lurp?" The driver smiled and nodded his head "yes." Then one of the 82d soldiers turned and asked us, "You guys goin' to a Lurp unit?"

We didn't respond.

"Do you know what a Lurp is?" he asked. We all drew a blank.

"You guys are going to a Lurp unit and you don't know what the hell a Lurp is? Mutha fucka!"

We stood there wondering what the hell he was talking about. Better yet . . . what the hell was a Lurp? The platoon of 82d Airborne soldiers loaded onto a waiting cargo plane, and we tossed our gear on the LRP truck and climbed aboard. The filling of the sandbags was an ongoing process, so we left enough work for the next group to complete the detail.

Things were happening too fast. We never got a chance to hear their explanation of a Lurp. But I was sure we'd find out soon enough. The battle-weary platoon of paratroopers did manage to get off an echoing parting volley as our truck pulled away. . . .

"All you John Wayne motherfuckas are gonna die in Vietnam!"

The ride to "God knows where" gave us a chance to take in this strange and incomprehensible country. I couldn't help but notice all the Vietnamese ARVN (Army of the Republic of Vietnam) soldiers joyriding on their cute little motorbikes when they should have been out defending their country. Whose war was this anyway?

Soon we were outside the city limits on a long stretch of road. The open deuce-and-a-half truck gave us a chance to take in the country landscape. We traveled by rice paddies and hamlets and the terrain went from flatland to rolling hills. The United States had poured billions of dollars into this underdeveloped wasteland to make it feel more like home. The primitive manner in which the rest of the country continued to operate was readily apparent. When you see how the rest of the world lives, you figure "home" isn't such a bad place after all.

Who were these people, and why was it so important for the Allied forces to try and exterminate them at the cost of so many American lives?

We arrived at a military camp where the sign over the front gate read, CAMP LINDSEY-LATTIN CO. F LONG RANGE PATROL 51ST INF. (ABN) NO WAR STORIES PLEASE.

I wondered what they meant by NO WAR STORIES PLEASE. I was surprised by the sturdy structure of the barracks and how well kept they were. As we rode further into the compound the entire company area came into full view. I never expected to see a full-length outdoor movie screen and theater stage in the company area. The truck pulled to a stop in front of the CQ office and we dismounted and fell into formation. A tall, husky first sergeant greeted us.

"Welcome, gentlemen," he bellowed in a deep raspy voice.

"Welcome to Company F 51st Long Range Patrol. My name is First Sergeant Walter P. Butts. Some of you men have volunteered to be part of the best fighting outfit in Vietnam. Company F Lurps are proven warriors in this war, and there is no braver soldier in this man's army. Forget all the bullshit you learned in basic training, because that shit does not apply here. We will retrain you to fight like real airborne soldiers. If you are able to handle the training and you do what you are told, we will get along fine. We are an all voluntary unit, so you are welcome to leave at any time. Those of you who haven't yet volunteered might be wondering why the hell you were sent here. You were picked from your individual profiles, and all I can say for you is, may God have mercy on your souls. All of our operations here are classified. That means, you do not write home to your mommies, daddies, or your wives to tell them what goes on over here. We will treat you like gentlemen . . . or like the good soldiers you claim to be, until one of you fucks up. Then we'll ship your ass out of here bag 'n' baggage to one of those shithead 'leg' outfits! Now to my left here is Sergeant First Class Barajas and Staff Sergeant Carter. They are your platoon sergeants. They will assign you to your platoons and team leaders. I will say this to you only once . . . do not cross these men, because when you cross them, you cross me. And when you get me pissed off, I ain't easy to get along with. Gentlemen, do we understand each other?"

"Yes, First Sergeant!" we barked.

"Now, when I dismiss you, I want you to fall out and get a haircut at the company barbershop whether you need it or not! That goes for Lottie, Dottie, and everybody! Do you understand?"

"Yes, First Sergeant!" we snapped even louder this time to show that we wanted no part of his ill temper. I couldn't help it, but I felt an immediate allegiance to 1st Sgt. Walter P. Butts on that first day in Company F. His naturally loud voice and strong personality added a harsh edge to his presence. First Sergeant Butts had a gregarious way about him, turning everything he said into a joke, but at the same time you knew he was dead serious. He had promised to treat us like gentlemen, but he warned us not to piss him off. I realized I had nothing to worry about. The last thing in the world I intended to do was put myself in a position to piss off the "first shirt."

After the Vietnamese barber butchered what little hair we had left on our heads, we filtered outside the small barbershop and jockeyed for a spot in the shade. The hot sun beating down on my neck felt like a magnifying glass laboring at optimum focus. I found a spot next to a watercooler and sat down, shielding my face from the direct sunlight. I started to reflect on my military training. I recalled all the endless hours of classrooms and physical training. I asked myself . . . was I really ready? Would I remember the right training under extreme pressure? I saw my situation as the "final test," the army's "final test." This final exam would determine whether or not I passed or failed in Vietnam. If I failed, it would mean a funeral back home. The more I thought about this scenario, the more I realized that I was in big trouble and my future was in serious doubt. I remember thinking at the time, "Wouldn't it be nice if I could go to someone and tell them that I was just kidding about this whole army thing . . . can I go home now?" A pipe dream of course.

While we waited for Sergeant First Class Barajas to return and assign us to our teams, the compound came alive with activity. A siren sounded in the company area. We watched as a team of helicopter pilots scrambled out to the chopper pad to warm the engines on their hi-tech war birds. Soldiers with weapons were scampering from every direction, all running toward the helicopter pad.

Suddenly, like a well-choreographed ballet, the team of helicopters simultaneously lifted off the ground and zoomed single file over the berm that protected the compound. We new arrivals wondered what all the excitement was about.

Like a bad rumor, word swirled around the compound that a dozen new replacements were in the company area. And like a pack of wolves, a group of short-timers soon emerged from their dens to sniff out the new meat. Four very tan and unshaven hardcore-looking Lurps swaggered toward us, each parading his own particular charm. They wore sunglasses, cutoff shorts, and sleeveless T-shirts, and a couple of them wore Ho Chi Minh sandals made of truck tire treads. I didn't know it at the time, but the Ho Chi Minh sandals were war trophies worn only after making a kill. They removed the sandals from the bodies of the enemy and wore them as a badge of honor. Each one of the Lurps had a weapon strapped to his body, including pistols and knives of various sorts. Some of these Lurps were formidable, much different from what I had expected.

Personally, I expected to be in the middle of a firebase deep in the boonies, running around with a steel helmet and wearing a combat flak jacket. I envisioned myself protecting the company perimeter with machine gun fire. Well, Company F was nothing like that. The atmosphere was casual, laid back, almost garrison-like. We heard loud music, yelling, and laughter coming from every other hootch along the path leading to the farthest barracks.

"What's the siren for?" I asked the tall, husky soldier who appeared to be the leader.

"One of the teams in the field just made contact," he replied. "They blew away three gooks on a trail. We had to send a reaction team in to get their asses out of a world of shit! The three gooks they hit were the point element for a platoon of NVA. Big Al's got a nice little war going on out there." They read the question marks on our faces.

"Oh, don't worry 'bout dem guys," he said in a cocky tone. "This company's got the best damn Lurps and best damn chopper pilots in the whole goddamn country of Vietnam. You motherfuckers are lucky. This company is great. We never pull any hard guard duty and no KP. All we have to do is go out in the field and fight for five days and when we come back, we fuckin' party! It's a fuckin' three-day weekend! The worst job you can pull around here is the shit-burning detail, and nobody gits out of doing that."

"Oh boy, I can hardly wait for that!" I sarcastically replied.

"Yeah, you guys are lucky you are not in the highlands with a line company like the Herd or the Chokin' Chickens. Those guys are gettin' the shit shot out of them. Here, we're doin' the shootin.' Hell, they love shootin' gooks in this company. That's why we joined the Long Range Patrol. Check it out. . . ." He continued almost in confidence, "I know you guys are new and everything, but let me give you young bucks a word of advice. . . . I shit you not, this place is like the old west, like Dodge City. Just be careful of what you say and do around here. Most of these guys here think they're real bad asses, so if you get into a fight or something, don't carry a grudge, just shine it on . . . it don't mean shit! Because when you start threatening these fools with bodily harm, that could mean your ass. These guys are used to shooting motherfuckers, and sometimes they don't particularly care who they fuckin' shoot!"

"War's hell," one of the cherries chimed in.

"War is hell, my man! But mostly profitable."

A short, stocky guy with really bad acne said, "We hit a gook paymaster yesterday and took about sixty-five hundred dollars off his sorry ass. Now I see three days of R & R in our immediate future. Three whole days on the white sandy beaches of Vung Tau!"

They pounded each other's fists in approval.

"Where the little French Vietnamese women love me for a long time and this war is just a memory," the short, stocky guy added.

"Yeah, a memory until a mortar round falls on your ass," his friend noted.

"Don't mind him, he's a cynic. C'mon, I'm too short for this chitchat bullshit anyhow! We just came out to see what our replacements looked like. 'Tee-Tee time!'" He indicated with a tiny space between his index finger and thumb.

"Thirty-three days and a wake-up. Hell, I'm so short, I might have to do battle with the insects to get to the airport. I'm so short, I'm gettin' little man's complex! I'm so short . . ." His buddies started pulling him away. "I may have to use a baby seat to ride in the helicopters. Short! Short! Short!"

We laughed at their comedic antics. I guess they could afford to be amusing, they were going home soon.

But the mysterious part was, I never saw those guys again and I don't have a clue who they were. "Don't threaten anyone." Well, that was a bit of valuable advice that stuck with me forever! I think they were only trying to scare us, but still, it made sense. If you are going to "kick someone's butt," you don't threaten them, you just do it.

These guys brought a whole new perspective to this style of fighting a war. Three days of R & R and extra money included for shooting a paymaster. I would call that a pretty good incentive.

Company F wasn't bad at all. No KP and no guard duty. Not to mention, the compound had everything, EM club, NCO club, TVs, movies, barbershop, tailor, mess hall. Hell, these guys were living like the air force flyboys . . . minus the air-conditioned barracks, of course. If I was going to be stationed overseas in a wartime environment, then Company F 51st LRP outfit is where I wanted to be!

Finally, SFC Catalino Barajas emerged from the TOC (tactical operations center) bunker and marched us off to our newly assigned accommodations. The music coming from the 2d Platoon hootch was blaring.

"Turn down that noise, Sergeant!" Barajas barked. Lying on a bunk was a tanned, small-framed, wiry, hippie-looking soldier reading a sci-fi book. The kind of quality stuff where the aliens are taking over the universe. He hopped up from his bunk and made his way over to the record player to turn it down.

"Mike, I got your warning orders. Meet me at the chopper pad at 1500 hours for your overflight." Barajas paused. "Sergeant Mike Frazier, this is PFC Emanuel. He'll be going out with you on your next mission. You two get acquainted."

Barajas turned and escorted the rest of the troops to what would become their new homes for the next twelve months. Hopefully . . .

"My close friends call me Brazzaville," said Frazier.

We shook hands. Mike asked, "Where are you from, Emanuel?"

"California . . . L.A.!" I declared proudly.

"Cool! I'm from Northern California. Do you dig good music?"

"Yeah!" I replied enthusiastically.

He lit up a Marlboro and took a deep drag, exhaling the smoke through his mouth and nose. He continued his thought. "I like listening to music before each mission. I'll play a few favorite songs over and over again, so if it starts to bug you, just put a pillow over your head or something. Or, you can go with it. Who knows, maybe before long you might be asking me to play 'Buddy Miles and the Electric Flag' before going into the boonies." Mike took another long drag from his cigarette.

"Music helps me to meditate before a mission," he said as he exhaled.

"Who is that?" I asked, referring to the music already playing on the record player.

"This group is called Love. You've never heard of Love before?" he asked, almost surprised.

"No," I said, shaking my head. "I'm more into jazz and R&B."

"Well, grab a seat and tell me what you think of this." I found a seat on his footlocker as Mike worked his way over to the record player, hopping over a bunk in a cubicle small enough to fit only four beds. This area was normally reserved for NCOs.

I made a quick scan of Mike's AO (area of operation). It was neat and clean, everything in its proper place. I took notice of the stack of science fiction books on a makeshift bookshelf assembled over the head of his bunk. Mike caught me mouthing the titles of his books.

"My mother got me hooked on reading when I was real young. But I love reading this sci-fi stuff. I dig this one." He handed me a book entitled *Lord of the Rings*. Mike was a bit ahead of his time. He gently placed the needle in a different groove on the album. The song was titled "Signed, D.C.," by Love. It was a suicide song. The artist sings about a junkie who overdosed on smack because he didn't feel loved. The junkie signed the suicide note with his initials, the letters "D.C."

"Interesting," I said, not really knowing how to react to the type of music that gave him pleasure. Mike had an interesting taste in his reading and the kind of music he listened to. The melancholy song became a fixture, almost an anthem in the hootch of the 2d Platoon. I quickly figured Mike's music played a large part in his Vietnam experience. I am often amazed at how the different songs in Vietnam left such an indelible mark on those who were there.

Just then I heard Thad Givins calling my name from outside.

"Emanuel! Emanuel! Where are you at?" he yelled.

"In here!" I yelled back.

Thad poked his head in the doorway. "We gotta pick up supplies at the quartermaster, you comin'?"

"Yeah, I'm coming," I replied.

Before I left, I got Mike to agree to listen to a copy of Sly and the Family Stone and the new Hugh Masekela album when he got back from his mission. Just maybe he would enjoy some jazz and rhythm & blues for a change. Mike had survived two tours in Vietnam and was getting ready to extend for a third. I certainly didn't want to upset his delicate balance, I just wanted to help brighten up the musical mood in the 2d Platoon hootch.

It wasn't tough to figure out that Sgt. Mike Frazier marched to a different drummer. I also knew right away that I would get along well with him, seeing how we were both from California. Mike Frazier had a profound yet morbid intellect, and I found him remarkably fascinating.

Thad and I took off toward the supply room in the sweltering heat. The hot sun was roasting us as we walked the long path between the barracks. The temperature had to be at least 115 degrees.

"Look what I got," Thad said with a smile.

He pulled out a nice-sized marijuana cigarette from his cargo pocket and palmed it in his hand.

We immediately made a beeline and slipped behind the berm next to the firing range to give the joint a whirl. We'd heard the "berm" was the place where the potheads would go after evening chow to smoke dope and reminisce about being back home, "back in the World" as they referred to it. We fired up the joint, and after just one hit I realized that I had just puffed on some of the most potent shit I had ever smoked in my life. I can't say I was an authority on this stuff, but sure as shit, after that one hit we were totally smashed! It was obvious that the heat had a lot to do with the effect of the marijuana in our systems.

"Damn, this is some powerful shit!" I confessed.

We stood there wobbling and dazed. We tried to compose ourselves, but it was useless. We were stoned out of our minds.

"You think they'll notice?" I asked.

Thad looked at me and broke into an uncontrollable laugh.

"You are fucked up!" He guffawed. His laughter became infectious. I started laughing at him because he couldn't stop laughing at me. I had to sit down before I fell down. After a few minutes of silliness, we finally gathered our composure and again headed for the supply hootch, this time floating on air.

When we reached the supply room, large floor fans were blowing cool air, aided by an air conditioner. The sudden temperature change gave much relief from the outside heat. We tried to stay inside the cool air-conditioned room as long as possible.

The quartermaster sergeant loaded us down with camouflage fatigues and floppy hats, OD green underwear, LBE (load-bearing equipment) web gear, duct tape, a banana clip magazine, K-bar knives, rucksacks, fat-rat water bottles, pill kits, survival kits, first aid kits, a signal mirror, and a compass. And that was only the first load.

We grabbed our gear and headed back to our hootches without incident. We couldn't walk fifty yards before breaking into a profuse sweat. By the time we reached the hootch we were drenched and still stoned out of our minds. We dumped our inventory on the concrete floor. Just as we sat down to sort through our belongings, Barajas showed up wearing cutoff fatigue pants and no shirt. His skin glistened with a dark golden brown hue from the Vietnam sun.

"All the new troops who arrived today, fall out for PT!" he announced. Thad and I looked at each other and muttered in unison . . . "Oooh shit!" We were both thinking the same thing. I knew I was way too high and it was definitely too hot for any form of physical activity. I tried to think up some kind of excuse or even a good lie to get myself out of this predicament. I couldn't come up with anything fast enough. I reluctantly joined the group and our fearless leader outside in the blistering heat.

There we were, twelve "green" cherries . . . trapped and marching toward the front gate like a herd of cattle being led to slaughter.

"Double time . . . Hurrach!" the sergeant instructed. The lean-bodied warrior took off running at a fast pace. He ran in the direction of the thirty-four-foot tower that was used to teach rappelling. We ran past the helicopter mock-up where we would learn the fine points of team insertions and extractions. I was out of breath by the time we started up the hill and then down the hill, around, and through the jungle area, which was used for LRRP training. My tongue was dry as dirt and felt like it was dragging on the ground. My feet felt like they were stuck in mud. I could feel the marijuana bubbling and boiling its way through my blood-stream, multiplying and unleashing oxygen-deprived blood cells into every vein in my body. I honestly felt that I was going to keel over on that hot dusty road. My pulse rate was going through the ceiling. Before that day, I had con-sidered myself a super-duper paratrooper in great shape. Hell, I was "airborne," for crying out loud! I should be able to run all day, every day, no sweat! As I struggled for my life, I glanced over at Thad to see if he was going to give up. Not a chance! He was probably waiting to see if I was going to fold. Not me! My pride wouldn't let me quit. I took a determined attitude to finish this run even if it killed me. From the way I was feeling, that idea wasn't too far-fetched.

When we reached the turnaround point, I was absolutely positive Barajas enjoyed torturing us, because he did it so well! Breaking in a bunch of eighteen- and nineteen-year-old soldiers and helping them survive the perils and pitfalls of a war took a great deal of responsibility. It was evident Barajas took his job seriously, not to mention the fact that he was in excellent physical condition. SFC Catalino Barajas was an American Indian, and I thought he had probably seen every Jim Thorpe movie ever made. He ran as if he was in a race with ol' Jim himself.

"Keep up!" he repeated at irregular intervals. By the time I thought my heart was going to tear through my chest, the company arch came into view. Stride for stride, Thad and I were out in front of the pack, charging for the threshold of the main gate.

"Quick time . . . Harrrach!" Barajas ordered, after crucifying us with the inaugural "Vietnam phlegm run."

"Thank God!" I gasped aloud. I was ready to collapse from heat exhaustion. It was an easy run for the sergeant, but for the rest of us greenhorns, we were ready to spew our guts. After the last straggler rejoined the group, Barajas went into a rage.

"If you ladies perform like that out in the field, you ain't gonna be going home standing up!" he scolded. "In this company you will be required to fight Charlie in his territory, in his backyard, in his base camps and on his trails, so you'd better be ready for him. Being 'ready' will mean the difference between you living or dying. Sometimes you are gonna have to carry more than a hundred pounds of supplies into combat. If Charlie gets in after your asses, you gonna be in goddamn big trouble. Look at you, wheezin' and coughin' like a bunch of little girls! Charlie can run all day and all night. He travels light and eats only when necessary. The least you can do is be ready, stay fit, stay alert. It might save your lives!" He took a long pause for effect and added, "Another thing, I want everybody to know we are on duty until 1800 hours every day except Sundays."

I got the uneasy feeling Barajas was talking directly to Thad and myself.

"Now, get back into your hootches and continue squaring away your gear. Group . . . Atten-hut!" he growled, and we came to a rigid stance. "Dismissed!" he belted with authority.

I'll never really know if Sergeant Barajas had seen Thad

and me go over the berm to get high or if he was just laying down the law. I did learn a couple very valuable lessons on my first day in Company F. Always expect the unexpected. . . . The second lesson, never, ever go up on the berm to get high before quittin' time!

CHAPTER TWO

My First Mission

It was a week later before I saw Sgt. Mike Frazier again. When he returned from his mission, he rested for a couple days, then packed to go out again. The turnaround came much too quickly. Just like before, SFC Barajas came down to the hootch to give him his warning orders. I was starting to get familiar with the routine. I heard Barajas tell Mike to meet him in the briefing room at 1300 hours.

I was the only cherry in Team 2-3 (2d Platoon, 3d Squad). Mike took the time to go through my gear. He showed me the importance of properly packing my rucksack for a mission. Every man packed differently according to his habits and physique. The object in packing is to place the weight as close to the body as possible to make it comfortable, with no bulges or sharp protrusions digging into the wearer's back, and having armament placed in the most accessible positions.

Pronounced Lurp, a complete Long Range Reconnaissance Patrol mission lasted five days and four nights, but we prepared to stay longer just in case. For reasons of not giving away information to the enemy in the event we were captured, or letting on that we were working in the area, other than dog tags we weren't allowed to carry any identification: no pictures, no insignias on our clothing, nothing. We were not allowed to carry paperback books, but we did. We had to do something while waiting to blow away the enemy.

A LRRP team carried an arsenal of weapons into combat. We packed enough ammo and supplies to replenish a platoon of soldiers. Depending on the type of mission, the team carried:

1. Five M-16 rifles w/3600 rounds of ammo (one noise suppressor)
2. One M-60 machine gun w/1000 to 1500 rounds of ammo
3. Forty to fifty fragmentation hand grenades
4. Six claymore mines (with time-fuse pencils)
5. One M-79 grenade launcher w/36 assorted rounds of ammo
6. Six willy peters (white phosphorous grenades)
7. Six knives (K-bars)
8. Four to six pistols (sidearms w/120 rounds of ammo)
9. Three LAWs (light antitank weapon)
10. One shotgun w/20 to 60 rounds of ammo
11. Twelve trip flares
12. Ten Toe poppers (antipersonnel mines)
13. Six one-pound sticks of C-4 (plastique explosives w/primer cord)

Individual Survival Needs

1. Map
2. Compass
3. SOI (signal operating instructions)
4. Signal mirror
5. Emergency UHF radio
6. Pen gun and flares
7. Signal panel and night flares
8. Head mosquito net
9. 35mm camera
10. Medical kit
11. Serum albumin (blood expander)
12. Squad radio (two men)
13. D-ring or snap links
14. Binoculars
15. Strobe lights
16. Insect repellent

17. One extra radio battery (per person)
18. Two smoke grenades (per person)
19. Ten Lurp rations (two meals a day per person)
20. Two gallons of water (per person)
21. One poncho liner (per person)
22. Duct tape (two rolls per team)
23. One starlight scope (night-vision unit per team)
24. One rucksack w/frame per person
25. One LBE (web gear and pistol belt w/ammo pouches) per person.

In F/51st, most Lurps lugged two different types of weapons into combat. Numerous rounds of ordnance were distributed equally among the team members. In a firefight we could conceivably hold off a large enemy force, engaging them with intense small-arms fire for at least thirty minutes. That would be enough time to get the support helicopters airborne and into the combat zone.

The Vietnam-era LRRPs were basically small groups of specially trained soldiers who practiced the art of enemy field surveillance. They were taught to infiltrate deep into hostile territory, sometimes operating well beyond radio contact and artillery support.

In Vietnam the combat forces needed accurate and timely intelligence about enemy forces, terrain, and weather. The line battalion commanders had to make fast and accurate decisions in order to have the right force in the right place at the right time. Their decisions were partly based on information gathered by Long Range Patrol intelligence sources. It was an advantage to put LRRP teams behind enemy lines for "eyes on" intelligence gathering assignments. The Long Range Patrol units were aggressively trained and given the latest equipment to gather this type of field intelligence. Lurps also pinpointed enemy targets and called in artillery or air strikes as needed. Vietnam LRRPs were especially skilled in initiating ambushes and carrying out (heavy) twelve-man harassment raids, where they captured prisoners and wreaked havoc on enemy personnel and fortifications. We were the first on the scene to recover downed airplanes and helicopters. On occasion, Lurps got the assignments to conduct top secret, high-level field assassinations. Our PFCs and Spec Fours were entrusted with combat knowledge equal to that of a first lieutenant. When it came to medical emergency procedures, Lurps had medical training equivalent to the first year and a half of medical school. Most of this specialized training was OJT (on-the-job training). I can objectively describe our job as one of the most hazardous and surreptitious in all of the Vietnam War. We spied with the purpose of eradicating the enemy.

Obviously, serving as a Lurp in Vietnam was not for everyone. If you were easily rattled or couldn't handle stressful situations, you were quickly identified and weeded out of the company. It happened often. I'm sure that fact alone is what drove me to work harder to achieve my goal of staying a Lurp.

Being a member of Company F gave me a sense of "empowerment." Oddly enough, for the first time I felt in control of my life. In the boonies, because I was a Lurp, I always felt like I was playing on offense.

The U.S. Army afforded me the opportunity to acquire special skills, but, Company F 51st LRP gave me the opportunity to be accepted among the "elite" fighting men of Vietnam. The desire to belong became a very powerful stimulant.

I once read a poignant characterization of a "Lurp" written in the yearbook issued by Company F 51st. It reads:

He has a caustic tongue and a definite to hell with it attitude. Inside the compound he's undisciplined and pointedly individual. He's rabidly anti-politic and fairly irreligious. The enemy to him isn't necessarily a soldier of uniform but rather something that has to be erased. He dislikes regimentation and authority is repugnant and abused in his eyes. He won't recognize anyone that isn't a

Lurp. He is, frankly, famous with a case of beer and can't remember any clean jokes. I wouldn't want one to go out with my sister. But they are unmatched in the field. We've lived with the word professional for so long that it tends at times to become dogeared, but there simply isn't another way to convey him. In the bush it isn't necessary to instruct, because he knows what has to be done and does it. He can assume command at any moment. Deprivation, fear, and fatigue are part of the mission and readily shared. Everything is shared. You never worry about him in a fight. Care of his wounded is paramount with him and he won't leave a dead partner under any circumstances. He knows the mission and the price, pays it and accomplishes it. He invented loyalty, and he's confident in his staying power. He may or may not accept our policy in Nam, but his attitude toward demonstrators, dissidents, malcontents and the like we can't print here. He wants to be left alone, live through the war, go home, get married and go into debt for some kids. He's a strange individual. Fortunately.

The description fits most. One thing is for sure, these guys were looking to live life in the fast lane. These Lurps were a special breed of airborne infantry soldiers who knew the risk and stared death in the eyes every time they took a mission.

It was comforting for me to know that Mike Frazier was a stickler for clean weapons, as was I. If Mike didn't physically see someone clean his weapon during the course of our stand-down, he would make it a point to check the weapon himself before the mission.

According to the terrain and conditions of the mission, Mike made sure we carried whatever was needed for the survival of the team. We prepared and taped our equipment so nothing rattled or clanked. We made sure that nothing shone or stood out visually. Our very lives depended on our ability to hide. The muzzle of each weapon was taped shut to prevent dirt or debris from entering the barrel. The M-16 ammo magazine clips held twenty rounds, but we used eighteen rounds of ammo in each clip to prevent the weapon from jamming. All the important pieces of equipment like bandoliers and claymore mines had quick-release knots for rapid deployment. Hand grenade pins were secured by mashing them flush to the primer heads; the exposed rings were taped down to prevent them from being snagged on a branch or other object. Everything was assembled on the rucksack and LBE belt, all neatly and methodically done.

Around 1300 hours the day before my first mission, I found myself standing at the gate where the helicopter pad was located. There was a lot of air traffic that day. I watched the teams of Lurps come and go. I was totally engrossed in the flying prowess of the pilots and the hovering capabilities of their aircraft.

The ATL (assistant team leader), Ted Godwin, came to me and asked, "Did you know you were supposed to be at the briefing?"

"What?" I shouted over the loud noise.

"You missed the briefing!" he repeated, at the same time scolding me for my ignorance. "Barajas is looking for you and he's got a real case of the ass!"

"Oh, shit!" I started to panic. I was never told to be at the briefing. I had no idea the meeting included myself as well as the rest of the team. Just then I felt the heat of Barajas's presence. Like magic he appeared from around the ammo bunker. SFC Barajas looked at the ground as he slowly walked toward me, stopping just short of bumping into me. He slowly tilted his head back, revealing those piercing dark eyes from underneath the edge of his floppy hat. We came together in eyeball to eyeball, nose to nose contact.

"Where were you, soldier?" he calmly asked.

"Out here watching the helicopters, Sergeant," I nervously responded.

"Didn't you hear me say to be in the briefing room at 1300 hours?" he snarled.

"Yes, Sergeant," I answered, not sure of any of this shit. "I thought the briefing was for the team leaders only, Sergeant."

I could see it mattered little what I said, he wasn't going to buy my defense. The sergeant now had me trembling in my jungle boots.

"Troop, you gonna dig me a goddamn six by!" he wrathfully snorted. "I'll teach you to miss a briefing on my watch! I want you to get your ass over to the supply room and draw a pickax and shovel and go out to the graveyard and dig me a goddamn six-by-six foxhole! You will not stop digging until you've finished. You got that, soldier?!"

I looked into his dark, half-closed, beady eyes and thought, "Boy, he is really pissed! What the hell have I gotten myself into, anyway?"

No one had mentioned that I was to be at the briefing, but I certainly wasn't going to stand there and argue with him about it.

"Yes, Sergeant," I quickly replied. I was only too happy to get out of his face. Then I put my tail between my legs and scampered off to the supply hootch to pick up my tools of punishment.

When I returned to the chopper pad, Sergeant Barajas was still waiting for me at the gate. He walked me over to the area where Company F buried their enemy kills and said, "Dig!" And so I dug. SFC Barajas turned and walked toward his hootch.

As I continued to dig, the ground became harder and harder. The first two feet weren't bad, but the next two feet were nothing but rock and gravel. The deeper I dug, the harder the ground became. After a couple hours my hands started to blister. By the time I had dug up to my waist in the hole, my hands were covered in blood. The sun was setting and I was starving. I had missed chow. A few hours later I saw a light off in the distance coming toward me. I could see it was Barajas walking toward me with a flashlight to check on my progress. He seemed to have calmed down. I had only a foot to go. I showed him that I had hit solid rock and could barely chip enough earth to fill a shovel load. He noticed the blood running down the handle of the shovel and figured I'd had enough. I couldn't have agreed more. Besides, we were to be inserted the following afternoon on my first mission. That alone was enough trauma for a rookie Lurp. Maybe I had gotten off easy, and maybe not. The worst possible punishment he could have given me was sending me to Vietnam. But he couldn't very well do that. I was already there!

Sleep didn't come easy that night. My hands burned and my back throbbed with pain. The artillery company next door to our compound was pounding out a fire mission. All night long they fired H&I (harassment and interdiction) rounds. The 175mm and the 8-inch guns belched out rounds every few minutes, one right after another. The thundering guns jolted you out of sleep, if you were lucky enough to even get to sleep. In between the fire missions I laid in my bunk and listened to the amplified whines of the Phantom jet turbine engines warming up for takeoff at Bien Hoa Air Base. The high-pitched screams intensified into angry roars as the aircraft climbed away into the darkened skies at all hours of the night.

The next morning at around 0830 hours there was a heavy tropical overcast. I rolled out of my bunk groggy and still aching all over. I slipped into my camouflage fatigues. Because we were going on a mission, I was minus my skivvies. Lurps never wore underwear out in the boonies. It felt strange not having that extra layer of cushion, but the purpose was for easy access. Also, skivvies didn't dry out like fatigues, so not wearing them prevented us from getting raw and chafed skin.

I dragged myself over to the mess hall for chow. I couldn't resist loading my plate down with eggs, bacon, and oatmeal. I ended up sitting at a table in a half empty mess hall ogling my food. I was unable to eat a thing. My stomach was jittery and I had a lump in my throat. I wasn't hungry after all.

I left the mess hall and headed back to the hootch to grab my M-16 rifle and a few magazines of ammo. I walked over to the firing range, which was only about a hundred feet from the 2d Platoon hootch. I found a group of sandbags and fashioned them into a comfortable formfitting firing position. I remembered how Frazier had emphasized the importance of having all sharpshooters on the team. I had not test-fired my weapon yet and wanted to make sure it was set up for my eyesight.

I propped up my weapon on the sandbags and fired off three rapid rounds. I made a quick adjustment to the range and windage and the next three rounds were right on the mark. It was the first real intimate meeting with my weapon. I began picking off targets eighty meters out. The weapon actually felt like she belonged to me. Most Lurps deadened the metallic sound of their weapons by wrapping them with some type of material or tape. I camouflaged mine, too. But the name "Wanda" was blended onto the stock of my rifle with green duct tape. Wanda was the name of the girl back home I had fancied as the "one and only." When I think about it, it was apropos to name my weapon "Wanda" . . . if you knew Wanda. When I squeezed the trigger, it made sounds much like "Lucille," blues singer B. B. King's guitar. It was music to my ear. As the relationship between a musician and his instrument is sacred, so is the weapon to a soldier.

Frazier instructed the team to meet him on the firing range at 0930 hours for "immediate action drills." This drill was used when a patrol inadvertently moved into an enemy ambush and needed to quickly break contact. The exercise taught us to respond instinctively to a sudden enemy attack and return an aggressive wall of fire (fluid suppression), then break contact and disappear under the flash, fire, and smoke of a willy peter (white phosphorous) hand grenade. The team would *di di mau* (run) to the rear and set up security to counter an attack. A spectator watching this drill under live fire conditions would truly be impressed. I only hoped we would never have to use the drill in combat, because it usually meant that the enemy had the drop on us and the point man and others more than likely had been hit.

During the initial two week company training course, I tried to assimilate as much valuable information as I could from each one of my teammates. Every day we worked on different aspects of patrolling. I soon found out that some things you couldn't prepare for; you just had to experience them for yourself.

At 0930 hours, exactly, the rest of the team showed up. We spent another twenty minutes fine-tuning our skills and test-firing weapons on the range. I felt like a prizefighter shadowboxing before a big fight rather than a soldier preparing for battle.

When we were dismissed from the detail, I went back to the hootch to write letters home. I sat at the end of my bunk and began to reflect on the predicament I had gotten myself into.

I was now going into combat. All I had trained for was finally at hand. This was it! Whether I was ready or not. I had never been sure of my progress. There was a lot to know and learn in a short period of time. I felt overwhelmed. I lay across my bed and began visualizing myself coming back from the mission. I saw myself sitting in the door of the helicopter as it touched down on the chopper pad. This practice would become a ritual of mine before every mission.

Mike Frazier's music played in the background, over and over again, just like he said it would. I dozed off with the lyrics to the music sewn into the back of my mind. Before long, I came to know all the words to the song "Signed, D.C."

Time passed. Frazier finally turned off the music.

"Okay, let's saddle up!" he said loud enough to wake the dead. I bolted straight up from a semiconscious state, feeling like I had been asleep for more than an hour, but in fact

it had been only thirty minutes or so. We sat around on our
bunks and footlockers painting our faces with a camouflage
grease stick. The mood change was radical and abrupt. The
sudden transformation sent everyone from gregarious to all-
business. Mike became "Sergeant Frazier." There was no
more joking around and absolutely no horseplay. We spoke
only when necessary. Talk about your game face! In Vietnam we actually applied our game face. The team quietly
prepared for the danger surrounding their work. It dawned
on me, this is what I do for a living now. This was my job!
Instead of me braving the freeways of Los Angeles every
morning, I had been flown off to the jungles of Vietnam to
make a kill. And, for this, I got paid. Go figure.

We moved outside where our heavily armed web gear
and rucksacks were leaning against the bunkers for safety
reasons. When I strapped on my bulky rucksack, I couldn't
believe how much more my equipment weighed compared
to the first time I had put it on. It had to weigh at least
ninety-five to a hundred pounds.

At 1300 hours we started toward the chopper pad. The
troops in the company area came out of their hootches, taking pictures and shouting words of encouragement and ex-
changing "thumbs-up" for good luck. It was a dramatic
gesture of solidarity and a very moving experience. Today
that same scene would choke me up, but at the time I was so
green, I didn't know what to think.

We boarded the chopper, three on each side of the door
with our feet dangling outside the craft. The pilots were still
being briefed, so we sat and waited. This had to be the most
eerie time of any mission, sitting, waiting, and thinking of
all the possibilities. It was too late to say, "I quit!" Not that
it mattered, but the "I quit" joke was frequently used around
this time to break the tension.

The pilots eventually emerged from the briefing room
along with the company commander, Lt. Col. Joseph J.
Zummo. His call sign was "Six Killer." He was a short,
skinny officer who appeared out of place among this elite
group of soldiers. He walked by, never once looking up from

his maps or acknowledging us. The wind vortex from the Cobra helicopters kicked up and ruffled the lite colonel and his heap of maps attached to his clipboard. Zummo climbed aboard the command and control helicopter and continued to read from his clipboard. It was my first time seeing him in the flesh. I'd heard a lot about his behavior as a leader. Also, the many alarming rumors about him leaving teams in the field after they made contact. But at that moment I was more concerned about surviving my first mission.

For reasons unknown our company commander was never satisfied with reports that the teams had made contact unless they brought back a body. The teams in the field would cater to Lieutenant Colonel Zummo's psychotic practices with an occasional stiff or two. The dead bodies gave him the opportunity to view the information firsthand. At least, that's what I was told.

"This is going to be an interesting convoy," I said to the Spec Four sitting next to me. "Three Cobra gunships and three Huey slicks." I raved like a kid at Disneyland. It was my first time ever riding in a helicopter. The pilots boarded and began going through a preflight checklist, with the switching of toggles and the turning of dials . . . then came the whine of the turbine engine. The lazily rotating blades started to pick up rapid speed. My heart began to pound uncontrollably. The nervous tension was unreal. Under the circumstances, that whining sound from the helicopter became one of the most frightening and thought provoking sounds I would experience while serving in Vietnam. And still to this day, I conjure up horrible visions and noxious thoughts when I hear the starting whine of a helicopter's turbine engine. "The sweet sounds of success," I used to jokingly say. Why that name, I have no idea. Maybe it was a nervous mutter.

The team insertions were the most dangerous and most crucial times of a mission. You never knew what to expect, but we were trained to expect anything and everything. Team insertions also rendered all participants vulnerable, everything from the helicopter and the crew to the Lurp

team. It was also a time that usually caused a great deal of
personal anxiety. I glanced over to the faces of my teammates. The moment gave me a chance to get inside their
heads and read into the strengths and weaknesses that faces
sometimes reveal. I rubbernecked to scan the faces of my
teammates seated behind me. I have to admit, I was impressed by their poker faces. I couldn't detect a trace of
open apprehension. They were veterans at this game, and
they made it easy for me to adopt the same courage and confidence they typified.

The helicopters finally lifted off and whisked us up and
over the earthen berm that signified our sanctuary. I tried to
remember the landscape and landmarks along the flight
path. In case the disconcerting need to "escape and evade"
ever came up, at least I would have a clue as to where I was
going. The ship climbed to an altitude of about twenty-five
hundred feet. We flew over the Dong Nai River, numerous
small villages, rice paddies, and roads leading nowhere.

About twenty minutes out we were deep into the triple
canopy jungle terrain, thirty miles from our original starting
point. Vietnam appeared so peaceful twenty-five hundred
feet up in the sky, you'd never know a war was being fought
below. The jungle floor looked like a thick, lush carpet spotted by bomb craters made by B-52 "Arc Lights" (bombing
missions). The sparse vegetation and openings in the jungle
terrain were used as LZs (landing zones) for Lurp insertions.

Suddenly the helicopter banked hard right and we started
to swiftly descend. I was sitting in the doorway with my feet
hanging outside the chopper. You would think by the steep
angle of the craft, we'd be falling to our demise. But cen-
trifugal force literally pushed us back into the cabin of the
helicopter.

"Amazing!" I thought. I was enjoying the amusement
park ride. The helicopter leveled out and continued at top
speed. We dropped down just above treetops, skimming and
contouring the jungle. The helicopter cast a fast-moving
shadow on the ground below, trailing us in a race to destiny.

The tail of the chopper abruptly lowered, changing the pitch of the rotor blades. We had reached the predetermined LZ. The loud popping and thumping sounds of the powerful flying machine caught my attention as it hovered effortlessly only a couple feet off the ground.

Simultaneously the entire team burst out the doors in a violent sprint for the tree line. Even with mud up to our knees, it was an all-out dash for cover. I threw my body into overdrive to catch up and assume my position in the team march. As I ran past teammates, I couldn't help but recall my high school football coach back at Centennial High in Compton, California. Aaron Wade coached us to one of the top two high school football teams in the entire nation during the '66 and '67 seasons. There were times he would stand over me on the seven-man football sleds and scream, "Emanuel! Git yer ass in there and drive like everybody else! That's what the hell we mean by teamwork. Everybody works together!" The "team" concept was the only philosophy taught at Centennial High school's football program.

By the time I got to Vietnam, I regarded myself as well versed in the theory of "teamwork" strategy long before I became a Lurp. Coach Aaron Wade in his esoteric way was toughening me up not only for football, but for life in general. His direct tutelage proved to be my advantage. Thank you, Coach Wade, you were right! Football training did follow me for the rest of my life. Well . . . certainly to Vietnam. It was easy to equate football with fighting a war, except we didn't get shot at in football games.

After we cleared the LZ, Mike pointed the team in the direction of a short steep hill. My first minutes on the ground were filled with concentrated fear and uncertainty. Anxiety and rapid heartbeats became my constant companions. We moved deeper inside the tree line until the sound of the choppers faded into the distance. Frazier held up our movement with a raised fist. We went down to one knee and "lay dog." The pause gave the team a chance to listen to the jungle and determine a correct compass heading.

When it was time to move out we did so, muffling the sound of the team advancing in tactical formation. We moved in the same order in which we had trained: this way we always knew where everyone was at all times. The order of march was:

Point man—Early warning, brush breaker, shock absorber.
Compass man—Kept the point oriented, high cover.
Patrol leader—In the center for control.
Radiotelephone operator—Next to team leader, with PRC-25 radio.
Pace man—Kept accurate count of how far we moved.
Assistant patrol leader—Rear security.

On this particular mission I was the "pace man." We started up the steep incline, using the trees and branches to pull ourselves up the hill. The team maneuvered to a semi-flat area that had enough cover and concealment so we could disappear into the foliage. We formed a tight perimeter and waited to see if Charlie was on our tail. Sergeant Frazier checked the radio commo and SOI (signal operating instructions); the team drank water and rested for ten minutes. Then Frazier gave the nod and we picked up to move out again. We headed in a northeasterly direction, our movement in the thick brush painstakingly slow and tedious. We made sure not to step on trails or bare patches of dirt, never leaving a trace or indication that we were in the area. Every man assisted another in order to squeeze between tight spots. We were careful not to break any brush or snap a twig, no unusual sounds to alert the enemy.

The sounds of the jungle were strangely different to my ears. I had to quickly learn the new and peculiar indigenous sounds that filled my new environment. There was not much difference between a dog barking and a bird cawing. I had to discern between the "fuck you" lizard or a pissed off gook shouting obscenities. In Vietnam they both sounded the same.

The team used hand signals and mouth-to-ear whispers to distribute information. We practiced hand signals in training, but once in the field the team conveyed information more profoundly. It was a language all its own. Sometimes it was nothing more than telepathic eye contact and body posture. Unless someone whispered directly into my ear with different instructions, I imitated the moves of my teammates.

The triple canopy and heavy ground foliage kept the air from circulating. The high humidity and thick air made breathing laborious. Sweat soon started to melt the camouflage paste from my face. Trying to stop the flow of sweat from dripping into my eyes was a personal battle. We moved toward an open field virtually bare of trees. On the other side of a nearby ridge, a shot rang out. Immediately we went into a one-knee crouched position. An AK-47 signal shot had been fired close by. I learned that the firing of a signal shot was the enemy's way of letting others know that intruders were nearby. Make no mistake about it, once you hear an AK-47 fired in the jungle or in the field, you can distinguish its sound from any other weapon. Rather than a pop or bang, the AK-47 makes a crackle sound. Apparently Charlie knew we were in the area, but he didn't know exactly where. The team lay dog for a few minutes. Frazier moved us out cautiously. He began to set a false trail to confuse any stalkers. If we were being followed, eventually we would wind up following our trackers.

Sgt. Mike Frazier studied Charlie's every move and had become proficient at the game. He had taken on the duties of my teacher, and his valuable lessons were learned. . . . Charlie never booby-trapped his own personal trails unless he wasn't using them anymore. When we came upon a high-speed trail (a frequently used trail), we could tell what type of enemy we were tracking by the footprints we found. If the shoe tracks were tire soles, more than likely they were VCs, and if the soles were boot prints, they were probably NVA soldiers. He could also tell how much equipment enemy

troops were carrying by how deeply embedded the footprints were. Footprints also revealed the number of enemy
and how fast and in what direction they were moving. If the
"toes" were embedded, they were moving at a rapid pace.
When there were no trails to speak of, broken vegetation
told the story. Animals break the bush at knee height, but
when arms and shoulders are used to squeeze through thick
foliage, they make distinctive markings about five feet
above the ground.

As a rule, Lurps never walked directly on trails as our
boot prints would surely have given us away. Uncle Ho
himself could determine if we were in the neighborhood if
we made those types of clumsy mistakes. Lurps always
moved parallel to enemy trails. Slipping undetected through
the jungle was an art, and the LRRPs of the Vietnam era
mastered the technique.

We trusted Mike's two years of Vietnam experience. His
Recondo savvy put him in a completely different class than
the rest of us. Mike was only twenty years old, but boy, did
this guy know his shit! I also came to the conclusion that
Sgt. Mike Frazier enjoyed leading a Lurp team. If it hadn't
been the Vietnam War, it would certainly have been some
other war in some other time or place where he could hunt
down a warring adversary. I often wondered if Mike had a
"death wish" or if he was just plain unafraid to die. Mike actively and aggressively pursued the enemy with zeal. He
wasn't one to go out into the bush and hide for five days.
No, not him. Mike always wanted either a kill or a prisoner
for his efforts. His fellow teammates acted robotically, following him without question, however ridiculous the job.

Around the company area Mike was becoming a legend
for his gung-ho, convoluted tactics. That type of aggressiveness separated our company from the other Lurp companies
in Vietnam. Most Lurp companies in Vietnam were Long
Range "Reconnaissance" Patrol. We were "Long Range Patrol," which meant we were not only watching the enemy
but, when it was safe and necessary, Company F got its
body counts.

"Humping" was an expression used for moving you and your supplies from "point A" to "point B." Depending on the terrain, we humped an average of about three klicks (kilometers, five-eighths of a mile) in eight hours to get to a plotted ambush site. Keep in mind, each team member was carrying about a hundred pounds of equipment. My first day in the boonies, I can easily say we "humped" until the sun went down!

Little by little, the stress of the mission and the high humidity took a heavy toll on my novice body. My fatigues were saturated with sweat. The straps from my rucksack had worn deep gouges into my shoulder blades.

I had heard about the "wait-a-minute" vines. Finding your way through an accumulation of this stuff was indeed a daunting task. The vines hung down from the canopy of the jungle, sprouting sharp barbs at one-foot intervals. I learned on the first day in the boonies that you have to cover up all exposed skin because the "wait-a-minute" vines would always triumph when it came to the slice-and-dice battle. It was unbelievable how badly the vines or even tall blades of grass could cut up your arms and hands, anything that was exposed. The barbs from the vines would hook onto your clothes or equipment and pull you backward down to the ground when the slack played out. The "wait-a-minute" vines were one of nature's many annoying jokes designed only to piss you off.

"Rest!" We all looked forward to our moments of intermission. It was a welcome break from hunting the prey. When we took our breaks, we spent most of the time trying to replace lost body fluids by drinking enough water to keep ourselves hydrated. Each Lurp carried enough water to last six or seven days, and it didn't take much to run out if you weren't careful.

Around 1600 hours the job of finding a suitable RON (rest overnight) was becoming apparent. Before the sun completely disappeared from the sky, we had to settle into our planned ambush site. Mike picked a spot next to a well-used foot trail. Personally, I thought we were much too close to the freshly used footpath, but what did I know, I was a cherry.

We established a six-man half-moon perimeter, with a 180-degree "field of fire." We were able to see the trail with only a few obstructions like bushes and branches. The vegetation growth in the area was sparse. The jungle was barren of big trees or anything we could use to protect us from incoming bullets. But still the team was able to hide with the confidence of not being spotted.

The sun was just beginning to set. We made sure to put out our claymore mines completely around us in a 360-degree perimeter. My teammates looked fairly confident that we were reasonably safe. I began to breathe a little easier after settling in for the night. I opened a package of spaghetti Lurps for my dinner. The Lurp rations were the wonder of the U.S. Army. "Dehydrated foods!" They came in assorted flavors like chili con carne, chicken stew, beef and rice, and chicken and rice. They were nutritious and lightweight, and it was easy to carry enough chow for five or six days. To consume these tasty delights, all you had to do was add a little water and stir. Wait about twenty minutes for the food to absorb the water, then devour. Yum! Yum! It made me hungry for real food.

Around 1900 hours, just after twilight, the jungle became so dark, we couldn't see a star in the sky. Zero visibility! I couldn't see my hand six inches from my face. The only visible sign of light in the entire jungle was the illuminated dial on my Casio watch that I had just bought at the PX. I quietly tore a piece of duct tape from my Lurp bag and covered the watch face.

I became affected by the medley of indigenous sounds . . . sounds I had never heard before, but which were now suffocating the evening air.

That night, "fear" took on a whole new meaning. The trial we were watching seemed to have come alive. I spotted what I thought was a person walking along the trail smoking a cigarette. It seemed that every ten feet the cigarette became illuminated as though someone was taking a puff while walking along the trail. I looked around to see if my teammates were watching this event, but no one was paying any particular attention to the occurrence.

I thought, "Don't they care that someone is walking by our position having a smoke?" I clutched my weapon and silently thumbed the selector switch to "rock & roll" (automatic). Suddenly the cigarette light took a different attitude and flew off in another direction.

"Aw shit!" I thought. It was evident that I was really green at this job! I was getting ready to put down a firefly! The truth was, I was from the city, and even in training schools I had never seen a firefly before in my life.

Then it hit me like a ton of bricks! I was in the middle of a pitch black jungle with only five other guys and more than thirty miles away from the nearest friendly support base. I realized I didn't have enough experience to distinguish the difference between a human being sneaking up on me or a damn firefly flitting silently down the middle of the trail.

Not far away a large tree crumbled to the ground, making a loud crash. I began to wonder if it was Mother Nature discarding one of her lifeless trees or if we were getting enemy movement.

I began to worry about the "what ifs!" "What if" we get into a firefight and I am wounded so severely that I can't get away? Or "what if" we get in a running gun battle and I am separated from the rest of the team in the pitch dark jungle? What would I do? And "what if" I were captured; do I just give up? I had a laundry list of terrible uncertainties crawling though my mind. "What the hell have I gotten myself into?" That first night in the jungle, fear and anxiety were replaced by outright terror. Nocturnal creatures made loud angry noises, and the silence became even more frightening. I could hear twigs snapping and movement all around.

Late into the night, I peered out in the direction of our field of fire. I was sure I heard a group of Viet Cong sitting there having a meal about twenty-five feet away.

"This can't be happening," I thought to myself. I eased my way over to Frazier and whispered in his ear.

"Sarge, someone is out there." I said it with a crackle in my voice. Mike said nothing. He just sat up to listen. After a few minutes, he lay back against his rucksack. I'd moved back to my rucksack and continued my vigilance of the area. Now I was certain I was hearing conversations and the clanking of flatware. I moved back to Frazier's position and again whispered in his ear.

"Sarge, Sarge! Somebody is out there!" Frazier waited until I had moved back to my position and leaned against my rucksack. Then he straddled my body on his knees. He slowly unholstered his Walther PPK pistol and pressed it hard against my forehead and whispered forcefully in my ear, "If you make another move or make another sound, I will blow your fucking head off!"

Mike calmly moved back to his position and lay against his rucksack. There was no doubt in my mind that he was serious! I almost pissed myself. Needless to say, I didn't utter another word for the rest of the night. But still, all that night I watched and listened in sheer terror as Charlie attended his nighttime gathering.

The following morning, surprisingly, we were still alive. The sun slowly burned off the drifting shroud of ground haze. I scanned the area where I believed I'd heard the sounds. I saw no signs that would indicate previous activities. Could I have been hallucinating? Did that first night in the jungle play tricks with my mind? Maybe it was the anxiety of being a young soldier in a wartime environment; certainly that can impair one's judgment. I began to wonder if I was cut out for this type of work. Clearly my confidence was shaken.

Around 0830 hours, Mike called in the morning "sitrep" (situation report). And, as we had the day before, we ate in shifts. Four team members watched the trail while the other two gobbled down breakfast. I was exhausted from not sleeping that night. It didn't matter who was on watch throughout the night, there was no way in hell I would have fallen asleep. I was tempted to go into my pill kit to pop a couple of dextroamphetamine tablets to stay alert, but then I fought back the urge. Besides, I had been warned against taking those things gratuitously. They would keep your mouth dry, which meant drinking more water. Not a "good" thing.

It didn't take long to find out that "sleep deprivation" is what being a Lurp is all about. You learned how "not" to sleep for days at a time.

I was surprised that no one in the team ever mentioned or made reference to my "first night" in the jungle. Maybe the "first night" panics had happened to one of them, or maybe there was really someone out there that night and they didn't want me to alert Charlie with my shifting around. I never knew for sure. My main concern from that point on was to become a good Lurp and learn the ways of survival.

Around 0930 hours it was time to move out. We sterilized our area to make it look as though it had never been inhabited. The thump in my heart got heavier every time we had to load up our gear and move out. I looked at my compass. We were headed 180 degrees due south to our next objective.

Our primary mission was to find a suspected sapper training camp. Our intelligence sources claimed to have documents showing the enemy was running a sapper school in the area. (Sappers were enemy soldiers specially trained to creep inside military perimeters to wreak havoc by blowing up personal and tactical installations.)

We crossed a field of elephant grass, the blades of grass reaching more than eight feet high. Spinning a web from tree to tree was a large spider. The web spanned over seven feet in diameter. In the middle of the web was a big black and yellow spider whose body was as large as my fist; the legs were at least six inches long. It was an unbelievable feat of nature. Some of God's creatures grew incredibly large in Vietnam.

We arrived at the vicinity alleged to be an enemy training camp. The G-2 (intelligence staff of the U.S. Army organization) information had been right on the money.

Under the triple canopy trees the point man spotted a series of enemy bunkers surrounding the camp area. The bunkers were ruggedly constructed of mud and wooden logs. They looked like mounds of dirt with portholes facing outward. The bunkers were covered with brushes and twigs and placed about twenty-five feet apart in a complete circle.

We sat in the bushes and observed from a distance, listening for anything "indigenous." For hours there was nothing, not even a small animal, and still we waited. Finally, we moved in to explore the interior of the bunkers and found huge rats had taken up residence inside them. After further inspection of the grounds, we found no enemy. Frazier pulled us back about fifty meters into the thick jungle to set an ambush on a trail leading to the bunker complex.

We picked our way through the thick undergrowth and found a natural cavern commonly referred as a "bamboo room." A little plot of land with ample bamboo trees, concealing anything or anybody wishing to hide from the sun . . . like snakes, wild boars, and this time, Lurps.

Getting pricked by the sharp bamboo thorns when entering was commonplace. Space inside these areas was generally limited, but this particular bamboo room had ample space and an accommodating field of fire. Excellent choice! Frazier and I exchanged thumbs up. The team lined the perimeter with claymore mines and settled in to wait. Mike got a fix on our position from "Aloft" (fixed-wing L-19 observation airplane). Teams on the ground were able to get a more precise fix on their position by flashing a mirror at the aircraft flying overhead, and having the pilot pinpoint their exact location on a map. Then he'd relay that information back to the team, the TOC, and the nearest support base. Aloft also relayed orders back to us from the TOC instructing us to "avoid contact at all cost." We were told to sit tight and monitor movement and activity. Two different teams in the field had made contact at the same time and all the choppers were up in the air and working. For the next few days and nights we listened and observed.

On the third night, not more than a few meters from our position, we counted twenty-four heavy mortar rounds leaving the tubes. Charlie was so close we could smell his body odor. Because of the thick foliage of the bamboo room, we weren't able to get a visual of the enemy. Mike radioed the TOC, letting them know several mortar rounds were incoming.

Throughout the night we monitored truck engines roaring, wood being cut, and constant hammering. We could see electric lights glowing through the jungle. Charlie was more adapted to the night environment and did his best work when the sun went down. The enemy's approximate position was plotted by the compass azimuth and we estimated the distance of the voices and noises. In the jungle the sound carried a great deal farther at night.

After sitting in the same spot and roasting for five days, Mike got the call to pack up and prepare for an extraction. We assisted each other with pulling in our claymore mines. One Lurp stood watch while another recovered our equipment.

The LZ was just a short distance from our RON. We worked our way through the jungle until we reached the extraction point. We hid just inside the tree line until the helicopters were inbound. After a while we could hear the extraction choppers in the distance. The Cobra gunships appeared first and circled the area to protect the inbound slick. We flashed a fluorescent signal panel to show the Cobra gunships our position and also to prevent them from mistakenly firing on us.

Minutes later the extraction helicopter swooped down out of the glare of the sun, flying fast and low. We sprinted from the the security of the wood line out to the inbound chopper. Because of our constant practice, every team member knew exactly where they were to sit aboard the aircraft. Before the chopper was able to completely settle, the team dived aboard. We timed the rendezvous perfectly. The pilot flew the ship out of the area just as fast as it had come in. I was amazed at the proficiency of the whole operation.

"This is too cool!" I said to myself. At the debriefing we learned that the area was being subjected to a B-52 strike. And, just as I had envisioned while lying on my bunk five days earlier, I had survived my first mission.

CHAPTER THREE

Going Home Too Soon

The third week in Vietnam was damned unsettling for me. All that week I had a strange premonition that something bad was brewing. Sure, it would've been unimaginable to be in the middle of a war zone and "not" have those peculiar feelings. But there was an unusual gnawing in my gut, the type of feeling that served as a constant reminder that something ominous was lurking.

We had gotten our warning orders. We were to continue patrolling the area officially known as War Zone D, and within War Zone D was an area esoterically referred to as the Catcher's Mitt. I took the time to find out as much as I could about the Catcher's Mitt AO. I also took the time to find out any information concerning my new company. The Catcher's Mitt AO was a major enemy staging ground and infiltration route into Saigon, Bien Hoa, and Long Binh. It had been the mission of Company F 51st Infantry Long Range Patrol to find and help shut down enemy supply lines into those regions.

Our company history indicates that on September 25, 1967, F Company 51st Inf. Long Range Patrol (Airborne) was reactivated in Vietnam. Twelve other Long Range Reconnaissance Patrol and Long Range Patrol companies throughout Vietnam were also getting started. General Westmoreland presided over the dedication ceremony of our company on November 22, 1967, the day Company F became officially combat operational. Out of the thirteen

LRRP and LRP units deployed in Vietnam, only two units operated on the Field Force level. We were one of them.

Company F 51st was formed as a tactical self-sufficient combat unit with the mission of running intelligence gathering operations utilizing Allied and indigenous personnel. We were the eyes and ears of II Field Force Vietnam. The insertion of Company F Lurps into War Zone D disrupted and decapitated enemy movement in that region. Before we moved in, Charlie ran amok, virtually unhindered and undetected. Company F was the new sheriff in town and we aimed to change all that. We soon had an extraordinarily accomplished record in patrolling and compiling intelligence for II Field Force.

The Long Range Patrol soldiers in Vietnam saw and fought a very different war than was reported back in the States. We were in a war where we totally dominated the enemy. We routinely used the "element of surprise" against the enemy in his own backyard. We were beating them at their own game. As a unit we actually felt we were making a difference, and from our perspective we were winning this contest hands down.

Counterinsurgency warfare was essential to the successful prosecution of the war in Vietnam. At one point, Special Forces and other special elite units were grudgingly tolerated. That situation changed dramatically when President John F. Kennedy took office. The president was the first to realize the historical significance of winning a war through counterinsurgency and "direct action units."

In a 1960 speech the president stated: "This is another type of warfare, new in its intensity, ancient in its origin, war by guerrillas, subversion, insurgents, assassins. War by ambush instead of by combat. By infiltration, instead of aggression, seeking victory by eroding and exhausting the enemy, instead of engaging them. And these are the kinds of challenges that will be before us in the next decade if freedom is to be saved, a wholly new kind of strategy, a wholly different kind of force, and therefore a new and whole different kind of military training."

In the early 1960s, Ho Chi Minh controlled some fifteen thousand Viet Cong guerrillas in South Vietnam. To turn back the communists, Kennedy put his faith in counterinsurgency units. He believed they could do more to stabilize Indochina compared to what conventional military forces could accomplish.

In January 1961, President John F. Kennedy remained true to his words by exercising the power of his presidency and placing into operation "direct action units" such as the U.S. Army Special Forces (Green Berets). In May 1961, President Kennedy sent four hundred Special Forces soldiers to Vietnam to expand present operations in the field of intelligence, unconventional warfare, and political-psychological activities.

These intelligence units were part of the general buildup of U.S. forces in Vietnam. By 1965 the largest concentration of intelligence personnel was in MACV (Military Assistance Command, Vietnam).

Other military intelligence groups were spread around the country with both intelligence gathering and counterintelligence duties. Besides an intelligence center in Saigon, there was also a center for interrogation and analysis of enemy documents and material. The Long Range Reconnaissance Patrol units provided tactical intelligence, often at the cost of casualties.

Years after President Kennedy had given his personal stamp of approval, the Special Operations units were able to flourish. In 1966 the 5th Special Forces Group spawned and trained the Long Range Patrol companies to fight the Vietnam War.

The typical Long Range Patrol volunteer soldier was looking for more excitement and better training than what was offered in the regular line combat units. Approximately

thirty-nine hundred U.S. Army soldiers served as
LRRP/LRP/Rangers in Vietnam. The specialization of these
small teams of maverick soldiers was aptly viewed as an
"acquired profession."

The name "Lurp" was never established as a "handle" in
the real world. I had always thought of the "Long Range Patrols" as Special Forces, SEALs, Recon Marines, Rangers,
SOG (Special Operations Group, or Special Operations and
Studies), snipers, commandos, and mercenaries, all rolled
into one. All members of the same "special" family. For the
most part, Lurps in Vietnam were trained and did perform
the same duties as all those units mentioned.

"Lurping" was soldiering with an attitude. We were the
army's bad boys, the rebels, daredevils, and sometimes the
misfits. We were the young, arrogant soldiers who felt privileged to belong in one of the army's elite fighting units.
Lurps were aggressive eighteen to twenty-five-year-old athletes, perhaps in the best physical condition of their lives.
The Long Range Patrol soldiers were the standouts in the
training classes, the ones who had supreme confidence in
their ability. Lurps were the kind of people who took
chances when others didn't. We were always searching for
ways to separate ourselves from the regular GIs in the army.
The majority of Lurp units in Vietnam were all-airborne
companies. The airborne soldier was by far better disciplined and more highly motivated and physically fit than the
average grunt, which sometimes resulted in a far superior
warrior. All paratroopers had little tolerance for anyone who
was not "airborne." It was a prerequisite to the membership
into their prestigious club and the basis of a very powerful
bond.

For me the Vietnam experience became a game of
knowledge, and knowledge was time. The missions weren't
gauged by time, but by the intensity of the mission.

It didn't take long to realize that my survival depended on
how much I knew. I also understood that good training was
the best insurance for survival. For the first time in my life I

started to pay particular attention to details. I learned how to value concepts such as "efficiency" and "proficiency."

It was also necessary for me to understand the effectiveness of our unit. My curiosity for that knowledge steered me to the company museum, which was conveniently located in the company compound. The museum was a room separate but adjacent to the orderly room. It was a modest twenty-by-twenty-foot gallery filled with mementos from successful raids and ambushes of past missions. War trophies adorned the four walls. Displayed for all eyes to see was shot-up Russian and Chinese web gear, a mangled communist flag, and various small-arms weapons, other ordnance, and booby traps. Displayed about the room were several plaques and pictures, including a few convincing photographs of Uncle Ho's nephews reaching for the sky. If this museum could talk, it would say: "Company F was out there whipping somebody's ass!"

On my first mission I couldn't help but be impressed with my teammates. It was invaluable to watch them work. I got a chance to witness "proficiency" at its finest. They were "professionals" in the truest sense of the word. Every man was totally competent, thoroughly trained, comfortably knowledgeable, and astute in both recognition and reaction. My desire was to be just like them.

I had an unquenchable curiosity to know more about the men who had fought and died while serving in Company F. This curiosity led me to discover the origin of the camp's name, Lindsey-Lattin. Sp4. Daniel H. Lindsey and 1st Lt. John II. Lattin. The names of two brave young soldiers who were the first to die in combat for our company. Their names were chosen for posterity. They were the sons of parents who paid the horrible price of having their sons' names enshrined with honors. The names of these two soldiers were arched high over the threshold of Company F. They served as a constant reminder of the type of gallant men who answered our nation's call. Sp4. Daniel H. Lindsey, Killed In Action December 5, 1967, and 1st Lt. John H. Lattin, Killed In Action December 15, 1967. They both died

with the proud distinction of being "Lurps." They will never
be forgotten.

Company F Lurps did not build a reputation out of luck,
but it was one of the strange attributes that continued to cir-
culate throughout the company and was sometimes deemed
an unspoken phenomenon. It was a common thread shared
by everyone in Company F. We all believed that we were
shrouded in a protective mantle of unbelievable good luck.
Yeah, yeah, anyone can be lucky, but we were quick to
point out that we had phenomenal luck. As for myself, I
stand in testimony to the authenticity of this phenomenon.
Still, an incredible fact remains . . . between the dates of
December 16, 1967, to August 11, 1968, there were no
deaths in the company. We had a lot of Lurps wounded during that eight-month stretch, some of them severely, but
none died. You bet I call that phenomenal. I also acknowledged that efficiency and professionalism are not accidental.
Quite frankly, we had a damn good company!

At the time I arrived at Company F, the racial mix was
approximately 40 percent black and 49 percent white with a
small number of Latino soldiers. And, if you did the math,
you'd discover that the government was involved in a form
of institutionalized genocide. This revelation was my first
discovery into the government's Big Lie. Another Big Lie
was the fairy tales Uncle Sam continued to perpetuate
throughout the history of the war. Such as, "We are fighting
to help the South Vietnamese people to exist without the
threat of communist influence." Or, "We are fighting to
keep America free."

In Vietnam the military mission was never clear. The
fighting forces didn't have the full commitment of our own
political leaders. It didn't take long to realize that thousands
of lives were being lost for the sake of the Big Lie. As a nation and as soldiers, we had been "had."

It's been said numerous times, the Vietnam War was a
different kind of war, and it called for a different kind of

soldier from any other wars. If you were to disregard the caustic personalities of these young Lurp soldiers, you'd quickly find that they were a select group of top-notch volunteers the army conveniently deemed as "expendable." The profile of the men needed to become Lurps, called for tough and exceedingly well-trained, gung-ho soldiers who were sometimes "hard to control." The army would prove that even the most incorrigible of characters could be harnessed into a positive entity when the right reinforcements and motivations are applied.

On the day of my second mission, at 1300 hours, we once again donned our war paint, and the routine of challenging the foe began. We boarded our choppers and headed for the Catcher's Mitt AO. The helicopter flight path had become a familiar route. After only one mission, I remembered the landmarks along the way. Our insertion was clean. That was the good news. The bad news . . . that the nagging premonition was still eating at me. Against my will, my mind started to replay this one song over and over again. The lyrics set the tone for my anxiety. "Danger, heartbreak dead ahead." I couldn't get the Marvelettes song out of my head. It was a song I hadn't heard in a long time, but it was now prevalent in my subconscious mind. "Danger, heartbreak dead ahead."

Once safely away from our landing zone, we worked our way through the always mysterious confines of the jungle. I tried to concentrate on the mission at hand, with no success. I even tried to replace those lyrics with another song, or different kinds of music. It was no use. I wondered what it all meant. "Danger, heartbreak dead ahead." It wasn't going away.

The rugged and steep terrain made the mission all the more difficult. The thick dry underbrush made for slow and noisy movement. We finally reached our ambush site and set up an RON. I was learning my job well. The routine of the missions was becoming second nature. In this business you learned your job fast or chanced putting the team in peril.

*   *   *

Around 1600 hours Mike got a radio message from Tactical Operations Command. He turned to my post with a strange look on his face.

I thought to myself, "What?! Why the hell are you looking at me?" Mike motioned me over to the radio. Instantly, I thought of SFC Barajas. "I'm out of the company," I feared. Mike handed me the handset and the voice on the radio said, "We will be extracting one Edwin L. Emanuel in two-zero minutes, the slicks are on the way." I gave the handset back to Frazier and he continued to talk. They didn't give any other explanation. I couldn't figure out why they would be pulling only me out of the team. We gathered our equipment and the team headed about a klick to the nearest LZ. As a team, we were again put in more danger with the unscheduled extraction. We hugged the tree line inside the landing zone until the ships were inbound. I heard the helicopters in the distance.

"What the hell did I do so wrong to be snatched off a mission like this?" I'm sure everyone on the team was just as puzzled as I was. When the helicopter appeared over the landing zone, I ran out to meet it before it was able to touch down on the ground. I hopped aboard and sat in the doorway. As the ship elevated away from the ground, I watched my team disappear back into the jungle.

The helicopter lifted up into a cloud-filled evening sky. I gazed out at the horizon. My heart was pounding. I tried not to think about what could have gone so horribly wrong. I had never felt so alone.

You know that feeling you get when someone is staring at you. I could sense the door gunner staring at me from over my shoulder. I looked up and shot him a nervous smile. I couldn't see his eyes because of his black helmet shield. He returned a weak nod. It was a long flight back. No matter how hard I fought to free myself from speculations, a hundred scenarios continued to flash through my mind.

Twenty-five minutes later the chopper landed at the company compound. SFC Barajas was already at the helipad gate waiting for me. The helicopter engine shut down to a draining whine. I collected my equipment from the deck of the chopper and hesitantly walked over to Barajas.

"Emanuel, do you have a relative . . . a cousin in Vietnam?" he asked. I knew right away what it was. Something happened to Ricky! My heart began to race. My cousin Ricky Riley was serving with the 1st Marine Division in I Corps.

"Your cousin died five days ago . . . your family and the Red Cross request that you escort his body back to the States." My knees buckled like an anvil had been dropped on my head. Barajas shouldered me to a chain-link fence that separates the company area from the helicopter pad.

"You are on a two-week leave to go home as of now. I'm sorry, son," he said, trying to comfort me from my gut-wrenching grief. I was moved to weep openly. SFC Barajas didn't know that Ricky was my best buddy in the whole world. We had grown up together and Ricky, quite frankly, was one of the funniest and most compassionate people I ever knew. He was a real jokester, a real character, my best friend. And now he was dead!

Ricky Vaughn Riley had been killed in action on June 29, 1968, during a mortar attack by hostile forces while on patrol in Quang Nam Province. He had sustained massive fragmentation wounds to his head and body. Ricky had little more than three weeks in-country. Now, I would be escorting his body home. I never expected my cousin Ricky to die in Vietnam. Anyone else . . . yes, but not Ricky.

His death was an enormous shock to my callow life. It was my first encounter with a death in my family. I loved my cousin very much and there were times when we were practically inseparable. During our high school years we had an unspoken accord that was essential to each other: I had his back, he had mine. Growing up together in Compton, we needed the security of each other. Ricky and I had our share of scrapes and scraps, but we also had indestructible trust and respect for each other. . . . We were best friends.

*   *   *

After I left the helicopter pad, I walked in the general direction of my hootch. I passed PFC Madison Flowers during my indiscriminate drift. I tried to mask my tears as I was too embarrassed to show that I had been crying. I suppose PFC Flowers saw through my charade; my inadequate acting led him to realize something was wrong. I told him what had happened to my cousin and that I was under orders to go home to accompany his body. I asked Flowers to tell Thad and the others that I would be back. I had to come back. I now had a score to settle.

The EM club had just opened for the day. I could hear the nasal twang of country/western music coming from the jukebox. I had an immediate need to get numb in a hurry. I was ready for a few shots of anything . . . straight! I was still dressed in my camouflage fatigues with grease paint on my face and reeked from the pungent scent of freshly applied insect repellent. I bellied up to the empty bar to have my way with a half-quart bottle of Jack Daniel's. The jukebox inside the EM club was filled with those real annoying country songs like "I Want to Go Home" and "Wolverton Mountain." I stood alone at the bar and drank Jack Daniel's until I couldn't take the "shitkickin'" music anymore. While I was still able, I stumbled out of the club toward my hootch, which was about seventy feet away. It was just turning dark as I staggered into the half-dark hootch and crawled onto my bunk. I curled into a ball and wept. Ricky was gone. I'd remembered the very last words I'd spoken to him. "Don't take it easy when you get to Vietnam!" The infamous last words! Ricky and I always said our good-byes to each other followed with, "Take it easy!" Our last words would be different on our last meeting. His death came suddenly, and it was so final. I missed him already. I cried myself to sleep.

The next morning I woke up hoping it was all a bad dream. It wasn't. It was far too real. The realities of the war had now taken a personal toll.

Preparing for my long trip home was just a matter of

stuffing my belongings into a duffel bag. All the other teams in the 2d Platoon hootch were out in the field, so I took the moment to stand in the middle of the empty hootch for one last look. This might be my last time to ever see this place. Who knew for sure! I slammed shut the door to my wall locker and headed for the CQ.

At exactly 0830 hours I was standing before First Sergeant Butts. He was an old soldier who knew the pains of war firsthand. The first sergeant was eminently sympathetic. In his compassion, he treated me like he would his own son. "Top" told me to take as much time at home as I needed.

First Sgt. Walter P. Butts was special to his men. He was unwavering in his convictions as a soldier. He stood up and protected his troops with vigor. We as soldiers knew we could trust "Top." Today I am a better person just having known him. For many years I always wanted to express my appreciation and let him know how much my family valued his thoughtfulness. At the 1998 Ranger Rendezvous (LRRP/Ranger reunion) at Fort Benning, Columbus, Georgia, I finally got a chance to thank 1st Sgt. Walter P. Butts in person.

First Sergeant Butts had a genuine love for his boys, and I'm sure if you ask any of the four hundred plus paratroopers that crossed the threshold of Company F 51st, they would concur. In return, we all loved him back.

My orders were already cut and a jeep was waiting outside the CQ ready to take me to Tan Son Nhut Airport. I said my random good-byes and took off for the airport. During the lonely ride to the airport, I thought about my team still in the field. I had become very attached to them in such a short period of time. I knew they would understand my leaving them.

I was booked on a direct flight to San Francisco International Airport. My destination was in the Bay Area, a small Marine base called Treasure Island. Among other things,

Treasure Island was used as a holding station for deceased Marines being shipped stateside from Vietnam.

My trip home was bittersweet. I was glad to be going home, but not that way. I would have given anything to talk to my cousin again. I thought about my aunt Eloise, Ricky's mother. The news must have destroyed her. Ricky was her youngest baby. She was crazy about Ricky, as we all were. Ricky was always the life of the party. He was the type of person who could fill a room with laughter. Ricky was only eighteen years old when he died. He stood a proud six-foot-six and weighed 230 pounds. He was a man-child. Ricky wanted so badly to be a good Marine. Surely he had been a courageous Marine.

In one day my whole life had changed, and I felt older than my years. In the course of a person's life we are all confronted with situations such as this. This was unquestionably one of the most defining moments of my life. I had come to realize I wasn't a kid anymore, I was suddenly growing into an adult. The growing pangs were just another opportunity to take more serious stock in my own mortality.

One of my revelations was that the U.S. Army spent a lot of time and money to make our little group of Lurps feel as though we were invincible. At nineteen and twenty years old, we believed the hype.

I questioned my cousin's reason for dying in Vietnam. Did he die for the adventure of fighting for his country in a war, or did he die because he had really swallowed the propaganda crap, "The Big Lie"? Did he really believe in the reason he was fighting? Out of my selfishness, I say, no matter the reason, the price couldn't begin to pay for the life of my cousin, Ricky Vaughn Riley.

It felt strange to be boarding a commercial jet headed for home so soon. The smiling faces of the flight attendants were a bona fide indication that I was going back to the World. Halfway through the flight I took a few of the little pink pills inside Darvon capsules and downed them with my complimentary beverage. Within the hour I was out cold. The flight home was a blur. I remember waking up only to eat and go to the restroom. I slept halfway around the world to forget the reason I was flying.

Yeah, I was depressed, but I wasn't nearly as depressed as I was pissed off that Ricky was dead.

After I woke from an eighteen-hour stupor, the jetliner touched down to the chill of San Francisco in early July. Violent winds heaved punishing arctic air across the Pacific Ocean. It was an extreme contrast in weather conditions. My summer khaki uniform was no match for the cold.

The processing had begun; checking in, signing papers, getting fitted for this and that. The U.S. Army machinery went to a lot of trouble to make me look like a real paratrooper for Ricky's funeral. They decked me out in an army "dress green" uniform, Corcoran jump boots, and instead of a tie I wore an infantry-blue ascot. They even "okayed" me wearing the "unauthorized" Ranger black beret. I was the best-looking paratrooper on the whole damn island, not to mention that I was the only paratrooper on the island.

Meanwhile, I had to live among the jarheads in their barracks on Treasure Island. I was assigned to a holding barracks with about forty other Marines who were waiting to be shipped to different parts of the globe. Most of the Marines in the overcrowded barracks were on their way to the Republic of Vietnam as replacements.

During my brief stay I took an occasional earful of catcalls administered by the Marine residents, sometimes in jest and other times, just because. I did my best to keep my temper in check and go along with the harmless jokes, but I was not to be intimidated.

The second day on the island, I walked between a group of jarheads who were congregating and blocking the entryway leading into the barracks.

"Well, lookit here!" a husky redneck Marine corporal announced as I tried to slide by unnoticed.

"A soldier boy wearing a cute little black beret!" he said, snatching the beret off my head. I figured this little scene could really get ugly fast. So before we puffed up and compared testosterone count, I explained to the Marine that we were all on the same team, except for the fact he was a "fucking leg!" I further deciphered for the Gomer that a "leg" is anyone who isn't "airborne," pointing to the jump wings on my chest.

"Hell, boy, didn't you know, the only thing that falls from the sky is birdshit and fools?" It was a big joke to all of his Marine buddies. I snatched my beret from his grip and went into the barracks and lay on my bunk. I figured at any moment a good fistfight would be in order. A couple of minutes passed, and the thick-necked Marine showed up standing over me. He hesitated a moment, then offered his hand in apology. I sat up and we shook hands.

"Hey, uhmm, I didn't mean anything. . . . I was just trying to get you to talk. You haven't said a word since you've been here. Listen, my name is Bayer, Corporal Bayer, but people around here call me 'The Bear.' These guys are in my squad and we're waiting to be shipped to the Nam. Shit, we're going fuckin' nuts in this place just sittin' around here and waitin'. Hell, the war will be over by the time they ship us over there!" After he got started, I couldn't stop the Marine corporal from talking my ear off if I'd tried. Turns out, the compunctious Marine was a pretty decent person, he just wanted to have a little fun at my expense but found out I wasn't in the mood. I guess he, like everyone else, was curious why an army soldier was lodging at a Marine base.

I told him about my cousin who had fought and died with the 1st Marine Division. The group of Marines was probably even more curious after learning I had just left the jungles of Vietnam. They continued to joke and rag me about my camouflage jungle fatigues, the likes of which some of them had never seen before. My attire had become an unavoidable subject. The topic gave me a chance to tell the Marines about Lurps in Vietnam, which I was more than happy to do. We chatted and argued endlessly about the history of the war and other things just as stupid.

The evening reveille sounded. The Bear and I stood at attention shoulder to shoulder and saluted Old Glory being lowered. Dinner chow was being served. Corporal Bayer

offered to buy me a beer at the EM club, but I was more interested in a burger, fries, and a thick chocolate shake, anything
but military chow. We walked to the nearest off-base water-
ing hole to eat and awaited the arrival of his buddies. About
an hour later the Marines landed. That night we instituted
what became now and forever the "Pre-Vietnam Drinkfest."
I had never drank so much beer in my life. We guzzled
brewskies until it got sloppy. We had a good time comparing
army and Marine screwups and telling awful "Johnny
Gross" jokes. By the time we closed the place down, we had
empty beer pitchers lined from one end of the table to the
next. That night I remember driving the porcelain bus home.
But even a good hangover must come to an end.

It took three days of processing before they would release Ricky to my possession. On the third morning I got orders to dress in a Class A uniform and depart for Los
Angeles International Airport. I was transported to the flight
line, where I stood and watched the flight crewmen load
Ricky's flag-draped container onto the aircraft. Three other
Marine crates were being shipped home unceremoniously,
and no one was there to attend them. It was small consola-
tion, but I locked my heels and saluted them as they loaded
the deceased Marines into the airplane's cargo bay.

It was afternoon when I arrived at LAX. I found my aunt
Eloise and my cousin Joyce at the airport searching for me. I
had mixed emotions; I didn't know whether to be happy or
be sad. It felt appropriate not to articulate either. It was a
difficult time for our family. Ricky's death seemed to bring
my family closer together, as deaths in large families sometimes will. I have always thought of Ricky as my brother
rather than my cousin, but in reality we represented a generation of first cousins and relatives removed from Shreve-
port, Louisiana, our mothers' birthplace. My mother Willie
Mae and his mother Eloise Shelton were sisters.

The twenty-five-minute drive home from the airport was
somber. Aunt Eloise remained strong as she tried to conceal

her emotions behind her fashionably stylish sunglasses. She drove faster than usual, wheeling the big blue Lincoln Continental onto the Los Angeles street traffic and freeways. That 1966 Lincoln was my favorite car to drive when I did small chores for her popular paint and body shop.

During the drive home Eloise entertained us with an occasional humorous quip. Other than that, there was not much conversation. I spent most of the ride home looking out the window and scanning familiar areas. I'd left Compton less than a month ago. It seemed so empty now. Most of my buddies were either in the military, in Vietnam, or dead as a result of Vietnam.

I knew it was not going to be easy not to think about the war now that I was home. The war and all the ill effects of the war were still fresh in my memory. When I was in Vietnam, I thought about home, and now that I was back home I thought about nothing but going back to Vietnam. It was hard to shake the idea that I would be sentenced to go back to the Nam in just a couple of weeks.

I had the feeling Eloise wanted to ask questions about Vietnam, but I could tell she was unsure if she really wanted to pursue it. I wanted to break the ice and tell her the story about the "song" that had entrenched itself into my mind on that dreadful day. But I just couldn't bring myself to talk about the unpleasant premonition. I rode home quietly immersed in my own inner hell.

"Danger, heartbreak, dead ahead." The mystery was over: "Danger" was the mission, "heartbreak" was Ricky, and "dead ahead" was his death. I would never share that premonition with my aunt Eloise. It seemed so futile at the time.

That afternoon as we pulled into the driveway, family members and school friends were waiting at the house to greet me. I learned the plans for Ricky's funeral. The following Tuesday at 10 A.M., with full military honors, Ricky would have his final day.

I absolutely dreaded any notion of going to the funeral home. I knew I wasn't ready to see my cousin lying inside a box, nor was I ready to accept the fact that he was really dead. I had secretly hoped the Marine Corps had made some lame mistake and Ricky was still alive, running around Vietnam unaware he was supposed to be dead. But that was not to be. I was there when the funeral director uncrated the box and opened the casket. If I had to describe that exact moment . . . it was like taking a hard punch in the face when I first saw Ricky lying there. I became violently ill to my stomach and experienced heat flashes and nausea.

Poor Ricky, he appeared as though he was just resting. Somehow the whole thing just didn't seem real. I stared at my cousin's mangled body, wondering what his last thoughts were and hoping he hadn't suffered. I wanted to reach in and touch him, but Ricky was encased in a Plexiglas-top casket that prevented anyone from making physical contact with him. The fatal mortar round had apparently exploded extremely close to his position. His upper torso was a lot smaller than I remembered. His body appeared broken up and distorted from the concussion blast. The Marine Corps had done a good job patching him up and making him presentable for an open casket funeral. His face was spotted with thick patches of makeup where the mortician had tried to hide the spray of shrapnel that hit him in the head. I never learned if Ricky died instantly or not, but he couldn't possibly have lived for long in that condition. Maybe he didn't suffer at all.

I found myself completely oblivious to anyone or anything going on in the room. As I stood over the casket staring at Ricky . . . I flashed on the last time I saw him alive. He had come home on leave dressed in his dress blue uniform. He looked so impressive as he swaggered around with his tall statuesque build, proud to be a Marine. The Marine Corps had turned Ricky into a different person. He wasn't the same funny, full of jokes "Ricky" I had known for so many years. I also got the feeling from some of his random remarks that he knew things were never going to be the same again after the war. In our last meeting together, Ricky kept saying to me, "If something happens to me, remember I love you." I could only remind him that we were both coming home alive to start our Corvette car club. I don't think he believed me.

Suddenly I had a terrible urge to leave. I walked out of the funeral home never to return, and never to view my cousin lying there again.

For the time being at least, I had made my final peace with Ricky's death. I knew I would never forget those moments in time that made our growing up together so wonderful. I still miss him today.

Time went by fast while I was on leave. I could feel my days of freedom dwindling minute by minute. I found myself absorbed in a thirst for life like there was no tomorrow. To amuse myself, I made a concerted effort to hit the same nightclubs Ricky and I used to hang out in when we were running the streets of Los Angeles. I visited the trendy LA party spots like Maverick Flats, Marty's on the Hill, and, with the help of my uniform, I was able to sneak into the Lighthouse, a really hip jazz nightclub.

No matter what I did to entertain myself, I felt a sense of restlessness and abandonment. Caged deep inside me was constant anxiety. Life wasn't the same without Ricky there playing his jokes and coming up with some wisecrack to make me laugh. I found myself becoming withdrawn and way too serious about life in general. It became increasingly difficult to have fun.

On the day of the funeral the sun darted in and out of the puffy cumulus cloud cover. I was one of the honor guards standing sentry over the proceedings. We were called to attention. I had to work rigorously to fight back my tears. I knew I had to be in control of my emotions, as it wouldn't look very prudent for a paratrooper to cry in formation. I glanced over at the audience and saw my family members and friends weeping. It hurt me to watch my relatives suffering so.

The military proceedings concluded with three salvos of gunfire and the playing of taps. I watched Aunt Eloise fight back tears as the Marine officers approached her. It was unfortunate, the only tangible items she had to show for the life of her son were a bunch of pictures and the folded military flag she was presented with the day of the funeral.

After we returned home from the awfully depressing funeral service, Eloise revealed to me that she'd wanted to punch the Marine major when he handed her the flag. Who can blame her? The Marine Corps got her son killed in a pointless war. I'm surprised she didn't get in a shot or two.

Ricky's maternal brother Albert "June," who was two years older than the both of us, was becoming more volatile with his drinking and combative antics during this period. Albert June started on a 151 rum–drinking binge, which led to him getting into fistfights and other mischievous deeds. He was on a collision course to self-destruct. I had seen June pull stupid pranks before, but never with such aggressive behavior. It was probably his way of grieving and dealing with the death of his brother. I tried to spend more time with Albert June to show him he wasn't alone with his grief. But nothing I did helped, he was out of control. His bizarre misconduct convinced him to start carrying a pistol. I usually saw the gun when he was in a threatening or aggressive posture. He'd flash his little piece of shit "Saturday night special" every chance he got. I knew it was just a matter of time before his erratic and irresponsible actions would catch up with him. I had to take the position of avoidance. And the more I tried to avoid him, the worse he'd become. At times I even feared for my life.

One day Albert June snuck up behind me and put me in a compromising choke hold. He began choking off my breathing. The more I moved, the tighter he'd squeeze. In between gasping for air, I calmly informed him that if he didn't let me go, this would become a fight to the finish . . . his finish! Like his brother, Albert June was also an impressive figure. He was a lean six-feet-two and weighed 190 to 200 pounds. Even though Albert June was my cousin, there was absolutely no doubt in my mind what I would do to protect my life. Albert June understood the seriousness of my convictions and finally let go of me.

A couple of years passed, and Albert June persisted with his menacing lifestyle. One day he made a costly mistake. After he had moved to Seattle, Washington, he got involved in a physical altercation with one of his neighbors. Albert June chased his fleeing neighbor into his home to kick his ass. Well, that turned out to be the last time he'd pull a stunt like that. His neighbor unloaded on him with a waiting shotgun, hitting June in the chest. Albert June died instantly. Albert June Riley was not a bad person, and I defy anyone who says otherwise. But I believe Albert June sealed his violent fate the day his brother died in Vietnam. Ricky's death affected a generation of people.

I was getting pretty good at staying home and away from the army. It became more and more difficult to entertain leaving the comforts of home to go back across the ocean to fight a war again. I remembered that First Sergeant Butts had told me to take as long as I needed. I needed another week. I needed to bond with my family longer, just in case I didn't make it home alive. We never talked about the war at home, and I never told anyone in my family what I was doing in Vietnam. They only knew I was fighting.

During my short leave I spent time trying to make brownie points with Wanda Burton, my then "future ex-wife" whom I was almost dating. I had taken Wanda to her high school prom before I left for Vietnam. While I was home on leave I made sure to visit her often. I suppose I was looking to get an inkling of support or affection from her.

From the beginning of time, every soldier who ever fought in a war needed someone he could hold on to. He needed someone to write to, to find a mutual connection. Wanda was that person for me. Unfortunately, she didn't think so. Wanda was attractive with a great body, and if that weren't enough, she was smart with an enthusiastic ambition to do something important with her life. She had plans to conquer the world after receiving her master's degree from the University of Southern California. I admired her drive and ambition. Wanda had a serious no-nonsense personality. In other words, she was a tough cookie and I was getting nowhere fast. Wanda had a profound way of keeping me guessing. I couldn't figure her out.

On one particular visit I spent most of the day being treated like I didn't exist. That night after leaving her house, I drove to a public telephone booth and made a call to Dena Simpson to let her know I was in the area. Dena was Ricky's high school ex-girlfriend and one of my good friends as well. Ricky had a knack for finding and dating the most beautiful girls. He also encouraged me to do the same because, as he explained, "Beautiful women need love, too."

I'd borrowed Eloise's new Lincoln Continental, and Dena and I decided to go for a long drive along the coast. We reminisced and laughed for hours about classic Ricky stories and shenanigans. Memories of Ricky had become a big part of both of our lives and seemed to have created a genuine and intense bond between us.

I will never be able to explain exactly how it happened, but one thing led to another and we ended up spending that night together at a hotel. We made the most beautiful love I had ever experienced in my young life. To this day, nothing else has compared. We held each other tight and wept uncontrollably the whole time we were absorbed in the act of passion and profound lovemaking. That night, my life's journey had led me to understand what God intended when he conceived the "union" between man and woman.

The night ended much too soon. We took the coastal route back home. The sun rising on the ocean revealed a glimmering a new day. We had no real need for words. I felt an unspoken love and true fondness for Dena. She looked into my eyes and gently clutched my hand, squeezing it with affection. Our time together was euphoric. I will cherish those moments forever with no regrets, no remorse, and no guilt. Somehow, I believe I've been chasing that feeling

ever since. Dena Simpson left only pleasant memories in
my heart.

After that night I never saw her or heard from Dena
again. I guess it was our quiet way of saying good-bye and
moving on with our individual lives.

Nonetheless, my hunt for true love was put on hold. I
was due back in Vietnam and already a week late. Before I
left the States, Wanda and I agreed to write each other when
I got back to the Nam.

CHAPTER FOUR

Okay Charlie . . . Here I Come!

In late July, duty called. I was aboard a commercial plane headed back to South Vietnam. This time I was determined more than ever to finish my tour and come home alive. The heartbreak my family suffered because of Ricky's death was more than I could bear. I didn't want to add to their pain.

During the long plane ride back to Vietnam, I was seated next to a group of GIs who were taking turns reading each other's palms. Perhaps it was for the sheer pleasure of entertaining themselves or maybe it was an attempt to convince themselves of their own immortality while serving in Vietnam. I couldn't help but notice the few who walked away from the readings upset and disappointed. Maybe they had gotten bad news or perhaps they didn't agree with the interpretations. It only made me more curious. I asked the group to take a gander at my palm and forecast my future. I'm not sure if it really mattered what was predicted, I always knew my fate was in the hands of God. I just needed to partake in some healthy banter to get my mind off my immediate problems. In my readings I was advised that I had a long lifeline and didn't have anything to worry about. The interpretation was a comforting thought for the moment. . . .

The exhausting flight back to Vietnam gave me time to finish up a letter to Wanda and her brother, Gerald Burton. Gerald was one of my closet friends. He had plans to marry my sister after his Vietnam tour was completed. I had much sympathy for him. Gerald was also in the Marine Corps and an intricate part of our small group of friends. He and I went to rival high schools, but we all took the pledge to join the military at the same time. The little circle of friends included George Wallace, Jr., who was fighting in the Central Highlands with 173d Airborne Brigade. George wrote me after hearing of Ricky's death. He mentioned in a letter that his unit was moving into Dak To Province. I knew from the *Stars and Stripes* newspaper that Dak To was crawling with large enemy forces primed for battle. After attending the funeral of my cousin, our bond as a group grew stronger. I worried for the safety of Gerald and George. I prayed for them often. Our small group had dwindled by one, and it would have hurt pretty badly if our group had gotten any smaller. We had big plans after the war. "All" would return home . . . in one piece and "all" would buy Corvettes and name the car club The Vette Set. For me it "all" fell apart when Ricky couldn't make the membership. Everything changed. I looked at life and death differently, and my values changed along with my ambition in the military. Nothing became more important than getting in a few licks and going home alive and in one piece.

I owed it to the guys to let them know where I was, how I was doing in Vietnam. And I expected the same from them. I also expected to get the types of letters both Gerald and George sent me, warning me against doing something stupid like getting back at Charlie out of revenge for Ricky's death.

The jetliner landed at Tan Son Nhut Airport. I was back in the war again. Around 0930 hours I arrived at Company F. The early morning weather was dreary and overcast. The unforgettable scent of jet fuel oil coupled with the foul smell of burning human feces still conjure a strong recollection. The artillery company next door was launching a fire mission, and that also reinforced the reality that I was back in the war.

The first person to greet me was First Sergeant Butts. With genuine compassion, he welcomed me back into the company. He actually made me feel like I was home again.

"Top" never said a word about me returning late. He filled me in on the changes that had occurred while I had been away. Sergeant Barajas had DEROSed (Date of Estimated Return from Overseas) and my team leader Mike Frazier was back in the States on leave. Mike had signed up for another tour and would return within a month. I was quite relieved to learn that no one in the company had died while I was away.

After the usual paperwork and orientation, I was instructed by First Sergeant Butts to get a haircut and report to my new team leader. While home on leave I'd let my hair grow into a small "afro." First Sergeant Butts believed if you were in the military, especially in his company, hair should be worn tight to the scalp. Although I didn't always agree with him on the hair situation, those were his rules. No arguments! First Sergeant Butts himself had a clean, close cut at all times.

There were a few new faces in the company. But it was a good feeling to see all my ol' buddies again. I was assigned to a new team, Team 2-3. Sgt. Seferino R. Alvarado would now assume the duties as my fearless leader. I knew Alvarado by reputation only. He was a tough, scrappy soldier with a lot of combat experience. When you were new in the Lurp game, it meant a lot to have a competent and knowledgeable team leader. Sergeant Alvarado was as good as they come. Like Mike Frazier, he wore a Recondo patch on his shirt pocket. Those who wore the Recondo "V" insignia seemed to be the superior warriors out in the field. I had a tendency to look up to them.

After a few days I settled into the routine. I was amazed at how quickly I was able to get back into the flow of things. My first morning back in Vietnam, I found myself waking up to the familiar call of "Goooooood Morning Vietnam!" The Armed Forces Radio disc jockeys felt a need to entertain the troops in Vietnam with a cheerful beginning to the day. The "goooooood morning" commentary was for those "REMF" (rear echelon motherfuckers) who didn't have to go to the boonies and fight the war. Each morning that we had to listen to that noise, other Lurps and I routinely responded to the expression with a loud and vocal chorus of "Kiss my ass!" Yeah, it was easy for those REMF to have a good morning, they didn't have to face Charlie. Personally, I could have done without the animated commentaries.

However, the radio comedy episodes of "Chicken Man! . . . He's everywhere! He's everywhere!" became our entertainment while we lay in our bunks late at night.

It didn't take long before our team got a warning order for a mission. I joined PFC Thad Givins, Sp4. Ellis Gates, Sp4. Norman Reid, and Sp4. Miles Stevens at the supply bunker to draw gear for my first mission back. This time out I wanted to rethink my field weaponry. We were granted permission to pick our weapons. I elected to carry a brand-new M-60 machine gun, which was passionately referred to as the "big gun." I knew I would have to lug more weight into the field, but it was a fair exchange for the security of the team having the "big gun" spitting at the enemy if we got into a heavy firefight. I was a big fan of fragmentation hand grenades. As a rule, on any given mission I carried no less than a dozen hand grenades, sometimes up to twenty-four. It was Sergeant Alvarado who revealed to me, in an off-the-cuff conversation, . . . if he were in a firefight for his life, he would expend all but one of his grenades. That last grenade was just in case he was about to be captured. It would be his little surprise for Charlie. It was Sergeant Alvarado who also impressed upon me, "No matter what happens, Lurps do not get captured!" It was this type of attitude that had the enemy scared to death of the hard-ass Lurps.

The early morning briefings were the same as always, too early! We learned the purpose of our mission. G-2 reported unusually heavy night movement in our recon area. A couple of days before, the territory we were now entering had been saturated by B-52 strikes, the code name for these missions being Arc Light. Our team was called on to conduct a BDA, or "hot pursuit mission," which simply means "bomb damage assessment." This would be my first "bomb count" mission. I was excited to witness the kind of destruction the U.S. military forces could execute from the air.

At 0830 hours we were in the air and under way. The chopper flew high over the AO. I marveled at the eight-mile stretch of deep bomb craters that mutated into hundreds of individual pools lining the river. The tortured landscape was stripped of its natural beauty. Because of the rising water and heavy rainfall after the air strike, each bomb crater was overflowing with water.

This would be no normal insertion. In the briefing we were instructed to hold our position on the LZ until it was appropriate to move out. In a normal situation the team would sprint from the helicopter into the tree line and take cover. This time, because of the damage to the jungle floor caused by the B-52 strikes, that changed the entire picture of the landing zone.

The helicopter charged in hard and hovered five feet off the ground in between the bomb craters. Three team members went out the port door and Gates and I exited the starboard door. Before I'd realized what had happened, I was sinking to the bottom of a ten-foot-deep bomb crater filled with water. I was carrying close to 120 pounds of gear strapped to my body. My M-60 machine gun and the thousand rounds of ammo helped me sink to the bottom even faster. I remembered thinking as I slipped downward, "Oh my God, I'm drowning! Nobody knows where I am!" I also knew that in Vietnam it was always a safe bet to save your own ass when you were in trouble or you would die.

As incredible as it sounds, with all my gear intact and still strapped to my body, I went into a crouch position and with all the strength I could muster sprang upward to the surface and grabbed a branch that was hanging over the edge of the crater. I silently pleaded, "Please don't break! Please don't break!" It didn't. I began hoisting myself out of the bomb crater. When I reached the surface, I took a life-saving gasp for air only to swallow a lot of water and red ants. That's when I discovered that the branch I had latched

on to was entirely covered with millions and millions of red
ants, "fire ants" they were called. The ants obviously clumped
together on the branch for refuge to keep themselves from
drowning.

When I began pulling myself farther out of the crater, a
heavy cluster of ants broke away from the branch and hit me
square in the face. The millions of ants were immediately all
over me. I couldn't breathe, they crawled in my nose, eyes,
ears, hair, down my fatigue shirt and pants. Each and every
one of them took their individual turns biting and chewing
on me. The rest of the team was still on the ground where
the helicopter had dropped us off. Everyone was up to his
waist in water, hiding among the shrubbery. When I finally
pulled myself completely out of the hole, I began stripping
off my equipment and clothes with extreme urgency! The
team saw that I was in distress and came to my aid, hosing
me down with their bottles of insect repellent. The ant bites
left huge bumps and lumps all over my face, neck, and
body. The pain was excruciating. Even though I looked a
mess, it wasn't bad enough for us to scrub the mission. The
thought probably never crossed anyone's mind . . . but it did
cross mine.

We worked our way off the LZ and trudged through the
knee-deep water along the river's edge. We were in constant
pursuit of a dry spot to rest or set up a night perimeter. We
finally came upon a burned out base camp that had been
used as a weapons factory. We found a stockpile of old U.S.
ordnance that hadn't exploded during the B-52 air strike.
Charlie developed clever ways of using discarded ordnance
or anything else we didn't use, against us. Explosives inside
bombs were pulled out and planted elsewhere as booby
traps. We took particular pleasure in blowing up the remaining bunkers and ordnance and anything else we were able to
stuff with C-4 explosive.

Outside the tree line, the AO had areas where we could
stand and see for miles in every direction. We felt secure
moving from bunker to bunker. The bunkers were posi-

tioned out in the open rice paddies. If Charlie was hiding among one of these small fortresses, he would need scuba gear to move around. After further investigation, we found what turned out to be an elaborate underground tunnel network with chambers that intersected and connected to the aboveground bunker complex. These bunkers were designed to harbor and conceal LZ watchers. When a helicopter flew into one of these landing zones, the pilot would be fooled into thinking the bunkers were only anthills. Helicopters flying in would come under intense crossfire that sometimes resulted in the demise of the helicopters, the pilots, their crew, and the Lurp teams. We made sure these death-dealing bunkers were blown completely off the face of the map. Even if Charlie tried, he would have a damn difficult time rebuilding his fortresses.

Daylight slowly slipped away, and before we realized it, time had disappeared. We still had the ongoing problem of finding a RON. We found a dry mound along the river that served as a dike separating the river from the bordering rice field. There was no need to put out claymore mines because they would have been positioned too close to the team perimeter. Anyway, Charlie would have to swim to get to our position.

When night fell, the river started to rise. The higher the water rose, the tighter we huddled together on what was now about four by two feet of dry earth. By morning we were all soaking in about a foot and a half of water. My skin had turned into a wrinkled prune from sitting in water all night. We spent the better part of four days trying to escape the rising water.

Around 0930 hours on the fourth day, we got the call to pack up and prepare for an extraction. Somebody back at TOC at least had the common sense to get us out of there a day early before somebody drowned.

When we returned to the compound, we learned to our surprise that the entire company was preparing to move to the province of Cu Chi. Pronounced as it is spelled, in any language it spelled "bad news." Cu Chi Province bordered

Cambodia. It was a well-known stronghold for NVA soldiers moving through the safe zone from North Vietnam down through Cambodia and Laos, then infiltrating into the vicinity of Bien Hoa and Saigon.

One evening just before chow, we stood in company formation. In the course of the company commander's speech, he estimated that only two-thirds of the company's 150 Lurps would be returning from this operation. The rest of us would die or get wounded in the area called Hobo Woods. I had hoped this ghastly information that reverberated down throughout the ranks was just a ploy to put the troops on their toes.

That night the EM club and NCO club were full of drunken GIs. Small groups of fights broke out all over the compound. In Company F, getting drunk and fighting was a way of life. It was our way of blowing off steam. And if you couldn't hold your own around these knuckleheads, then you'd better get out of Dodge. But this brouhaha was different from the usual uproars. I knew things were getting out of hand when someone fired an AK-47 thirty-round magazine clip into the air on full automatic. The Company F overlords popped a few tear gas grenades in the compound to try and get the troops under control. That only created more chaos. They shut down the EM and NCO clubs early to stop the rampaging Lurps from drinking. However, that didn't help either. Everyone usually kept a bottle of liquor in their footlocker.

The party lasted until early morning. I've often wondered what was the proper way to react to the news that a good number of us were slated to die. It was more than enough pressure for any young soldier to endure.

The next morning at 0600 hours, First Sergeant Butts called a mandatory formation. It was highly unusual to take the long walk to the company formation area that early in the morning unless it was something serious. We assembled in a ragged formation. First Sergeant Butts paced back and forth, pausing long enough to inspect the battered and the bruised. Just about everyone in formation was swaying back and forth like palm trees blowing in the breeze. We could tell Butts was pissed.

"I have had enough of this high school bullshit!" Butts shouted. "I want you to know the very next time we have another incident like this, I will tear down that NCO and the EM club and build fucking churches in their places. Let this be your first and final warning! Now, get the hell out of here!"

First Sergeant Butts gave us a lengthier than usual ass chewin' that morning. I felt like a little kid getting a tongue-lashing from dad. He really wanted us to get the message that he wasn't pleased with our self-control and conduct. Butts finally turned and walked into the CQ office. One by one we broke formation and headed back to our barracks to sleep off the effects of the night before. After that morning, everyone stepped lightly around First Sergeant Butts for a while.

The army teaches you to pack and move on a moment's notice. The departure for Cu Chi was just a matter of stuffing all our belongings into a duffel bag. Because the entire country of Vietnam was a combat zone, we all wore our full web gear and hand carried our rifles. A squadron of Chinook helicopters soon lined up to transport us to our new home.

Our arrival at the new company area was much to our dismay. We stumbled into a dilapidated, rickety old base camp that had been left abandoned. Most of the hootches were leaning in different directions and barely standing on their own. It was a far cry from what we were used to back at Company F. The good news was, at least they weren't tents. The one thing that really caught our attention at the new camp was the B-52 bombing going on miles outside of the military installation. The B-52 strikes sounded and felt like a major California earthquake. It must have been a horrible feeling for the enemy to get caught in an air strike just before the lights go out. The ground shook violently and the thunderous noise was beyond terror even from a distance. The Arc Light strike was many miles away, but it felt like it was just outside the perimeter of the berm.

We were warned constantly to be on the alert for sapper suicide squads that had successfully penetrated the compound prior to our arrival. Sappers had been known to get past the fortifications of concertina wire and barbed wire. They were even able to get past the defensive land mines and sentries to detonate highly explosive satchel charges on strategic military sites and military personnel. While we were in the Cu Chi base camp area, we found ourselves sleeping with one eye open, which made our stay there a little uneasy and certainly unpredictable.

One evening after chow a ten-foot cobra snake made the mistake of crawling into the middle of the compound. The almost defenseless reptile incited unlimited assaults from the pistol-packing brigade. At first only a few Lurps took part in the target practice, but as others gathered, it became an all-out shooting gallery. It seemed that anyone who owned a pistol was out there firing on the pitiful snake. I watched the enjoyment in the soldiers' eyes as they fired repeatedly. Their contagious frustrations had now taken the form of a pistol. The snake was blown into several parts as it was riddled full of holes. The war had sunk to a new low.

The new AO was anything but disappointing, and it didn't take long for the shit to hit the fan. Almost every team inserted into the field made contact. The reports were right on the money, and the weather conditions were the same as at the old AO . . . extremely hot. The teams were making contact and bringing "pee" on the enemy strongholds. Some of the older guys who had been in-country longer were familiar with the type of terrain and conditions in the new area. Most of them had fought there before. Instead of fighting in triple canopy jungles, we were now watching canals and waterways, sometimes with very little or no cover and concealment.

Time after time the teams brought back their kills for

confirmed body counts. The documents collected from the enemy victims proved that we were making an impact in that region.

Somehow the enemy found out that Company F was operating in their area. Rumor had it, a very high price was being offered for the capture of a Company F Lurp team or any of its members. Wanted posters were positioned throughout the region for our capture. Again, we were a thorn in the asses of the communists.

Without any success, the enemy worked unrelentingly to figure out ways to neutralize our teams. Like in the Catcher's Mitt AO, we were effectively doing our jobs. The flip side of the coin was that the war was taking a toll on U.S. military personnel. The MASH hospital was receiving an overflow of wounded Lurps and helicopter pilots from Company F 51st.

In mid-August, I finally got a chance to meet up with Sgt. Jerry Brock, who had been away on a thirty-day leave. I had heard many great stories about his bravery. I respected him to the point that I was almost nervous about meeting him. Brock was only nineteen years old, but from what I understood he was an outstanding soldier. He was one of my real homeboys from California, hailing from the San Fernando Valley in Los Angeles. The scuttlebutt on Jerry Brock was, he had extended for another six months and was looking to put together a team of his own.

The first time I met Jerry, I personally let him know I was interested in working on his new team. Brock had an outstanding reputation as a smart leader. He was tough and paid attention to details. He wore the Recondo "V" patch like all the other team leaders in the company. He and I hit it off right away. We were able to talk about the same high schools, and we even knew some of the same girls. For us that was a helluva connection so far away from home.

After seeing Jerry Brock sporting his Recondo School "V" badge, I began asking questions, such as "How and when can I get into this Recondo School program?" I was

soon enlightened by those who knew. I would have to be in-
country more than six months before I could even be considered to go to the MACV (Military Assistance Command,
Vietnam) Special Forces "Recondo" School in Nha Trang,
Vietnam. That is, of course, if I lived that long. That policy
hadn't always applied; it gradually came into effect because
entry into the school became more demanding. I was also
informed that I would have to be picked by a superior, and
only if I showed leadership skills and ability. Hey, my mind
was made up, I was going to earn a "Recondo" patch.
Everyone I met in Vietnam who wore the Recondo "V" radiated supreme confidence, and I wanted to feel what I saw
in them.

I'd heard through the grapevine that Sergeant Brock and
the company commander, Lieutenant Colonel Zummo,
were occasional drinking buddies. The history between the
two seemed to have developed into mutual admiration and a
real friendship. I'd also heard that the colonel got Brock and
his team out of a lot of heavy shit out in the boonies, and
that Brock was eternally grateful.

After Brock returned from his leave, he and the colonel
went on another one of their notorious drinking binges.
Sergeant Brock asked Zummo if he would be allowed to
pick the members of his new team. Brock read a list of
names; Ellis Gates, five-feet-seven inches of smiling,
happy-go-lucky kid from Pennsylvania. Gates would become the team radiotelephone operator and sometimes point
man. Norman Reid, a hard-ass, streetwise New Yorker from
the Brooklyn area. Norman was drafted into the service but
volunteered to be a Lurp. He was about five years older than
the rest of us. Brock appointed him assistant team leader.
Thomas Mattox, a farm boy from Georgia, son of a share-
cropper, appointed rifleman because of his accuracy with
the M-16 rifle. Lawton Mackey, the youngest and newest
member to arrive in the company. Mackey was also from
the South, South Carolina to be exact. Mackey always knew
the right things to say when our spirits were low. He, too,

was appointed team rifleman. And then there was myself, Edwin L. Emanuel, *boo coo dinky dow* (very crazy) for being there in the first place. At nineteen years old, I appeared very unassuming, but certainly not afraid of a good fight "on or off" the battlefield. Brock made sure I carried the M-60 machine gun because of my size and because I knew the weapon like the back of my hand. I couldn't have been happier with his decisions.

By coincidence or perhaps by design, we all happened to be black or African-Americans or, as they called us in Vietnam, "soul brothers." I want to go on record saying I despised being called "soul brother" because of the stereotypical connotations associated with the name. Nonetheless, we were a collection of different soldiers with the same background, the same problems, and pretty much the same attitudes.

"All soul brothers, huh?" the colonel questioned Brock. "The Soul Patrol. We'll call them the Soul Patrol," he declared, never realizing we were the first of its kind in the Vietnam War or any other war for that matter. An all-black special operations Lurp team. The Soul Patrol! And so the dubious name stuck. Soon after, the bond of brotherhood was sealed.

It was obvious that Zummo had taken a professional liking to the clever buck sergeant. That turned out to be one of the advantages of being on Brock's team. When Brock called for assistance out in the boonies, his calls got the attention of Lieutenant Colonel Zummo. As we had a good team leader and we were all experienced veterans of the war, we felt pretty good about our chances of survival in Vietnam.

From time to time Team 2-6 was designated 2-5 or 2-4 depending on the mission. The Soul Patrol had a number of replacements when we were a man or two short. I can recall Franklin Swann, Thad Givins, Charles P. Sailes, John (Piggy) Millender, Henry Bonvillian, William B. Gray, Donald Mann, and Emerson Branch, Jr. joined the team when we needed a

spot filled. Although, it really didn't matter who was designated as a replacement, they could be black, white, brown,
or rainbow, we learned to operate as a team. For five intense
days in the jungle we learned to protect each other's lives
just as critically as we did our own.

I got wind of a .357 Colt Magnum pistol that was up for
sale. The owner had orders to DEROS back to the World.
When I found out I was going to partner up with the M-60
machine gun for the remainder of my tour, I put in a request
to supplies to get a government issue .45 automatic. There
was a long waiting list and I was at the bottom. I needed a
backup weapon in the field and a sidearm for my individual
protection. It made perfect sense to buy the .357 Magnum
pistol with a four-inch barrel. It was just short of standard
procedure for Lurps to carry two or more weapons into the
boonies in case their primary weapon was damaged or mal-
functioned in a firefight. I jumped at the chance to own a
"preferred" .357 Magnum pistol. I mean, how cool is that?
After I bought it, I wore the holster slung low on my right
side for a fast draw. That pistol had special powers; it was
able to transform me and others into a gunfighters like in the
Old West. I spent many hours working on my fast-draw
techniques and became very proficient at it. The first six
rounds in the chamber of the pistol were "dum-dum"
rounds, able to penetrate an engine block if needed. They
were my "just in case" rounds. The extra rounds were forty
to eighty of the regular .38-caliber rounds. I carried those
rounds in a box tightly sealed to keep out dirt. They were
seated at the bottom of my rucksack.

One hot, sultry August morning the Soul Patrol received
a warning order. We were handed another mission to monitor enemy traffic on a canal where the "bad guys" erro-
neously felt they had the privilege of using the river without
fear of intrusion. We were told in the briefing that a combat
cameraman from II Field Force would be filming our insertion into the AO.

Around 1600 hours the team filed out to the chopper pad.
A young Spec Four carrying nothing more than a 16mm
camera was already on board the chopper, waiting for us.
He began shooting film as soon as we turned the corner and
headed toward the helicopter. We were excited to get expo-
sure for the new "Soul Patrol" team. The cameraman sat in
the doorway of the helicopter. He continued to roll film as
he slid close to the door frame, giving us enough space to fit
our gear inside the cargo area.

The convoy of helicopters took off and the film kept
rolling. When we reached the AO, the team grew concerned
after realizing there was no place to set the ship down. The
entire area was flooded. As the helicopter lowered over the
water to let us out, we started receiving automatic weapons
fire on the side of the door where Spec Four Gates, the cameraman, and I were sitting. As film continued to roll, the enemy began to walk machine gun rounds up to the door of
the helicopter. When the cameraman saw the rounds hitting
the water and coming straight toward us, he backed into the
cockpit area of the chopper with quite a disturbed look of
fear on his face. We laughed at him as we randomly returned fire at suspected enemy targets. By this time in our
tours, we had been fired at so many times it was almost fun
to get this event on film. The helicopter pilots saw we were
taking on hard fire and flew the ship out of the area and back
to the base camp. We were told to wait for a first light insertion the following morning.

The next morning the cameraman refused to go back out,
claiming he had enough footage. But we had seen that look
on his face when Charlie fired on the chopper. I had a feeling we were not going to be seeing the likes of him the next
time out. The look in his eyes told us he wasn't going to
push his luck.

Nonetheless, we were inserted into another area filled
with streams and dikes. We were able to penetrate inside the
line of trees along the canal undetected. The territory was a
confirmed enemy stronghold. We expected to walk into a
base camp at each turn. The enemy diligently made every

effort to protect this refuge. We hiked deeper into the jungle of their community; you can call it their "backyard" if you will. The backyard canals provided clear and safe passage to move their supplies without the threat of being discovered.

Although our mission was recon in nature, the area was very hot and considered a safe haven for the enemy. And on the map it was listed as a free-fire zone. We would be hard-pressed to avoid contact.

We humped the better part of day to get to an active main artery of the river. We crossed a small stream to a dike. When I stuck my foot into water, I sunk in to my thigh. I struggled for a few minutes to free both legs. Eventually I pulled myself out and reached the top of the dike with the help of my teammates. I took a moment to catch my breath and happened to look down at my ankles. I had hundreds of big, fat leeches clinging to my pant legs and boots. I hated the bloodsuckers almost as much as I hated mosquitoes. I pulled off as many as I could, but we weren't able to stop and rid ourselves of all the unsightly parasites; we had to keep moving.

We made our way into a small opening in the vegetation that exposed a large section of the river. Brock chose a good spot for our night defensive position. Then the Zippo lighters came out. We began plucking leeches from our bodies by burning them off with the lighters. Preparing for a mission always included the routine of duct-taping the ankle area of our boots. The duct tape prevented the leeches from working their way inside our boots and having a "free" five-day meal. Somehow they always seemed to find a way into the most impossible areas. Out in the boonies we would peel our boots down only to the ankles to service that area. Completely removing your boots while in the boonies was not advised and rarely done unless absolutely necessary.

The RON (remain overnight) spot that was chosen provided us with ample coverage that also shielded us from searching eyes. I remember describing our location as "a good view of the war." We set up an ambush site, maintaining surveillance right in the midst of the enemy's busy waterway. The enemy moved about the canal in daylight just as freely as they did in darkness. We counted sampan after sampan, each with occupants carrying weapons and supplies. We could have had our pick of any one of the assorted-size vessels in the target-rich canal. Lucky for us and lucky for them, our mission was reconnaissance only. Still, we were truly awestruck by the heavy enemy population moving up and down the middle of the river. I figured we would have an easy mission sitting and hiding among the foliage on the banks for the next five days.

The daylight soon gave way to twilight. I had positioned myself and the M-60 machine gun closest to the water's edge. From a distance, I watched what looked to be a large "log" floating upstream against the river's current. However, it soon became apparent that the big log was a twenty-five-foot crocodile using the business end of its massive and powerful tail to propel itself onward.

Around 2100 hundred hours, in the dark and downstream but very close by, we heard voices and the thudding sound of a sampan working its way past our position. The lone sampan was traveling underneath the jungle overhang that we were using to conceal our position. We had no time to react. We dared not move, much less fire on them. The fourteen-foot sampan broke vegetation only a few feet in front of us. The boat carried a beacon lantern to guide the bow. The bright lamp also illuminated the front of the boat, revealing a female fighter gripping an M-60 machine gun. She turned and looked directly into our faces, but apparently she didn't see us. If she had, she never reacted, but simply turned back forward.

Behind her and side by side sat a host of Viet Cong wearing black pajamas with AK-47s and M-16s, all with their weapons trained on the nearby banks in our direction. The nine-member boat crew eased by our position hugging the bank to avoid being spotted by passing helicopters. They looked directly at us but never saw us. Or had they?

Often when the enemy saw us in the field, they never

knew exactly what to think. Most of the time they thought
we were one of them, sometimes actually engaging us in
conversation until we raised our weapons and fired on them.

After the sampan passed by our position, I turned my
head back toward our team to see exactly what the boat
crew might have seen. I saw four heavily camouflaged human silhouettes with hats and weapons all blending into the
green and black jungle.

Then, farther upstream, we heard the sampan dock. "Oh
shit, they did see us!" We waited to see if they would come
back around, but the boat crew landed the sampan and began working around to our flank on foot. We immediately
prepared for an attack. To our advantage, Charlie would
have to make his way through the thick jungle vegetation to
get at us. The path leading to our position was a noisy and
difficult route, exposing Charlie to a classic ambush. We'd
packed a heavy supply of ammo for this mission and we
were ready for their asses.

We sat and waited for Charlie to make the mistake of
breaking brush in our direction. I had relocated my weapon
away from the river and aimed it in the direction of their assault route. The growing anticipation of battle was exhilarating. The prospect of firing on them became electrifying. I
broke into a light sweat. I lay on the ground tightly grasping
the pistol grip on my M-60 machine gun. It was almost like
having too much fun. I had never felt so alive in all my life.
My body tingled and shivered. I almost wanted to laugh
aloud from having such a morbidly good time. And yet I
was so terrified with fear I could hear the pounding of my
heart coming from my throat and mouth. Oh God, how I
loved that feeling!

I realized that my desire to cut someone down in battle
had become intoxicating. It was no secret that I had a nasty
appetite to get my licks in to revenge Ricky's death. That
night my cousin Ricky was heavy on my mind.

Sergeant Brock radioed the TOC to let them know that
Team 2-6 was in position and poised for an attack. The
choppers and reaction teams back at the compound were put

on "high alert." The TOC radio operators stood by waiting for the word "contact" to pierce the radio waves. And, we waited as well.

Twenty minutes passed, no Charlie. Then in the distance we heard a male voice shout repeatedly, *"Mau len! Mau len!"* In the Vietnamese language, it means, "Let's go! Let's go!" Moments later we heard the sampan take off up-river again. I was pissed! We had been primed for a big fight and nobody showed up. We continued our assigned five days of surveillance, and suddenly there was far less enemy traffic on the river after we had been spotted. Apparently the word had gotten out that Lurps were in the area. We completed the five-day mission without further incident.

Around this time, two Navy SEAL teams arrived at our base camp in Cu Chi. About fourteen SEALs showed up packing oxygen tanks, weapons, and other necessary items for a mission. They were assigned to their own hootch in a remote part of our compound. The SEAL teams stayed pretty much to themselves. I never really saw them socialize with any of our Lurps.

Even then we had heard a lot of "talk" about how tough the SEALs were, and I personally looked forward to working with them. It soon became apparent that their hype was all "talk." When we compared the high expectations we had for the Navy SEALs against the few light missions they pulled out in the field, Navy SEAL teams ultimately became the butt of jokes around the compound. The Lurps felt like the SEALs were out of their league when it came to fighting in the jungle. They certainly could not match the job we were doing out in the field.

I'm sure that at the time it was nothing more than interservice rivalry between the two branches of the military. But the real fact of the matter is, we had heard so much about the SEALs and their operations that when we did get a chance to work with them, we were disappointed. The Navy SEALs spent their time trying to impress us with their untimely morning physical training exercises. Around 0600 hours every morning they would form a circle in the middle of the compound and start shouting exercise cadences. Each morning when they woke us up, we responded by shouting obscenities and sometimes threw whatever we could get our hands on at them for disturbing our sleep. Our group of Lurps let the SEAL teams know, "If they spent more time in the field humping gear and fighting, they wouldn't have the time or energy to do physical training every morning at 0600." The war was not about how many jumping jacks we could do, but instead, how we performed in the field.

Warning orders came down, on this mission our call sign would change from 2-6 to 2-5. We were picked to go on a tandem mission with one of the Navy SEAL teams. From our perspective the SEALs weren't battle tested, and that affected how we viewed the mission.

The briefing soon revealed that the teams would fly in separate helicopters, and both teams would be inserted into the same LZ at the same time. Both teams were to stay on the same radio frequency in case one team got into trouble. Then, either team would act as backup support.

When we hit the ground, the group of LRRPs and the SEAL team both disappeared into the tree line. The SEAL team made its way upstream through the jungle tree line about four hundred meters to blow up a bridge in order to stop traffic from moving supplies up and down the river. Team 2-5 would set up less than a klick downstream to look for trouble and make contact if necessary. We would observe and report the effects of the river's traffic after the bridge was destroyed.

The SEAL team swam across the large river in broad daylight. They set a charge of C-4 explosives that blew the forty-meter steel bridge from its foundation. With four loud booms the bridge fell into the water like a house of cards. Less than two hours later we monitored the radio extraction of the SEAL team. There's no question the SEALs' mission had merit, but it was typical of the soft missions the Navy SEAL teams pulled while they operated in our company.

Our team stayed behind for one of our routine five-day-and-four-night missions.

Since Vietnam, the U.S. Navy SEALs with their high-powered public relations firms have become the most publicized "direct action unit" in the world. Over the years the U.S. Navy SEALs and their BUD/S training (basic underwater demolition/SEAL) program have turned out a respectable special operations unit for the U.S. Navy. But there is a lot to be said about the Special Operations groups that are not publicly known, such as today's LRSD (Long Range Surveillance Detachments). They are the direct descendants of the Vietnam-era LRRPs. Even our own U.S. military forces know very little about the LRSD and their operations. It's that kind of stealth that gives them the edge in combat and surveillance operations.

I mean no disrespect to the navy SEALs, but it is difficult for me not to be biased being an army Lurp. It goes without saying, the U.S. Army Special Operations units and their schools are the absolute best on this planet. It is no wonder that the U.S. Navy SEALs and all the other Allied Special Operations military forces around the world attend "U.S. Army" Special Operations training facilities.

It became clear to me later in my tour that the only way for the Long Range Patrol units to understand the ways of the enemy and fight them on their own terms would be to spend time living in the jungle. Our survival depended on our depth of knowledge of the indigenous Vietnam surroundings.

Most things regarding jungle life had to be experienced, and it would be virtually impossible to teach everything we needed to know. Lurps were forced into living, thinking, and reacting like their adversary, thereby gaining the opportunity to outmatch the enemy in a head-to-head confrontation. The Lurps were also more effective warriors than their enemy because we were better equipped, better trained, and better informed.

A complete learning process of indigenous reconnaissance

training took place while we practically lived in the boonies.
All the right entities had to be in place before I was able to
understand the "art of discernment." We had to train ourselves to hear and study all the different sounds the jungle
possessed. An impressive note was how fast we were able to
learn and pick out the sounds of all the different weapons
and mortar sizes.

Rifles were especially tricky; they made different sounds
out in the open than inside the jungle.

It was also essential for us to understand the ecology of
the jungle and how it worked. More important was how vi-
tal it became to understand how the enemy worked within
the jungle. Charlie routinely moved and ate at certain times.
He used trails that were easily exploited by LRRP teams.
We observed them and found their weaknesses. Charlie became a creature of habit and frequently paid for his mistakes
with his life. As Lurps, we did what was essential for the
team's survival or we died, it was just that simple. As it was
preached so many times before in training, "There are only
two types of soldiers in the jungles of Vietnam, the quick
and the dead." We were the quick.

Just after the Navy SEAL teams departed, two teams of
Aussie SAS (Special Air Service) joined our company. Now
these were the fightingest, drinkingest, most hard-core bastards you'll ever meet in your life. This group of fighters
was not pretentious. They loved fighting Charlie! Fighting
in Vietnam was nothing more than a big-game hunt to them.
And the fact that the game could and did shoot back made
their adventure that much more exciting to them.

One evening after chow I passed by their hootch while a
couple of these wild men were entangled in a brawl. A lone
Aussie was sitting outside the hootch, trying to get away
from all the crap going on inside. He called me over to share
in his quart-sized bottle of Johnny Walker Red and several
large cans of Foster's beer.

"Hey mate, do you know what they call this stuff back
home where I come from?" He swayed back and forth,

justifying a case for sobriety. He handed me the drink. I took the bottle, wiped the top clean, and took a few healthy swigs to prove to him that I could drink, too, then handed the bottle back to him.

"No. What?" I said, gasping from the effects of the alcohol.

"They call this shit 'Legopner!' "

" 'Legopner?' What the hell's that?"

"You know, Legopener! Leg opener! For the girls! Leg opener!" We both laughed. Just then the screen door flew open and the fight inside spilled outside on the grass right in front of us. The two combatants were throwing blows over a bullshit poker game. I figured it was time for me to leave, I certainly didn't want to get caught up in that mess. I headed back to my hootch to tell everyone what "Legopner" meant. The funny name became synonymous with all bottles of liquor.

In early September the monsoon season was rapidly approaching. Huge, puffy clouds were showing up daily. Our team got a warning order. Before I drew my supplies, I headed for the latrine wearing a pair of shower sandals and accidentally stepped on a piece of metal, slicing my foot open. I returned to the hootch bleeding like a slaughtered pig. I tried to convince Brock that I could still do my job effectively by tightly bandaging my foot and keeping it dry, but Sergeant Brock didn't buy my plan. He knew that once infected, my foot would take forever to heal. He filled my position on the team with a "cherry."

I was taken to the hospital and the first words out of the mouth of the nurse when we walked through the door was, "Here comes another one of those Lurps from Company F!" The wound wasn't serious, requiring only twenty stitches. The injury was probably a breather for the doctors, who had been inundated with stitching up more serious wounds. The doctor made a few bedside jokes and sent me back to the company with a medical profile, ten days' "light duty." It was almost like being on a two-week vacation.

The jeep dropped me off at the company area. I reported

to my platoon sergeant, who was now Staff Sergeant Carter.
When I limped back into the company compound, the hit
song "Say It Loud, I'm Black and I'm Proud" by James
Brown could be heard blasting from a nearby hootch. Located right in the middle of the company area was the 4th
Platoon hootch. One of the brothers was testing at maximum volume his brand-new pair of twelve-inch Sansui
speakers. Staff Sergeant Carter didn't see me come through
the door. He was standing at the window buck naked with
his back to me shouting at the top of his lungs, "Turn that
goddamn nigger music off!"

The cantankerous team leader had just returned from a
five-day mission and was trying to get some sleep in the
middle of the day. Judging from his remarks, Staff Sergeant
Carter didn't particularly care a whole lot for James Brown
and the Famous Flames. From that day forward, word came
from the top banning black soldiers from playing "Say It
Loud, I'm Black and I'm Proud!" in the company area. And
after that incident, I also noticed that this particular song
was never played on Armed Forces Radio.

Later that day, at around 1500 hours, Team 2-6 was inserted without me on the "big gun." It didn't take long before the company siren sounded again. Word resonated
around the compound that Brock was in trouble! The team
had never gotten off the LZ before coming under fire. A reaction team was already at the chopper pad and taking off
for the AO. After forcing my injured foot into my boot, I
grabbed my weapon and rushed out to the chopper pad.
Usually when the siren sounded, more than enough troops
showed up to support the teams in the field. Because of my
injury, I was adamantly turned away at the last minute. I
hurried back to the hootch to listen to the firefight on the
PRC-25. The radio already had a group of listeners huddled
around it.

Brock's insertion helicopter had come under heavy fire.
It was knocked out of the air just after the Lurp team was
safely on the ground. Team 2-6 was pinned down on the
landing zone without cover. Every extraction ship that went

in came under antiaircraft fire, .51-caliber machine gun fire, and small-arms fire. The command-&-control ship arrived on the scene and was circling the action. While the C&C ship was in the air, it took a few large rounds to the hydraulic system and went down in the middle of the LZ. The reaction force was deployed immediately. They were dropped behind the fight and soon became the focal point of the battle as they worked their way to the center of the action. The reaction team presented enough of a distraction that other choppers were able to go in and pull out the downed crew and Lurp team from the hot LZ. In that fight our company suffered two KIAs and four wounded in action, and we also lost two Huey helicopters. It was a bad day for Company F 51st Infantry.

For a while it seemed that every time the siren in the company area sounded, we found ourselves crammed around a PRC-25 radio dialed in on the frequency of the teams in the field.

Midday, August 12, we clung to the radio listening to a vicious firefight already in progress. A sizable group of concerned paratroopers sat around listening helplessly. We were all absorbed in the intense situation over the radio. I can still remember the horror and the fierceness of the battle as the firefight in the field continued to escalate. Every time the RTO (radiotelephone operator) keyed his handset, we could hear explosions and sporadic automatic weapons fire in the background. The Lurp team ran into a large group of hard-core NVA on the move to a base camp. We monitored the command and control airship racing to the scene to direct the helicopter gun runs from overhead. The helicopter pilots above the firefight reported receiving .50-caliber machine gun fire and small-arms fire. During the battle, the enemy's ground-to-air firepower eventually disabled a helicopter, knocking it from the sky. The commo line was filled with cross-talk. I found myself totally wrapped up in the tragedy. I remember sitting on a cot with a my chin resting in the palm of hands, thinking about my family and my deceased cousin. I shared much grief and sympathy for my fellow Lurps who were entangled in the gruesome firefight. I knew firsthand how their families were going to take the coming news. I realized this episode was just another day in the life of a Lurp in Vietnam. And it was just another rude awakening to the hell of war.

My thoughts were disrupted by horrifying shrieks for help. The Lurp's cry over the radio brought a momentary silence to the usually heavy air traffic cross-talk. The team's RTO was in a fight for his life. He was trying to hold off numerous attackers and maintain radio communication all at the same time. The team was surrounded, outnumbered, and had already taken heavy casualties.

Suddenly over the radio, all hell broke loose. We heard a relentless burst of automatic weapons fire. An enormous explosion distorted the radio speaker. We actually heard the enemy shouting over the weapons fire. Then the Lurp radio transmission abruptly ended. White noise filled the airwaves. A few minutes later the radio came alive again, and we all sat and listened in shock as a male Vietnamese voice screamed garbled and unintelligible remarks into the handset. Then, once again . . . silence.

Sergeant Brock switched over to another frequency. We were able to monitor the reaction team's radio talk as they fought their way to the Lurp team's position. The command-and-control helicopter was now orbiting over the firefight. The reaction team described their findings to C&C and advised them of the seriousness of the situation.

It became evident that the five-man Lurp team had put up a courageous fight. Because moments later, the reaction team again radioed to C&C, apprising them of finding numerous dead NVA soldiers all around the team's perimeter. The Lurp team had been shot up pretty badly, sustaining two KIAs with the rest of the team wounded and left for dead. I remember that day well, August 12, 1968. My friends, Sp4. Jan V. Henrickson and Sp4. Kenneth R. Blair, fell victim to a platoon of NVA regulars, possibly out for revenge because of all the damage our company had inflicted on them while working this AO.

On that day I realized I had become overly sensitive to the war. I knew that in order to "win" in this war . . . meaning, to go home "alive" . . . I had to assume and maintain a superinflated sense of toughness. I had to find another level of survival, what I called my "survival mode." Even after the war as a civilian, I found times when I had to employ my "survival mode" to stay alive or motivate myself out of trouble. It's a mind-set that remains useful from time to time. Believe me, with some of my knucklehead antics, my survival mode still comes in handy.

In early September the Soul Patrol received a warning order for a high-priority mission. We had a new addition to our team. Besides the presence of Brock, Reid, Gates, Mackey, and me, Sp4. William B. Gray was assigned to our team. He was one of the few caucasians who went out on an occasional mission with us. Someone remarked while we prepared for the mission, "Whenever we take a 'white boy' on one of our missions, we are almost guaranteed to get in a big firefight." I never gave the comment much thought. As far as I was concerned, it was just another off-color joke. I had certainly heard worse remarks.

When we showed up for the intelligence report that morning, the briefing room was darker than usual. The single forty-watt bulb, which gave barely enough light to fill the room, was aimed at the map board. Not much information was discussed other than the routine points of interest. The helicopter pilot pointed out LZs on the briefing map and touched on insertion procedures. Brock went over the recon sites and the radio frequencies and artillery support. After he presented his plan, Brock asked for questions. For reasons I couldn't explain at the time, the mood in the room had become noticeably different. However, what really caught my eye was the peculiar way the map was displayed on the large board. Rather than laid out end to end, as was customarily done, the map was folded into a small square, the same way we read it in the field.

The briefing ended, we headed to the chopper pad with our usual anticipation and apprehension. The flight to the

AO seemed a lot longer than at any previous time. The insertion point was in an area that seemed to be about forty to fifty miles from our base camp.

When we flew in over the AO, it became alarmingly apparent how barren the terrain was, even more so than the map had indicated. It was SOP (standard operating procedure) for a team leader to do a "flyover" and plan the insertion points as well as the mission in general. I wondered if Brock had made an overflight before inserting the team into this vicinity, and if he had, the situation begged the question, "Whose choice was it to recon this spot?" Whoever had made the decision to put a Lurp team into this area was nuts.

Our insertion was clean. The team couldn't travel on foot for very long because the cover was basically nonexistent. We had to find a place to hide at once. Only, there was no real cover to speak of for miles, just open flatlands with rice paddies and dikes, and a few bamboo trees lining the canal. We humped about a hundred meters to the bamboo area and set up an RON.

With the aid of a new relay station, our objective was to find out if we could establish and sustain PRC radio communications with the new Tactical Operations Command.

We set up an ambush site on the edge of a crystal clear canal that seemed to go on forever. A cluster of ten-foot-high bamboo stalks sequestered us from the sun and the river. It was a perfect spot for a Boy Scout outing, an even better spot for hitting an unsuspecting sampan meandering down the stream. PFC Lawton Mackey and I volunteered to pull a two-man recon. We dived into the water and swam to the other side of the canal to investigate. Before diving in, I stuck my K-bar between my teeth and dived in headfirst. I skimmed under the water to the other side. But putting the K-bar in my mouth and diving into the water was a mistake. The water rushed into my nostrils, my mouth, and then into my stomach. When I reached the other side, I found myself gagging and coughing excess water from my mouth and sinus cavity. . . . It wasn't a pretty picture. Obviously, those

Tarzan stunts worked only in the movies. They really didn't fare well in real-life situations. In all fairness, it was probably one of those silly mistakes others wouldn't make. But I was a nineteen-year-old kid living in a dreamlike nightmare. I tried to experience everything, however crazy.

Located directly on the other side of the canal was the entryway into an underground tunnel system. I threw a few hand grenades into the opening just in case some surprise guest was lurking about. It seemed terribly unlikely that any living human being would be within a hundred miles of this place.

Mackey and I both agreed that no one had inhabited the tunnel for a while. When the small recon job was complete . . . this time, with my K-bar placed safely in its sheath, I plunged into the water and swam back to the team's position. The short splash to the other side was cool and refreshing. It was one of those days when the temperature was a sultry 105 degrees. The humidity was high, and in the very next hour it would begin to rain intermittently.

As the sun began to fade from the purple sky, the remaining rays of sunlight reflecting off the bamboo stalks gave the illusion that we were being caged in.

Two days passed. Nothing, no enemy or anything was seen. The only sign of life was an annoying little freshwater crab that had apparently lost its right claw in its own struggle. The radio was constantly crapping out. Ellis Gates was frequently changing batteries to keep it alive. He switched over to the field-expedient antenna and we were able to establish commo with the relay station and TOC full-time, but at night only.

Depending on the time of day, we spent painfully long hours either laid back roasting in the sun or relaxing in the shade. It had been an arduous but uneventful two days. To put it mildly, we were bored out of our minds. We weren't able to move because there was no place to go.

At the end of the third day, the evening gave way to a perfect pitch blackness. We had ended another long day with absolutely no activity. The rising full moon toiled to break through the thick clouds. Gentle drops of rain started to fall. The rhythmic beat of the raindrops quickly matured into a torrential downpour. A half hour later, the pelting rain ceased as though a terrestrial sprinkler system had been set on an omnipotent timer. I heard Brock rustling with his gear. He was probably agitated at the idea of being dumped in the middle of nowhere for another boring five-day mission with not a soul in sight. Brock began to audibly show his disgust when he started swearing aloud. I admonished him with a firm, "Shhh!"

Brock snapped back at me angrily, "Ain't nobody out here! Have you seen anyone out here?"

Brock was right, we hadn't seen or heard anything the entire time we were out there. We were so remote from the rest of the world we rarely saw or heard a jet flying about. Just as Brock had started to settle down . . . *Boom! Boom! Rattatat, Rattatat! Boom! Boom! Rattatat!* The concussion shock lifted us off the ground. We had suddenly come under a vicious and relentless attack by an unknown force. A hail of bullets and numerous RPG (Rocket Propelled Grenade) rounds sent us sprawling for security. The startling intensity of the attack caught us totally off guard. Charlie had assembled on the other side of the river under the cover of the rainstorm, exactly where the bunker entrance had been located. Brock shouted over the noise of the unrelenting assault into the radio handset, "Contact! Contact! Team 2-6 under heavy attack!"

Yeah, he was right, Team 2-6 was under very heavy attack, and taking on real serious enemy firepower. The ground in front of us was spitting up dirt. For what seemed like forever, the enemy continuously poured firepower toward our position. The steady stream of green tracers was so fierce, it was impossible to raise your head even an inch without fear of getting it shot off. We sweated out nearly twenty minutes of earsplitting grenade explosions and continual RPG rocket fire. The concentrated machine gun fire kept us pinned hard to the ground.

Time crawled. Tracer bullets from the machine guns

wouldn't let up. They continued to pour in machine gun fire with a panning and probing pattern. The bamboo stalks in front of us snapped apart at the roots. Our limited protection was toppling down all over us. This time the element of surprise was theirs.

Right after the first rounds I had slipped down off my rucksack and lay flat on my back just in time to watch a shit-load of green tracer rounds scream straight toward my head, barely missing me. As the firing continued, I nestled flat to the ground, burrowing among the insects and earthworms. Green tracer rounds pelted the ground next to my head. The rounds continued to glow even after being embedded in the earth. The bullets sounded like bees as they whizzed past my ears. I remember thinking, "So, this is what it's like to die!"

At that moment, I concluded, the closer you come to death, the easier it is to accept. I wasn't giving up, but if I had happened to die on that night, I knew I had no control over living or dying. I remember giving everything up to God. I said, "God, if I'm to die now, I'm all Yours." At that moment, somewhere inside, the fear of dying seemed to disappear.

It has been said, "You have never lived till you have almost died; and for those who fight for it, life has a flavor the protected will never know." Most combat veterans know exactly what those words mean.

We lay silent and lifeless. No one moved a muscle and no one spoke. The electric stench of RPG rocket fire and the smell of gunfire filled the air. I figured, if any team members made it through the onslaught, they were probably thinking the same thing, "Where in the hell did they get all that fire-power?" Getting hit off guard was one of the worst things that could possibly occur, and here it was actually happening, exponentially!

I was concerned that our artillery support couldn't help us because the enemy was right on top of us. The rain was coming down extremely hard back at the company area, and the helicopter gunships were about forty minutes away. But I have to admit, it was always comforting to know that the

company recovery slicks and the "Playboy" 334th Aerial
Assault Squadron would fly through a nuclear blast to get us
out of trouble. Or that's what we'd always believed.

When Charlie finally stopped firing, my first thought
was, "Maybe they have expended all of their ammo." Then I
figured, "Naw . . . They're probably just exhausted and taking a tea break from carrying the arsenal they have un-
leashed on our asses!"

The haze from the explosions began to dissipate. A moment of silence hung in the air like a bad smell. The electric
residue and debris from the RPG rockets started to settle
onto our clothes and skin. I slowly turned my head to see if
any other team members were moving. After a few seconds,
I saw them moving around. Amazingly, everyone was still
alive! It was an absolute miracle! Somehow we had been
spared from certain death.

I turned over on my stomach and crawled back to my
machine gun. I peered through what was left of the bamboo
stalks. I was able to make out enemy movement on the other
side of the canal. Assisted by the intermittent moonlight, I
saw three NVA soldiers running toward the tunnel entrance.
When they reached the opening, they literally dived headfirst inside the tunnel. I fired about fifty rounds directly on
the entryway of the bunker and scattered two other enemy
soldiers moving from the opposite direction toward the tunnel entrance. After squeezing off a burst of about a hundred
rounds, my machine gun jammed. A cartridge had wedged
itself inside the barrel of the gun. I worked my hand inside
my rucksack to find a cleaning rod. In my haste, the rod was
nowhere to be found. In case the machine gun barrel got too
hot, I normally carried a pair of black leather gloves. Now, I
couldn't find my gloves either.

Meanwhile, Reid, Mackey, and Gray began to lay down
moderate fire and Gates assisted Brock with the radio. Moments later I saw Gates crawl over to the bamboo stalks to
join the return fire. I rolled over on my back and grabbed
about ten hand grenades and, while lying flat on my back,

commenced hurling them up and over the bamboo trees and across twenty feet of river. A few grenades landed short of the target. I heard the muffled sounds of the hand grenades discharging in the water. The grenades detonating short of their mark may have deterred Charlie from crossing to our side of the river. I threw about eight or nine more grenades before I drew my .357 Magnum pistol and popped off a few rounds at darting targets racing toward the tunnel entrance. The pistol shots were a joke compared to the firepower we had just survived. Our counterattack was disoriented and ineffectual, pale in comparison to the attack we had just endured.

While the fight was going on, the extraction helicopter radioed to Sergeant Brock to let him know that the support ships were inbound. Ellis Gates popped a flare to signal the team's position. We scrambled to gather our equipment. We had no idea what Charlie was planning, if anything. As a rule, when Charlie spotted a Lurp team, they would pull back and wait for reinforcements to arrive and then overrun the Lurp team with overwhelming force.

Out of nowhere the choppers appeared. I hadn't noticed the helicopters until they were right on top of us. Flying in under the cloak of darkness, the helicopters skimmed just inches off the surface of the water-filled rice paddies. Unprotected from enemy ground fire, the chopper hovered in the open, an easy mark for Charlie. I grabbed my weapon and my rucksack and headed for the helicopter. Brock yelled back instructing me to leave the equipment. Against my will, I obeyed his order. When I stepped over the dike into the rice paddy, I fully understood his reason for leaving the equipment. I had never realized just how deep, sticky, and gooey rice paddies could be until we moved out into the quicksandlike sludge. The more I struggled to free my legs, the deeper I sank. At times I was up to my nose in the mud and water. Single file the team plowed out to the thumping palpitations of the hovering helicopter. One by one, each team member disappeared into the bottomless muddy water, sometimes exposing only a hand beckoning for help. The door gunners on both sides of the ship and the bellyman assisted us by grasping our hands and hoisting us out of the watery abyss and into the swaying helicopter.

Wet, muddy, and exhausted, the entire team was finally aboard the chopper. Brock made a quick head count and, satisfied with the total, signaled to the pilot, "Everyone accounted for!" The helicopter banked away and accelerated across the field, quickly gaining altitude. I sat in the doorway of the chopper, the cool air rushing across my face. The smell of Vietnam at night haunted my soul. I flashed on the horrible ambush we had just survived. The team as a whole had sustained only two minor wounds, but the wound to our psyche was an entirely different story. Every thought I had about "war" had changed radically on that mission. Nothing could ever come close to the experience of actually being shot at for keeps. For me, war had become evil and revolting.

I watched the assault helicopter gunships make their presence felt by unleashing their brutal firepower. The C&C ship illuminated the sky by dropping flares. The Cobra gunships generated a hot glow against the dark skies with heavy rocket fire, minigun tracers, and twenty mike-mike (millimeter) explosions. From the distance, I watched the exploding bombs on the horizon get smaller and smaller. I had hoped the gunships would destroy the equipment we'd left behind.

We were long out of the area by the time the Cobra gunships completed their mission. I'll never know what became of our equipment or my M-60 machine gun, and I'm not sure if I really wanted to find out. They say "the truth will set you free," and to this day, I still have regrets for leaving my M-60 machine gun behind. I will always feel responsible for giving Charlie one more instrument to kill another GI.

After we finished the team debriefing in TOC, Brock huddled us inside the hootch and began lecturing us.

"We looked like shit out there, every one of us. We almost got our asses killed because we were too lax! From now on, no fucking around! On any mission! No matter where they stick our asses."

Brock's last comment caught my attention. What did he mean by, "No matter where they stick our asses"? A few days later I happened to be studying the map from the last mission when Brock walked into the hootch. I alluded to our insertion point on the map.

"Damn, Brock, according to this map, we were in Cambodia!" In classic Jerry Brock style, he replied, "No shit, Sherlock! Since when did it matter where they send us? What the hell do you think this is, a movie?"

Now I was pissed. If I was going to die, I at least wanted to know what country I was dying in. I couldn't hold back with a number of questions.

"Did you know that we were going inside Cambodia before taking the mission?"

Brock became uncomfortable with me quizzing him about details of the mission.

"How deep inside Cambodia were we?" I continued with the questioning. Brock breathed deeply, a serious look registered on his face. Reluctant to give up much more information, he lifted an eye brow and affirmed, "Deep enough!"

Technically we were not supposed to be there. It was a secret mission authorized by II Field Force. That also explained the odd fashion in which the map had been displayed on the board during the briefing. Brock's unusually quiet manner had made me curious, but I could tell someone had said something about the mission that he unequivocally would not talk about, not even to his homeboy. I promptly dropped the subject.

In spite of the damage to our confidence, Team 2-6 was able to survive and eventually recover from an operation that was far less than favorable. We had to learn that lesson. We were lucky to be alive. The entire team had been only a few feet away from total annihilation. Charlie was off the mark by a mere ten feet. The ordeal was like being in front-row seats at a fireworks show and having the whole damn thing blow up in your face.

*   *   *

A month after that mission I was taking a shower, and the scent of the RPG residue was still coming out of the pores of my skin. I could still smell it in my hair. I immediately flashed on the ambush. The frightening memories elevated my heart rate to a frenzy. It became obvious, the RPG rounds had a powerful and lasting psychological effect on its victims.

On a September mission, Team 2-4 (Soul Patrol) was inserted into AO Scout on a midday insertion. The long flight out to the LZ was always enough time to conjure a fair share of doubts and negative thoughts, especially since the last disastrous mission was still fresh in our minds. I found that experiencing this kind of "fear" kept us sharp and on our toes. At times it was easy for teams to get lax and begin thinking Charlie wasn't in the area. The "fear factor" gave us the instinct to survive, and we learned to use it routinely and knowledgeably.

The insertion went without a hitch; we hit the ground running for the tree line. The faster we were able to blend into the thick foliage, the better. The area was tagged by G-2 for having active heavy day and night movement.

The jungle was thick with triple canopy trees that grew large roots protruding from the ground. Some of the trees stood up to a hundred feet high. This type of jungle terrain was rare for this area. The ground was still wet from the heavy rainfall the night before. The footing was slippery. We were aware of leaving defined boot imprints in the mud. We decided to play it safe, and a course was set through the dense jungle. We walked only in areas that were littered with fallen foliage. We made a concerted effort not to step on trails. Ellis Gates was on the point. He shot an azimuth for twenty degrees. We followed what was believed to be an animal trail, a path that was exhaustively slow and precarious.

We paused briefly to lay dog and rid ourselves of leeches. We took a moment to listen to the jungle. I wiped the steady stream of sweat from my eyes. The team stayed on the twenty degree azimuth. We approached an area that was excessively congested with tall, thick trees. I counted a large tree every twelve feet in all directions. The area was also covered with heavy ground vegetation. We kept finding droppings that looked to be human feces. The smell was almost unbearable. That particular "red flag" usually signified that we were in or near an enemy base camp. Suddenly the silence and stillness of the jungle became noticeably irregular. Gates looked back to Brock as if to say, "Go on?" His face was a mask of terror. Common sense told us something wasn't right. Our steps became shorter, with more discretion and purpose. The suspense was numbing. We advanced carefully, sweeping and covering 360 degrees with our eyes and weapons.

Suddenly we were jolted by a loud commotion coming from the trees high above our heads. The tree branches began popping and breaking. Strange noises of bellowing calls were heard throughout the jungle. We immediately dropped to a knee and went into a defensive posture. Without hesitation we instinctively trained a couple of weapons toward the trees and the noise overhead. We didn't move until we found out exactly what was making the sounds. After a few seconds of evaluating the situation, we'd determined the noise was coming from a large family of gibbons living in the trees overhead. The angry apes had a violent reaction to our presence in their jungle and they let us know about it. Before getting back to my feet, I took a moment to give a silent prayer of thanks. While still leaning on one knee and waiting for Jerry Brock to give orders to move out, I looked over to Ellis Gates and Sp4. Norman Reid and nodded my head in disgust. I was thinking to myself, "Damn! They would have 'had' us! If Charlie had posted a lookout in those trees, that would have been our asses!"

In that type of terrain, the average tree grew fifty to sixty feet high. So much of our focus was watching for the enemy on the ground, there was not enough emphasis on the trees above. The gibbon "scare" was the awakening that brought attention to how vulnerable we had become from an attack overhead. It was another reality check.

At around 1800 hours our daily recon was winding down. We had moved about three klicks due north toward another LZ and were looking for a safe place to set up for the night. We picked another route through the thick jungle. I remember thinking how the four months of work in the boonies was beginning to pay off. I came to understand why it was so necessary for the Lurps to train so hard for survival. And why the army selected only young kids to do this kind of work. Lurping was extremely debilitating and taxing to one's body. Lurps had to stay in prime physical shape the entire time to operate at a high level. Plus the psychological factor, that a kid of nineteen or twenty-one years old sometimes believes he is invincible or bulletproof. . . . Well, that's what gave Lurps the edge.

I had always thought of Lurps as kids doing a grown man's job, but soldiers enough to believe we would prevail under any circumstance.

There came a time in Vietnam when I started to believe I was an animal. I was no longer human. I was an animal that lived and ruled the jungle. I had envisioned myself as a strong and mighty guerrilla/gorilla. I began to believe I was the king of all the jungle beasts, including "man." I dominated my immediate territory, and wherever I was in the jungles of Vietnam, I ruled!

I actually found comfort in the fact that I had adapted well to the environment. The jungle was starting to feel like home. Wild boars would be rooting and grunting right next to us. We didn't react to them and they never bothered us. We became so much a part of the jungle landscape, small animals would play about or walk right over the top of us as if we weren't there. Sometimes I felt safer in the jungle and preferred to be out in the boonies rather than in the rear area at the base camp.

That evening, as we looked to settle into our night defen-

Left to right: author Ed Emanuel, Seferino Alvarado, and Ellis Gates Jr. On the chopper headed to the boonies.

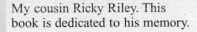

My cousin Ricky Riley. This book is dedicated to his memory.

Left to right: Brock, Emanuel, and Rodriguez. Gathered around the PRC-25, listening to our team being overrun on August 12, 1968, in Cu Chi.

Author Ed Emanuel.
Headed to the chopper for
another mission.

Author Ed
Emanuel after
Recondo
School.

Author on left and Brock on
right. Brock worried about
my gunplay.

Team headed to A.O.

Landing zone ahead.

Blowing bunkers.

Author Ed Emanuel when he was a cherry.

Author diving. Showing off at the hotel pool in Bangkok, Thailand.

The Brothers. Left to right: Branch, Willis, unidentified, unidentified, Mackey, Millender, and Givins.

Author Ed Emanuel set up on a trail and waiting to blow an ambush.

First Sergeant Butts.

This is what we saw headed to the A.O. "Vietnam from the air."

Vietnam from the air.

On the berm in the
evening, part 1.

On the berm,
part 2.

The author and Chico.

Thad Givins in Thailand.

The long path leading to the barracks.

The author and his .357 pistol.

The author reading in sleeping quarters.

sive position, we found a location surrounded by large trees. It was an ideal spot for protection against the rain and incoming enemy fire. To stay concealed, we made a point to reapply camouflage stick to our faces and hands.

The warm muggy night air was stagnant. The ear-buzzing mosquitoes were on a vicious attack, especially the big ones that could bite through our clothing. I hated those little bastards with a passion! They also caused many cases of malaria in Vietnam. Each time out in the boonies, I had to learn and re-learn how to deal with getting bit by the antagonizing mosquitoes, termites, and fire ants. There were other species of bully biting insects roaming the jungle floors, proving their dominion over my body. According to the Recondo School training that had been passed down to every Lurp, we weren't supposed to use insect repellent because of the pungent odor. That smell can easily give away a position. But if it hadn't been for those personal aids like mosquito head nets and insect repellent, I surely would have gone nuts out in the boonies of Vietnam.

We remained overnight at the base of one of these enormous one-hundred-foot-tall trees. The large roots of this one particular tree came to a V shape. The cover would be enough to shield us from at least two sides. After placing out the usual amount of trip flares and claymore mines for perimeter protection, we nestled among the tall timbers to rest.

Late into the evening, around 2200 hours, we were startled by single shots fired in intervals of five minutes apart. We estimated the distance to be less than a klick away. After a while the whole area became alive with activity. We listened to a large group of enemy soldiers yelling and firing weapons into the air as if they were taking part in a big rally. The rifle volleys echoing throughout the jungle were nerve-racking. From the sounds of the voices, it was estimated that more than a hundred, maybe two hundred spirited soldiers vocalized their emotions toward the war.

We huddled in our perimeter close enough to alert each other with a touch. I realized our worst fears were due east

and not far away. There was no movement in our immediate
area to report to TOC. But on the other hand, the movement
of enemy soldiers approximately a klick away was nothing
to scoff at. The situation was unstable at best.

It was eerie to know that such a large enemy force was
nearby. Each time they fired their weapons into the air, my
teeth clenched and my heart beat harder. It also became increasingly apparent that this large gathering of enemy
troops was well supplied with American-made weapons and
equipment. Along with the AK-47 fire, we also heard M-60
machine guns and M-16 rifles being fired into the air.

Around 2300 hours the yelling and cheering subsided.
Then Charlie fired off about twenty to thirty parachute flares
into the air, for whatever reason. The flares were fired off in
another direction but happened to drift over our heads, illuminating our small perimeter area. The lights from the flares
leaked through the triple canopy, disbursing enough bright-
ness to establish the camouflage faces of my teammates.
The flickering balls of fire sailed slowly across the black
sky. The reflection of light on the ground fashioned odd and
interesting shadows in our field of fire. In the boonies, you
never took anything for granted. If it moved, you watched it
until you were absolutely sure it was not the enemy. And at
night, rather than staring at a suspected target, you scanned
the area by panning your head from left to right and back,
but making sure your eyes were always sighted on your target area. I was almost confident the enemy was not looking
for us. Personally, I don't think Charlie had any idea we
were in the vicinity. But we were ... in his backyard,
watching and listening to everything.

As if things couldn't get worse, when all was quiet, a
large snake slithered over the top of my stomach and into
our position. I figured if I didn't move, the snake would
keep going. Mackey and Millender (Piggy) felt the snake
creep in our position, too, but they jumped and the snake bit
them. Brock was not able to analyze the seriousness of the
problem on the spot, so he played it safe by calling for an
unscheduled team extraction. None of us was sure of the

type of snakebite they had encountered; we never got a chance to see the reptile. For the sake of the two bitten Lurps, we kept a very watchful eye on their health as we moved discreetly through the totally black jungle to the LZ. The helicopters arrived out to the AO expeditiously. C&C was the first ship to reach us. We heard them in the air and on the radio. We were instructed at the last minute, turn on a strobe light to guide the inbound extraction helicopter into a small LZ. We carried the rucksacks of the two injured Lurps and helped them aboard the chopper. The helicopter lifted off into the night sky without incident.

When we arrived back at the base camp, we were debriefed for a short period of time and then dismissed to get some rest. I was unable to sleep due to all the excitement of the mission. That was the night I picked up the nasty habit of smoking cigarettes. I grabbed a pack of Kool cigarettes and quart bottle of Johnny Walker Red from my footlocker and went out to the bunker next to the hootch. Hosting a party of their own was a group of late-night drinkers and smokers who were already howling at the moon. I sat through the night and drank until the early morning, almost as if I didn't have to go back out into the boonies the next day.

That night at the hospital the doctors had determined that Mackey and Millender had been bitten by a nonvenomous snake, and they were cleared to return to duty. They were returned to the compound promptly to get some rest. But who in their right mind would be able to sleep after a night like that? Not to mention, we were conditioned to stay awake all night with only a couple hours' sleep. Eventually the entire team drifted out to the berm to talk about the eventful two-day mission. For some reason, a team talking about a mission was rare, unless it was an important subject.

In the middle of our conversations, the siren sounded off in the company area. That was always bad news. Night extractions were invariably a big concern to us all. Team 2-3 was in contact. Thad Givins was on that team. We brought a PRC-25 out to the bunker to monitor the radio talk.

Charlie had inadvertently walked into the team's position

and an intense firefight broke out. The RTO transmitted information saying they had two friendly WIAs (wounded in action), one with a serious head wound. Somehow I knew in my gut it was Thad.

"Damn, I hope Givins is not out there trying to be a hero," I said aloud. Don't get me wrong, Givins was not reckless, he was too smart for that, but he did what it took to help the team to survive, no matter the cost. That's the kind of soldier he was. On Team 2-3, Staff Sergeant Carter was the team leader, but Steven Miles and Sgt. Sandy Boyd were also on the team and they were all top-notch Lurps. Any one of them would be able to take charge and get the team out safely. I felt confident after considering those facts.

At around 0200 hours the helicopter landed at the company chopper pad. I ran out to meet them as they landed. The team of helicopters was landing at the same time. The chopper noise was loud and roaring. As the hovering helicopters slowly touched down, I shielded my eyes from the flying dust and debris. The team of Lurps off-loaded and passed by in single file. Thad Givins wasn't among them. I ran to catch up with Steven Miles after he passed me by.

"Where's Givins?!" I yelled over the deafening noise.

"He's at the hospital!" Miles yelled back, matching my volume. "The chopper dropped him off before we flew in here."

"Is he okay?" I asked.

"Yeah, he's fine! He took a gook round that ricochetted off his hard-ass forehead. Nothing can penetrate that shit!" I was relieved to hear that, but Thad managed to give me a good scare.

About an hour later, while we were still trying to drink ourselves asleep, the headlights of a jeep pulled into the middle of the compound. Thad got out with a big white bandage on his forehead and a big grin on his face. He strutted toward the bunker to join the party and announced, after coming to a complete stop, "Many of them tried . . . and many of them died!"

Typical Thad Givins! For a moment out there, I thought I had lost my good friend. I and the others were elated to see him standing there leading the banter as usual. Airborne, Thad Givins, Airborne!

The next morning at 0930 hours, our team gathered in the mess hall for chow. I found myself laboring with a nasty hangover. We carried enough Darvons in our pill kits to eradicate any small problem like a simple headache. One or two capsules down the hatch did the trick.

It was no surprise to us that we were going back out to the field that day. The word in the debriefing was "Charlie Mike" (continue mission)!

At 1500 hours that afternoon, the entire team again boarded the chopper and headed back into the same AO. But this time we were flown into a different LZ. No sooner had we secured a perimeter and put out the claymores than we started to monitor 81mm mortar rockets leaving a tube about four hundred meters west of our position. The destination of the rockets was unknown. Brock called in artillery and began probing the area where the mortar fire was originating. After we called in a "sitrep," our artillery fired a volley of rounds around our position for a good ten minutes with unknown results.

Just before midnight, around 2330 hours, we heard the roaring noise of a very large multiengine prop airplane flying low and moving slowly from the northeast to southeast at the altitude of about two thousand feet. The primary concerns that caught our undivided attention were the loud and awfully bright explosions of lights emanating from the aircraft every few seconds. From a distance, the bursts of lights made it appear as if the airplane was dropping bright illuminating bombs. The airplane turned and headed straight for our position. *Boom! Boom! Boom!* Just when the aircraft flew directly over the top of us, I curled into a fetal position, knowing this was the end of the line for all of us. I expected to be blown into bits when the bright lights exploded over us with more thunderous flashes. Surprisingly, the plane passed over us and continued on its same flight path, lighting up the sky. The huge airplane's engines trembled the ground as it flew past, leaving in its wake a trail of bright flashes of light and loud thunderous bursts. What a relief to find out that the airplane was an aerial reconnaissance and observation plane taking pictures for mapmaking. Brock immediately radioed TOC informing them of the situation. About an hour later, after confirming information with G-2 at II Field Force, TOC came back on the air and emphatically and repeatedly cautioned the team that the plane was "not" one of our own! This was a very unusual sighting; none of us had ever seen anything like this before. The airplane was enormous, and apparently not an American-made job. The aircraft made two small circles in the sky flashing pictures before moving on.

At 0350 hours we were stirred by the sound of enemy movement. This time they were looking for us. We observed two NVA soldiers checking the bushes with a determined effort to find Lurps hiding in their territory. They communicated back and forth with hand signals as they walked right past our position. Had they come any closer, or spotted us, we would have spanked them with automatic weapons fire. Brock mouthed the words, "Point element!" Sure as hell, ten minutes later, fourteen NVA soldier jogged by carrying weapons and clanking equipment hanging from their rucksacks. The area was way too hot to fire them up, plus we didn't want to give away our position. Brock let the soldiers move away about a hundred meters down the trail, then called for a fire mission to "Shocker," the artillery liaison officer attached to Company F. The artillery strike was aimed a hundred feet ahead of them and a hundred feet behind them, hoping to catch them in the middle. The rounds whistled in, smashing and uprooting trees. We were close enough to receive light debris and shrapnel. Real on-the-money shooting. I was alway amazed at the pinpoint accuracy of the artillery units. The fire mission had unknown results. Our team was extracted at 1700 hours due to the completion of the mission. I was glad to get the hell out of there.

When we returned to the company area, the choppers dropped us off and immediately turned around and went back out to the field. Another team on patrol had made contact and captured an NVA officer and an enlisted man. The enemy officer led the Lurp team to a cache of weapons and ordnance. The 199th Infantry Brigade was activated as our reaction team. About 75 to 100 soldiers were choppered out to the AO to secure and recover the weapons cache. The weapons consisted of mortar rounds of all sizes, Chi-Com (Chinese Communist) hand grenades, and crates of AK-47 rifles. Part of the cache was brought back to the company area to be displayed for the II Field Force G-2 officers, and also as a photo opportunity for the record.

The Lurp team delivered the two NVA soldiers to TOC for interrogation. While one of the enemy officers was being interrogated, the other was handcuffed to the steering wheel of a jeep behind TOC, which was located in the middle of the company area. The NVA soldier was wounded pretty badly in the right shoulder, the same arm that was cuffed to the jeep. The interpreters made sure the NVA soldier was able to hear the screams of his comrade, who was now telling all. The confessions from the enemy were a direct result of the Vietnamese NCOs Staff Sergeant Mot and Staff Sergeant Nghia, who were assigned directly to our company as "indigenous interpreters." Believe me, Mot and Nghia had ways of making the enemy talk. Enough said.

Thad Givins and I decided to walk over to the TOC area to see what the commotion was about and to take photos. Thad was still sporting that big white bandage on his forehead. A group of Lurps had already gathered around the jeep and the captured NVA soldier. The enemy soldier tried his best to endure the continuous taunting as he was absolutely frightened out of his mind. His eyes rolled to the back of his head and he appeared to be faking several fainting spells.

Over the voices in the crowd, I could hear Thad ridiculing the NVA soldier, "Uh huh, you shouldn't have been out there shooting at motherfuckers if you were going to punk out when your ass got captured, you faggot!" Just then, a loud, bearish voice on the other side of the darkened screen door grumbled out, "Get the hell out of here you bloodthirsty bastards! What the hell are you doing over here fuckin' with my prisoner!" The screen door whipped open and First Sergeant Butts filled the doorway. The group of soldiers scrambled away laughing and snickering, as the whole thing turned out to be a big sideshow to entertain the Lurps. First Sergeant Butts knew he would attract the troops if he cuffed the enemy to a jeep in the middle of the company area for all eyes to see. It was his way of putting his spin on the Vietnam War.

CHAPTER FIVE

Black Warriors and the Vietnam War

During the early sixties, a profound change in social awareness took place in America. The Black Revolution was gaining a foothold in black family infrastructures. In the military, young black soldiers were learning the true meaning of "unity" among their own kind. We began to pay attention when leaders such as Malcolm X, Dr. Martin Luther King, Jr., Huey Newton, Rap Brown, Angela Davis, Cassius Clay (Muhammad Ali), and other high-profile black people who spoke out against the war were either killed or disappeared from the spotlight.

I found myself caught between the new "black experience" and my own personal convictions. It never occurred to me whether or not fighting the war in Vietnam was right or wrong, I only knew I was young and compelled to do my own thing. At an early age, I was intrigued by the heavy sense of adventure surrounding fighting in a war.

Today, I remain steadfast in my beliefs . . . in 1968, I did the right thing. I, like my fellow veterans, answered our nation's call for duty. You can argue all of the issues, but once I considered the lifelong guilt and "excess baggage" of dodging the draft, I was more than determined not to let that controversial issue be added to my list of life's embarrassments. And, believe me, I do have a list!

I also have to go on record and say, I hold no grudge or malice toward anyone who found it necessary to circumnavigate his military obligations and tiptoe off to some foreign country. I feel those people did what they had to do for their own survival. Anyway, how can I or anyone else blame a person for not being willing to die for a fight they really didn't believe in?

I suppose some parents of potential servicemen saw the big picture and played a sizable role in protecting their offspring from war. Instinctively, those parents who had the means to safeguard their sons from a senseless war did so. The affluent held a certain advantage over the masses. They were simply better informed politically, which put them in a better position to defy the government. Personally, I'm glad some of those people never got a chance to see the inside of a military garrison.

I particularly wanted to be surrounded by those who were trusted and committed members of the team. I shudder to think what would have happened if we had to fight next to a person who refused to engage in battle. That would have been the quickest way for all of us to have gotten killed.

I do have a problem with those "cowards" who ran away from the fight and yet had the gall and audacity to ridicule the brave soldiers who considered it an honor to fight for their country. Our country's brave and dedicated soldiers sometimes gave their lives and limbs to an unappreciative nation of people who wouldn't show up for that unpopular war.

Today those same returning veterans who did fight in the Vietnam War gave more than body parts or their lives. Vietnam veterans are still in a perpetual fight long after the war's end. Some are fighting the crippling effects of PTSD (post-traumatic stress disorder). And still, some continue to battle the tragic consequences of Agent Orange, a lethal chemical designed to kill plants that also ravaged the young bodies of returning soldiers and even their children for decades after the war. How dare anyone spit upon these brave young men and call them "baby killers!"

In the late sixties and early seventies the United States was rapidly moving toward ending the war. With the Republican Party leading the way, our politicians charged returning Vietnam veterans with being traitors and accused them of turning communist simply because the vets didn't believe in their policies. The massive groups of veterans returning home at the same time had a lot to say about the way the war was being run. It was the veterans who were putting their lives on the line while the politicians sat on their fat asses here in the good ol' U.S. of A. imposing more policies. And how dare those politicians! The whole time, those same politicians were placing more and more GIs' lives in harm's way and scoring political and media points by adding up the communist body counts at the cost of American lives. We (the veterans) saw the atrocities firsthand. That alone gave returning vets every right to speak out against the unnecessary deaths of our brothers and fellow men.

It is my personal opinion that all wars are wrong. If I had a son, I would hope to be able to protect him from the evils of fighting and killing in a war. Although, the ultimate decision would be his own. On the other hand, I also believe if this country didn't have the thousands of soldiers who volunteered and ultimately sacrificed their lives in that war, America would have been substantially crippled for many years following the Vietnam War. If the sons of this country had not been willing to put their lives on the line during the volatile stages of the Cold War, a major victory would have been scored for the communists and their world propaganda.

The mental images of National Guard soldiers shooting students at Kent State are forever embedded in my memory. It proved to me that the United States would do anything to restore order, including killing innocent students who had the God-given right to protest against the war. It also proved to me that during the so-called "Vietnam intervention," anarchy was spreading and, politically, we as a nation were in big trouble with the younger population. They showed total contempt for our leaders, and with just cause.

The U.S. government had growing concerns that a large portion of America's youth was leaning toward communism. Our government also believed that a powerful influx of subversive entities was acting to undermine the United States government through the younger and impressionable generation.

By the time I got to Vietnam, the war had already been the longest conflict ever fought by the United States. The Vietnam War exceeded the U.S. participation in the two world wars and the Korean War combined. The United States was able to dodge physical devastation, but it suffered the loss of 58,000 lives (2,400 unaccounted for), costing approximately 150 billion dollars in direct expense to sustain the war.

The Vietnam War confused and divided the American public. It was the first war played out on television like a soap opera for the purpose of gaining national TV ratings and commercial buys.

The war in Vietnam had become a grim television spectacle. While I was home on leave, I watched the war unfold on a national stage . . . primetime television. The news services were pumping daily images of the Vietnam War, followed by massive student bodies clashing against the establishment and those who mandated war. The continued saga kept viewers glued to their television sets. The opportunist networks were not going to turn a blind eye to the climb in ratings.

The Vietnam War left our nation essentially and notably in great need of a population who believed serving one's country was the right thing to do.

At a time when racism was a biting social issue, economic grievances were chiefly to blame for blacks entering the military. African-Americans entered the service at a high rate during the late sixties and early seventies.

Over the years, I've been asked numerous times if "racism" played a role during my tour in the Vietnam War. I can only speak from a Lurp's personal experience. One thing is for sure . . . there was no such thing as a black, white, or brown Lurp in the jungles of Vietnam. We were all "camouflage green." Somehow, that way of thinking seemed to weave its way into the fabric of our everyday mien. The racial problems actually stemmed from our superiors, the very ones who did not have to face Charlie in the boonies day after day. Often, assignments given by the leaders would promote animosity among the troops. For example, the special missions given to one team over another would often create friction, or the favoritism used by platoon sergeants when delegating "unfair" details. Things like that usually fostered ill feelings within the ranks.

The black soldiers I knew in Company F 51st Inf. LRP made a conscious decision not to let racism become an issue. It had become apparent to everyone how important both team and individual survival was. As far as I could tell, the issues of racism hardly entered into the picture. This is not to say that everything was always jovial between the troops. Of course, the black troops were always cautious and took notice of those who had problems with black soldiers or black authority. Anyway, the closet racist would always surface when the drinking started. The inbred prejudices would rise like the South, sometimes by members of your own team.

Conceivably, alcohol explains why the social hours were segregated, as I will explain further in this chapter. But as far as I know, racism never found a home out in the boonies of Vietnam, where the Lurps spent most of their time. When you have to depend on the man next to you in order to exist, you don't have time to think about the color underneath his shades of green camouflage.

There's one thing most people in the military don't like to talk about or vehemently deny. A lot of people today would like to conceal the undeniable fact that black soldiers played a sizable and important combat role in the Vietnam War. Eventually black soldiers became a majority rather than a minority of the fighting force.

According to the Pentagon, from 1961 to December 31, 1972, a total of 46,163 men were either killed or fatally wounded in combat in Vietnam. Blacks comprised 5,672 or 12.28% of the casualties. In the U.S. Army, 30,627 were either killed or fatally wounded in combat. Blacks accounted for 4,000 of this total for 13.057% of the fatal casualties incurred from 1961 to December 31, 1972. The controversy over black casualties in Vietnam developed during the 1965–66 period when blacks, who made up 14% of the total U.S. Army, incurred 23% of the casualties in Vietnam. The explanation for the inequity was that blacks either volunteered or were selected (by standards testing) for service in the combat units. Consequently, by December 31, 1966, the actual percentage of blacks assigned to "combat occupations" throughout the U.S. Army was 17.2%. In elite combat units, such as the 173d Airborne Brigade and 101st Airborne Division, black participation was largely voluntary and exceptionally high. For example, when the average strength of blacks in Vietnam was 13.4% of all troops in 1965, blacks comprised 25.4% of the 173d Airborne Brigade and 23.9% of the 101st Airborne Division. The casualty figures reflect this disproportionate representation in combat units, so that during the first eleven months of 1966, blacks accounted for 22.4% of all U.S. Army troops killed in action. By 1969 this percentage had declined to 15%.

During the Vietnam campaign, blacks made up 10.6% or 275,000 of the war's population. More than 7,240 black soldiers died in Vietnam. Overall, blacks suffered 12.5% of the deaths in Vietnam at a time when the percentage of blacks in the military was only 13.5% of the total population.

Army Casualties in South Vietnam by Race

Army Strength by Race as of 30 April 1969

	Army-Wide	RVN
Total Strength Less USMA Cadets	1,511,017	378,797
Black Strength	180,917	44,000
Black Percentages	12.0%	11.6%

Percent Black Strength and Hostile Deaths
for Major Units in RVN (Strengths as of 28 Feb. 1969.
Deaths 1 Nov. 1965 thru 31 May 1969)*

	% Black Strength	Total Deaths	Black Deaths	% Black Deaths
Americal Div.	11.8%	254	30	11.8%
1st Cav Div.	11.8%	3,358	474	14.1%
1st Inf. Div.	11.9%	2,459	375	15.3%
4th Inf. Div.	12.9%	1,813	264	14.6%
9th Inf. Div.	12.8%	2,139	290	13.6%
11th Cav Regt.	10.9%	430	64	14.9%
25th Inf. Div.	12.9%	3,377	517	15.3%
101st Abn. Div.	9.8%	2,052	350	17.1%
173d Abn. Bde.	19.0%	1,160	224	19.3%
196th Inf. Bde.	13.2%	553	67	12.1%
199th Inf. Bde.	13.9%	474	65	13.7%
198th Inf. Bde.	14.8	455	53	11.6%
11th Inf. Bde.	13.8%	541	60	11.1%
3d Bde. 82d Abn. Div.	13.7%	161	21	13.0%
1st Bde. 5th Mech Div.	13.9%	107	20	18.7%
Total	12.6%	19,333	2,874	14.9%

Hostile and Nonhostile Deaths by Race in RVN
(1 Jan. 61 thru 31 May 69)

	Army	Blacks	% Blacks
Hostile Deaths	22,515	3,129	14.0%
Nonhostile Deaths	3,739	607	16.2%
Total Deaths	26,254	3,736	14.2%

*Strength and hostile deaths do not include attached units, some of which are listed separately.

One thing always struck me as odd. I found that Company F 51st had a few different "cliques." It was my guess that cliques band together because of the comfort zone nurtured by familiarity, in effect, creating self-imposed segregation.

The black groups and the white groups stayed pretty much to themselves. We worked well together, but in the evening, when duty was completed, the groups changed.

Everyone headed to their respective areas. The alcohol drinkers were predominantly white soldiers who customarily headed for the EM or NCO clubs after hours. The "pothead" crowd, seeking less confrontation and a more diverse gathering, headed for the berm to mingle.

Sometimes beer became a big part of these pothead gatherings, but there was rarely any fighting. On the other hand, the hard-core drinkers fought at least once a night or all night.

Even though black soldiers took refuge in bonding with their own, I personally think that gravitating to your own persuasion is a natural behavior. Although, sometimes it really didn't matter what race, religion, or creed a person was when it came to one of your best buddies. I will always say that Vietnam exposed a biracial brotherhood that proved to be the beginning of lasting friendships.

I had a white brother who was straight from the hills of Kentucky. I knew in my heart this buck sergeant was totally blind to color. I won't embarrass him by mentioning his real name (Barney). Perhaps the time and the place allowed the bond between Lurps and fellow soldiers to transcend the not-so-important barriers like "race." The time and place also gave us a chance to see the true colors; green . . . army green! Vietnam probably helped bridge the gap between the races in the late sixties and early seventies.

Being a part of the situation, I can see why the black Vietnam soldiers felt safer "yoking" and unifying with their own kind. The reasons were apparent. The black soldiers were faced with many perils; friendly fire, enemy fire, booby traps, the elements, indigenous creatures, shit happening, and on top of all that, "racism."

Keep in mind, I am talking about the late sixties and thousands of miles away from "real" civilization. The "good ol' boys'" club had a whole lot of big guns and sometimes they would do just about anything they wanted so far away from what we call real military justice. Case in point: Lieutenant Calley and the My Lai massacre. An incident where the frustrated lieutenant had his troops line up a village of Vietnamese and then began to execute them, only to be stopped by a couple of American helicopter pilots who sat their ship down on the ground between the villagers and the American troops who were doing the firing. Vietnam was a time and a situation that kept you alert and on your toes.

While I attended college in the early seventies, I had to write a term paper about the Reconstruction era. My research led me to uncover that Civil War historians made no attempt to hide their racial prejudice by maligning black soldiers. Well, times have changed since the Civil War. Recently I read a few "special operations" Vietnam books. Only one writer of this very popular book genre had the need to take potshots at the black soldiers who fought in Vietnam. The deep-seated racist slurs toward blacks continue to appear with words like shiftless, unresponsive, and scary, only when relating to black soldiers.

Over the years I have even heard that the Vietnam War was lost because the black soldiers wouldn't fight in the battles for whatever reasons. That kind of rhetoric is just one more ploy to continue the division between races propagated by those who are insecure with their own place in the real world. The average black soldier was a mere pawn on the military chessboard in Vietnam. The politicians and public opinion are responsible for losing the Vietnam War. The black soldiers I fought beside were noble, courageous soldiers who vaulted at the chance to make a difference for their race and their country.

I came away from the Vietnam War with the view that black soldiers were true warriors. Arguably, when it comes to raw physical agility, black soldiers were inherently superior warriors. Case in point: the NFL, NBA, the boxing associations. Who can deny the fact that black athletes are the better athletes? On a level playing field, black athletes are by far the leaders in most gladiatorial type arenas. Why should it be any different on the field of battle? Well, the fact is, there isn't any difference. Their tenacious fury shown on the fields of play could be and was mutated onto the field of battle.

Sometimes blacks Lurps were depicted as soldiers with bad attitudes. The truth was, they were no more incorrigible than anyone else. The commanders of these units came to realize that these soldiers had a street-smart toughness and "hard to the core" attitude that transcended oceans and environmental boundaries. Their toughness grew out of the need to survive in the ghettos. Most of these soldiers grew up in an atmosphere where they were in a perpetual fight for their survival.

Back on the block, if it weren't for this same person trying to do the right thing, he would be a considered a criminal. Most of the black soldiers I knew would have been tenacious warriors in any company in Vietnam, not just the Lurps.

Most black Lurps I'd come to know proved to be credible adversaries against the NVA and Viet Cong soldiers. I thought we matched up pretty well with our enemy. After months of pulling tough missions and having encountered the enemy wherever he dwelled, I began to have a profound respect for the North Vietnamese regulars and the Viet Cong soldiers. For that matter, I acquired a secret admiration for the Vietnamese people in general. In many ways the Vietnamese people endured the same harsh problems as the American black population. Both were victims of social and economic inequality.

For decades the Vietnamese were embroiled in defending their homeland against the world's most powerful war machines. The Chinese were the first to intrude on their country. After thousands of years of trouble with the Chinese, the French, the Japanese, and finally the United States and its mighty allied forces took their shot at dominance over the will of the Vietnamese people and their wealth.

Military history will bear me out when I say the French Foreign Legionnaires and Chinese soldiers were well-trained, hard-core fighters. And yet the Vietnamese soldiers whipped them soundly. They are not to be taken lightly. I have also come to admire the meticulous and methodical guerrilla techniques the North Vietnamese soldiers and Viet Cong used to fight off their opponents. Our company year-book sums up the enemy best:

They were tough warriors and difficult to figure out. They were constant, yet seldom if ever patterned. They were a mixture of Viet Cong guerilla and North Vietnam-ese Army Regulars. I have personally seen them as hard-core and unpredictable. Sometimes he was seen walking down trails with total abandon, "ditty bopping," convers-ing and even playing a loud radio. However, at other times he was in good military formation, controlled and alert. Uncle Ho's boys were always well-equipped, even if it was captured equipment. At times, on contact, he would blend into the bush. Other times he would stick around and fight like it was something personal. He was a daring soldier and a worthy antagonist. We generally held him in contempt and respect conjointly.

It was rumored throughout Vietnam that Lurps had boun-ties on their heads. That was one of the reasons Lurps dared not get captured. The Viet Cong and North Vietnamese Army soldiers were considered "first-class heroes" and held in high esteem if they either caught or killed a Lurp. It was the Lurp units that beleaguered the tough NVA soldiers. Lurp teams that focused on ambushing the enemy always presented problems for Uncle Ho's boys. The enemy also feared the Lurp units whose targets were only to hunt and report the whereabouts of NVA units, routes, and base camps. To counter the Lurp companies, the NVA created numerous antirecon units.

According to reports corresponding to their strategically critical war zones, the communists deployed a counterrecon-naissance battalion composed of counterreconnaissance companies. They dressed in tiger stripes and camouflage (like the Lurps). They were always well equipped with the latest recon and communications intercept equipment as well as dogs and trackers. Frequently their weapons and equipment were American made.

Their missions were to locate and hunt down to the death any Allied LRRP teams found. In addition, smaller counter-recon units were organized by the communists. It was authenticated through captured documents and prisoner interrogations that many enemy units established bounties on Lurps. Often the bounty was paid in the cash equivalent of one thousand U.S. dollars, the same bounty for killing a U.S. colonel.

The North Vietnamese Army trained and sent to the south a special team with the specific mission of directly countering the Lurp teams. The enemy team was composed of six men . . . just like its prey. Except in February 1972, the hunter became the hunted; a patrol from H Company Ranger ambushed and killed the NVA counter-LRRP team. Among the captured documents was information detailing the NVA team's mission and a picture of the six men taken in the North, holding their country's flag. According to their documents, they would each receive a small rice farm for the killing or capturing an entire Lurp team.

The Viet Cong and NVA soldiers called the elusive Lurps *bien rich du.* That is Vietnamese for "spies." The enemy also sometimes called us "ghosts," "men with green faces," and even "murderers." It was concluded that Lurps and other Special Operations recon teams were making a huge impact on the enemy's daily operations as well as the increase in the enemy body count.

CHAPTER SIX

The Mission from Hell

While the company operated in the Cu Chi AO, I became a seasoned combat veteran. Most of our missions were tougher than the one before, yet seemingly all too routine. The string of missions seemed to run together as each began to resemble the last one. By this time in my tour I had become very astute in the craft of Long Range Reconnaissance Patrol. I knew how to plan for a mission, call in artillery or air strikes, make field "situation reports," and pretty much run the team if necessary. I knew I didn't have all the tools or all the answers like the team leaders before me, but I was always willing to learn the next lesson.

Our premission briefings were beginning to feel much too routine as well. Some of the time I found myself not paying attention to what was being said. In the middle of the orientation I would find myself drifting off into other thoughts, like the insertion, which was always a reason for a concern or two.

I always made sure I knew the radio SOI, the LZ we were being inserted into, our rally points, escape and evading routes, and all significant information essential to our survival. When the Lurp teams were on the ground, they executed the mission pretty much at the discretion of the team leaders.

But there were times in the briefing room when things were said that made you sit up and take notice, especially when we were told we would be operating in the Hobo Woods. The Hobo Woods was not just a name, but an emotion.

To this day I am sure that name still strikes fear in the hearts of those men who fought there. This particular AO was located next to the Cambodian border. It was called Hobo Woods because of the damage done to the triple canopy jungle by the U.S. Army's chemical agents. Years before I ever saw the area, it was a lush green jungle that was eventually depleted by Agent Orange. The chemicals reduced the thick foliage into an open wasteland, rendering the area unfit to hold the name "jungle."

In late September 1968 the Soul Patrol received warning orders to operate in the Hobo Woods AO. I had heard many frightening stories about the sector before the company ever moved into the Cu Chi base camp. Hobo Woods was rumored to have a high concentration of enemy activity. The region was infested with elaborate underground tunnel systems leading from Cambodia into Cu Chi. It was a place we feared.

G-2 spotted heavy equipment being moved around at night from their infrared aerial reconnaissance photos. The grim reports of troop movements during the day didn't help our fears either; it only made us realize we were walking into something really ugly.

Our mission was simple: we were to watch a small section of a ten-mile stretch of road that obviously lead straight into the depths of hell.

I absolutely loathed everything about this mission. At 1800 hours we were to make a last-light insertion. I hated those late drops. It didn't give the team enough time to search out an adequate hiding place.

The helicopter flight out to the AO was awful. I was scared and sick to my stomach. The flight took about thirty-five minutes. We flew approximately twenty-five hundred feet up in the air. During the flight I had this insatiable urge to bail out of the helicopter into the river along the flight path and take my chances falling into the water below. My thoughts of suicide seemed to be a better option than facing the dreaded Hobo Woods.

On the map our insertion point was an area spotted with tall dried grass and sparse vegetation. This type of terrain always presented the team with concern. We would be in a constant strain to find an appropriate spot to hide. During the flight over the AO, the chopper pilots provided the team with a couple of "false insertions." By flying in fast and low, they pulled up at the last minute, then flew to another LZ and dropped us off. The maneuver would confuse potential enemy landing zone watchers.

As we flew high over the landing zone, I observed a Y-shaped river about three hundred meters behind our insertion point. The river's edge would provide ample cover, but the path getting there was through an open field.

Suddenly we dropped down to treetop level. The pilot set the helicopter down on a frequently used, wide dirt road. Sgt. Jerry Brock, ATL Norman Reid, PFC Lawton Mackey, Sp 4. Thomas Mattox, and myself exited the same side of the chopper with no tree line or cover for concealment.

Daylight was fading. We haphazardly chose an NDP (night defensive position) that was about twenty feet from the wide road that ran east and west. Our small perimeter was partly surrounded by a few flimsy bushes approximately three feet high. I had a small prone log lying in front of me that ran adjacent to the road. Just as I began positioning the M-60 machine gun on the road, four NVA soldiers with new AK-47s walked into my kill zone. They were probably looking for the Lurp team that had flown in over the area. I had a clear shot at all four. I turned to Sergeant Brock and begged for permission to light them up. Brock repeatedly waved me off by emphatically shaking his head "No!" I was disappointed that permission to engage was quickly denied. Somehow those soldiers sensed danger and scurried out of the area. Had we sprung the ambush, we would have been sure to get a few kills and at least one prisoner. Not to mention that TOC would be forced to pull us out of the field after having our position compromised. It was nothing more than a delusion to think of the possibilities of getting out of the boonies and having three days of R & R for capturing a prisoner. Brock's orders stood, no prisoners today.

From the time we hit the ground, Sergeant Brock was in constant radio contact with TOC. After we settled into our RON, Brock continued radio contact as if something were about to happen. Because we were only a five-man patrol, Sergeant Brock sometimes doubled as team leader and radio operator. He was very comfortable and capable of pulling the multitask. I couldn't help wondering why he stayed on the radio; I had never seen him do that before.

Around 2100 hours, in the darkness, we started hearing twigs snapping. It sounded like we were getting 360-degree movement. Brock was still on the radio. We were on high alert, every weapon at the ready.

It was evident the enemy knew we were in the area but was unable to track our exact location. We figured that the four NVA soldiers we'd seen earlier had come back to investigate what made them take off in such a hurry. Not long after, the noises made by the curious NVA soldiers suddenly stopped. I wondered if they had abandoned their efforts of finding us in the flimsy bushes.

About an hour later the first round whistled by our location, impacting the ground approximately seventy-five meters west of our position. Then, one by one, the rounds began walking directly toward us. The explosions dropped closer and closer, straight toward our tight perimeter. Just before the next round would have found our exact spot, the firing abruptly stopped and immediately started from the opposite direction, this time from the east. Another series of rounds began to walk straight toward our perimeter. Red-hot flying shrapnel tumbled over our heads, barely missing us. I noticed that Sergeant Brock was still in uninterrupted radio contact with our command post back at Cu Chi. With every explosion he whispered into the handset, as if directing an artillery fire mission. Then Brock simultaneously moved ever so slightly away from the center of our perimeter, like he knew the next round was going to be real close.

And just like before, the last rounds fell just short of a direct hit. The firing stopped . . . seconds later it started from another direction. Boy, if Brock were directing this fire mission, he was doing a fine job. I couldn't help but compliment Brock on his textbook artillery support.

"Damn, Brock," I whispered in his ear, "that's some nice shooting!"

"That's not us, that's them, you fool!" Brock exclaimed.

It was enemy mortar fire, not our artillery support! Well, whoever was doing the firing was doing one hell of a job. That's how our fire support should have been protecting us! It was time to be real concerned. Now the mission was turning into one of those ugly heartpounding events that made your chest hurt. Just then another pattern of rounds came at us from the north working their way to the south toward our position. And each time, the mortar rounds stopped just short of a direct hit. The mortar rounds slammed so close to our position that we were receiving hard concussion blows that knocked the breath from our bodies. Larger pieces of amber shrapnel scattered around us.

Each round became a gamble for our lives. The perfect pattern in which the mortar dropped made it easy to understand why I thought we were being covered by our own artillery firepower.

The rumors about Hobo Woods weren't rumors at all. This place was crawling with enemy activity. We lay among the thin bushy cover, sweating out an hour of constant and terrifying shelling. Then all at once the mortars stopped. The night air was warm and charged with electricity, punctuated by complete silence.

A couple of hours passed with no movement. It was like the calm before the storm. I expected the worst. Around 0200 hours, as we lay huddled in our small perimeter, Charlie snuck in close enough to throw an unknown object into our position. It could have been a grenade or a rock. Whatever it was, it landed near my right leg. I'd hoped Charlie was using one of their common tricks to hit a metallic object like a weapon or a radio, desperately hoping it was not a grenade. Sometimes the maneuver was a ploy to make us scramble and give away our position.

PFC Lawton Mackey was lying close to me on my left side. When we heard the object hit the ground, Mackey jumped, ready to bolt out of the perimeter. I quickly reached and grabbed a fistful of the front of his shirt with my left hand, forcefully holding him down, gesturing with my grip and the strength of my arm, "Don't move!" At the same time I reached with my right hand and began searching in the bushes to find whatever had been tossed. I knew I had only five or seven seconds at most to get rid of it . . . if it were a grenade. I also knew I had a fifty-fifty chance of getting blown up if it was one of their rusty, unreliable Chi-Com (Chinese Communist) grenades. While this was going on, the rest of the team lay perfectly still and completely silent. I remember thinking as I felt around in the shrubbery looking for the object, "If this thing goes off, I still might be able to live through this. I would be minus my right hand and leg, but I can still survive this."

I never found whatever landed near our perimeter. I surmised it was a rock and thanked God it was not a U.S. grenade, because that's what it sounded like. Charlie's intention was to hit something with a metallic sound, but they missed and we didn't move. I believed at that point that Charlie had determined we weren't in the immediate area and discontinued his search.

The Vietnam War was an equal strain on all body parts. On this mission I felt energy being drained from my soul. The stress of the mission wore me out. By this time in my tour I had learned how to go for days without sleep. This was one of those missions where sleep was not an option.

To be sure, our tribulations didn't stop there, that would have been too easy. It was exactly 0500 hours. Under the cover of predawn darkness, we were startled by someone calling out cadences in the Vietnamese language some fifty meters down the wide dirt road. The voices became closer and louder. We heard stomping footsteps marching toward our position.

Once in a great while, just when you think you've seen it all . . . That morning, to our amazement and disbelief, we witnessed hundreds of NVA soldiers marching in lockstep deliberation. They were moving from the east to the west on that wide dirt road only twenty feet from our position, and that far away from the barrel of my machine gun. Every single one of them was dressed in completely new combat gear with a full rucksack, all prepared for battle. The soldiers carried brand-new AK-47 rifles with red and blue tassels that dangled from the barrels of their rifles. Their weapons were securely placed on their shoulders with the bayonets erect and pointing toward the sky. They all wore high-top boots and helmets with the chin straps tightened beneath their chins. They were the mirror image of each other. Every soldier dressed alike in a beige khaki uniform with a red bandana wrapped around his neck. They looked like an arrogant elite army unit strutting their stuff with pride. With the precision of a dress parade, they all appeared to be showing off. The only missing ingredient was the marching band to accompany their lockstep movements.

We were so close we could hear the heel to toe crunch of gravel being pulverized underneath their boots. We watched in terror as this impressive episode of the war unfolded right before our eyes. I remember trying to will myself to be invisible.

The marching troops continued past daybreak. When the enemy came that close to us, I often wondered how and why they weren't able to hear our collective heartbeats.

Around 0730 hours the sun began to rise over the hilly ravine that ran along the road. The broken sunlight peeking through the trees was surely enough to give away our position. Again we were literally in the open! The only things concealing our position were a few shrubs and a small log lying in front of us. I knew that at any moment a few of their troops would stray off the road and trample into our area. Or by chance one of them would come by with tracking dogs that would sniff us out.

As I watched the endless march, I accepted that anything

was possible. I was mentally preparing myself for the worst, including my death. I had decided, if we were spotted, I was going to take as many of them as possible with the M-60 machine gun.

I slowly turned my head to look at my teammates. Their eyes showed what was going on in their minds. We were all witnessing one of the most horrific sights a Lurp could ever encounter. Even if we were lucky enough to live through this, who would believe it? No one would ever know the enormity of what we were experiencing. Never in my wildest dreams would I have believed that I would see anything quite as awesome as what I watched that morning.

They were easy to count; they moved by us in sets of fifties. The count was now up to 250 and still they continued to march. Out of my peripheral vision I happened to get a quick glimpse at Thomas Mattox, who was positioned directly behind me. I'll blame it on my imagination, but Mattox's eyes seemed to be bulging out of his head. I wanted to somehow gesture him to squint or close his eyes because they resembled a pair of '58 Buick headlights. I was afraid the enemy troops marching by would glance over and spot his high-beam glare. Silly me, I still managed to find a glimmer of humor during this most intense moment. Watching Thomas Mattox make visual commentaries with his changing facial expressions is something etched in my memory forever. Somehow I was able to muster a puny yet silent snicker.

The entire time, Brock had the PRC-25 radio handset practically glued to his head; it literally never left his ear. By squeezing the button on the handset, Brock was able to click or squelch out information to TOC. Information such as the enemy troop count and their direction of movement. I was sure Brock was transmitting other pertinent intelligence just in case we were spotted and wiped out. For me, it was little comfort that someone would know what had happened to Team 2-6 should the worst-case scenario play out.

Considering everything that happened, the power of

prayer became a very important part of the mission. And hindsight proved beyond a shadow of a doubt that we had an Omnipotent Power safeguarding our presence. Another thing, I also believe one of the reasons we weren't detected was because the enemy soldiers were marching in formation. With the discipline of a well-groomed unit, each eye was glued to the back of the head of the man in front of him.

If Charlie wanted to find us, all he had to do was "look." They would have come across a Lurp team that was frightened to death, but with the will to fight until their last breath of air. We knew that making first contact was out of the question, because our deaths would be inescapable. Like the Motown song goes, "Nowhere to run, nowhere to hide!" Well, that was us.

The river was about two hundred meters away. I had thought about running for the river if we were detected. But still, an accurate shot would have picked me off with no problem. I had heard about Lurp teams being overrun and never heard from again. I had already decided that I was not going to be taken alive. Sergeant Alvarado's words still loomed heavy in the back of my mind, "Lurps do not get captured!"

By the time the enemy count reached 350, I personally stopped counting. What was the use in tallying. We couldn't fight off a force that size anyway. So I sat among the small brush hoping and praying the nightmare would end soon.

Finally, around 0900 hours the march did end. After the last group of soldiers went by, our team sat in complete bewilderment. I was numb. Time and space didn't seem real. I felt like I was having an out-of-body experience. It was as though my soul had left my body and hovered over the situation. This was the closest I had come to death without being shot at.

Minutes passed and still no one spoke a word. It was a mystery "why" and "how" they had missed us. It just wasn't logical.

I remember how difficult it was to breathe; the adrenaline

rush was more than my body was able to handle. I tried to steady my heart rate and bring it to a normal beat, to no avail.

Brock looked up from his radio transmissions and motioned for us to pack up and prepare for an extraction. Ten minutes later we heard the glorious and welcome thumping sounds of the helicopters in the distant sky.

When the helicopter came within sight, it descended flying fast and low. The tail of the extraction ship lowered and kicked up a cloud of dust on the dirt road. We ran and dived headfirst into the cargo bay, yelling to the pilots, "Go! Go! Go!" The pilot wasted no time taking off. As the helicopter elevated to about a hundred feet off the ground, I sat in the doorway and began spitting at the ground and giving the area the "finger." I taunted over the noise of the chopper, "Fuck you, you sons of bitches! You missed me again, you motherfuckers!" After my brief outburst, we flew away from the Hobo Woods in a daze. I quietly watched the Vietnam landscape constantly change beneath our feet.

By the time we reached the helipad back at the company area, there was a host of Lurps waiting to greet and congratulate us. Everyone within earshot heard about the mission. TOC and the briefing room were buzzing with big-time army brass from II Field Force.

During the debriefing the team estimated that approximately 450 to 500 enemy soldiers had marched by us that morning. I remember the debriefing interviews being short and to the point. That was fine with me. I wanted to hurry to the mess hall for morning chow and then a nice cool shower.

Sergeant Brock stayed behind for more debriefing. The rest of the team hurried single file into the mess hall. When we entered, everyone turned and looked at us with admiration. The slobbering kudos gushed from our fellow Lurps. Even the cooks acknowledged us when we entered. They had never done that before. They, too, had heard about the mission. The cooks showed their approval by smiling and shoveling extra helpings of food onto our trays. Their acknowledgment was very inspirational. I remember thinking how proud I was to be a Lurp.

A couple of hours later Brock joined us in the hootch. The look on his face was especially interesting as he beamed with pride and accomplishment.

"I guess the term 'two regiment-size enemy forces' sez it all!" he said. "We found out where General Vo Nguyen Giap was holding his southernmost army division," Brock said, like I knew who he was talking about.

Who in the hell is General Giap? I questioned. Brock acted like he didn't hear me; he continued on talking about the meeting in the TOC. He was also told by a top G-2 officer that the company would be on "stand-down" status. The Hobo Woods AO was off limits for at least one week due to complete saturation bombing of the area.

That was the best news I had heard since arriving in that abominable country. The mission had lasted less than twenty-four hours. The command had no plans to stick us back into the field. It was standard procedure to put a team back into the field when a mission was cut short. Usually, after an abbreviated debriefing, we would be told to "Charlie Mike" (continue mission). Surprisingly, this time we didn't have to go back out to the boonies.

The mission turned out to be very good for Team 2-6, the Soul Patrol. Company F 51st Infantry had made a big impact and a great contribution to the war effort.

Only a few years ago I learned that Sgt. Gary Ford was on radio watch that night. He was the voice communicating with Brock throughout the night and the morning during that impressive display of enemy forces. This particular mission is mentioned briefly on page 167 in the book entitled *4/4: A LRP's Narrative*, written by Gary Douglas Ford.

Hindsight proved that Sgt. Jerry Brock was a smart and experienced team leader. He stopped me from firing on those four enemy soldiers on the road that day. Had I done so, hundreds of NVA soldiers would have surely descended on us and wiped us out within minutes. The episode on that morning is forever inscribed in my memory. Every time I think about that particular mission, I thank God for His presence and protection . . . I give Him praise. I prayed hard that night, and I am sure I was not alone. We undoubtedly had a lot of prayers going out that night from our folks back home. They would be happy to know that, on that mission, their prayers were answered.

The other upside to our encounter was that as a team we shared a sense of self-confidence and pride. I believed we could operate as a "Lurp team" in Vietnam or anywhere else on this globe. I had never been so proud of my teammates as I was the day we touched down on the chopper pad that thankful morning. Positive images of my teammates are forever stored. We performed just as we were trained. We were told by the II Field Force commanders that we had responded impeccably under those difficult circumstances. From that day forward, I knew that Team 2-6, the Soul Patrol, had become something special.

Thirty years later, all the things I saw and all the things I did in Vietnam do not seem real. I had a conversation with Thomas Mattox after many years of trying to not remember the Vietnam War. I asked him to reassure me that what we saw that morning was not in my imagination. Mattox told me it was all real and the numbers were all too valid.

I still have nightmares about that mission at least once a month since returning home from Vietnam. Today I am a completely different person than I was back then, with a host of memories and residual side effects from the past.

When we performed our duties in Vietnam, we never thought about the magnitude of our achievements while fighting the war. We were just doing a job. Besides, we had returned from one of those campfire missions. This was the kind of story that was told on the berm late at night. The Soul Patrol had just experienced a mission of absolute terror, but we survived.

After that mission I began to realize how numb I was becoming to the everyday trials and tribulations of the war.

Each time we experienced an intense mission, it would take an increased level of excitement to pin my heartbeat meter in the red. The horrors of war didn't surprise me anymore. I learned to take each episode with stride. I often wondered if others felt that way.

Many months later, subsequent to my leaving Vietnam and returning to Stateside duty at Fort Bragg, North Carolina, I had to make a mandatory parachute jump from a helicopter to continue my jump pay status. I'm sure those previous notions of suicide while flying over the Hobo Woods AO prepared me to make an easy leap from the helicopter. After a year and a half of not having to don a parachute, on my first jump, once the command was given to "go," I jumped without hesitation and was happy to do it! It was such a relief to finally jump from a helicopter while it was in flight.

CHAPTER SEVEN

Welcome Back to Bien Hoa

By early October the cycle of the seasons began to change. Summer had vanished and the monsoon season was in full swing. It had been pouring off and on for about ten days. The Huey UH-1 helicopters did not fly well in rainstorms and entire helicopter squadrons were put on a standdown status. That resulted in the teams not having to go into the field. For many reasons, the company stand-down seemed to be very timely for all.

Fighting in Vietnam was never a picnic, but when it rained it was dreadful. The rains presented a significant problem out in the boonies. Projectile raindrops blew in sideways and pelted you in the face. There were times during torrential downpours when we had to scale up and slide down the sides of hills slick with mud. The infamous red volcanic clay of Vietnam became an extension of our camouflaged attire. What made matters even more rotten was that we also had to sleep in the cold, gooey stuff. During the dark, wet jungle nights, monsoon rains beating down on you, your bush hat, and the vegetation around you, it was virtually impossible to hear the enemy sneaking up on your position. Team leaders in the field made sure to fortify their perimeters with layers of trip flares and claymore mines. The enemy used the rain to their advantage and the Lurp teams learned to counter those actions.

The monsoon season was here with a vengeance, and it was here to stay . . . at least for another four months. The rumor mill was working overtime. This time the talk was that the entire company would be shipping back to Camp Lindsey-Lattin in Bien Hoa. We would go back to working the old familiar AO, the Catcher's Mitt, with triple canopy trees, real foliage, and a real jungle. Certainly, fighting in that type of terrain was much more conducive to our jungle training than moving and operating in the open like we were doing at times in the Cu Chi AOs. The reports of going back to Bien Hoa gave most of us a reason to smile. That was the good news . . . the unconfirmed pesky groundswell of "bad news" concerning the company splitting up continued to gather momentum.

Most of the Lurps were starting to get bored from the lack of activity. Our weeklong stand-down consisted of me and a group of Lurps lifting weights during the day and writing letters home at night. There was not much to do in the way of details, except for filling sandbags and shoring up bunkers around our hootches.

After Ricky's funeral, I had made a conscious effort to stop smoking pot. The haunting effects of marijuana made me focus on Ricky's death, especially at a time when I was trying to put those agonizing thoughts out of my mind.

I want to clarify our position on pot smoking. Let it be known by every reader of this book . . . Under no circumstance did we ever smoke marijuana before going into the field or while we were in the field. It was absolutely not permitted. Back in the rear, as long as we didn't kill each other, minor offenses like smoking pot were overlooked. I'd also like to qualify that statement with . . . it depended on who caught you smoking pot. Some of the heavy-drinking NCOs had a real hard-on for anyone who did smoke pot, and they were more than happy to take away a stripe or give you an Article 15 (punishment under the Uniform Code of Military Justice) for the petty offense. But we Lurps policed ourselves in the field. When it came to getting "high" while operating on patrols in Vietnam, it just didn't happen!

Anyone who ever sampled army mess will know they didn't serve the greatest food. It was around this time I started to improvise our meals in the 2d Platoon hootch. I picked up the culinary art of learning how to prepare tolerable meals with the dehydrated Lurp rations, C rations, and goodies sent from home. Instead of a stove, we tore off about two inches in diameter of C-4 explosive and ignited it with a match or Zippo lighter. The C-4 tab burned a hot blue base, with a bright red flame that heated water inside a canteen holder very quickly. The best way to describe the effects of C-4 is that of "solid rocket fuel." It burns very hot with a lot of force.

With boiling water, a pinch of salt, a dab of pepper, and helpings from a large bottle of tabasco sauce, my chili con carne with Vienna sausage entrees turned out to be very popular among the guys.

During this time in the 2d Platoon hootch we were able to manage a few fun-filled rainy evenings in Company F, as much fun as anyone could expect in a wartime environment.

The holiday season was only a few short weeks away and the mail was dribbling in at a snail's pace. Wanda had not written back after the numerous letters I had sent her. I was getting anxious to hear from her. And as time passed, it seemed very unlikely that she was ever going to write back. When I didn't hear from her, her silence became a powerful focal point, so much that it became a distraction. My lack of concentration was beginning to show in my work. I received a couple of comments about my attitude and my overall performance in the field. The remarks came from those who knew me best. They were friends who knew when to pull my coattails regarding my "amour" problems. I was told by Thad Givins and Brock to "pull my shit together and get over her," or risk getting myself and others killed.

It was hell living in a war environment. I was always angry and always afraid. And to have that special girl back home snub me week after week by not writing or answering my letters made for a pretty disgruntled soldier. Wanda undoubtedly didn't understand the despair she was putting into a young soldier's heart.

After weeks of mail calls without a letter from Wanda, I

realized I had to toughen up and treat the situation like she didn't exist. It happened overnight. I made up my mind and "poof," she was out of my heart and my mind. But before I put the situation to rest, I lashed out at her the only way I could. I wanted her to feel my pain, so I wrote her that final letter. It simply read . . . "Dear Wanda, Fuck you!" And with that it was over, the pain was gone. My hurt vanished into thin air. Of course, I knew I wouldn't hear from her ever, especially after choosing such profound words to end our "almost" relationship. But I certainly felt better because the anticipation of the heartbreak didn't exist anymore.

In Vietnam, home was not only a great distance away, but it actually "felt" far away. The mental and physical pressures of the war taught me the difference between lonely and being alone.

In my opinion, those words had two intensely different meanings. In Vietnam, being "lonely" is what every GI experienced. My definition of being "alone" was a sense of total detachment from all things and everybody. I had come to believe that it was in my best interest not to get emotionally attached to anyone or anything, including my own life. Lurps couldn't help caring for each other. Deep down inside we understood and accepted the idea of possibly finding ourselves crouched over a friend's mangled body, weeping. Disconnecting my emotions from the very people I would take a bullet for became a bizarre practice. The emotional and psychological separation was unpleasant but necessary. It became clear to me, the impact of my cousin's death had an extreme effect on how I was going to live the rest of my life. The lessons learned in Vietnam continue to affect me even today, some thirty years later.

It's a fact, in a war idle time breeds low morale. It was something the military tried desperately to guard against. Just as our long, boring stand-down became unbearable, on November 4, 1968, it happened! We got orders to move back to Bien Hoa. I was tickled to be going back to Camp

Lindsey-Lattin. We did the nasty job of identifying and eliminating enemy sanctuaries; now it was time to go back to our real "home" in Vietnam.

Once again the Company F 51st LRP proved its worth as a "direct action unit" in Vietnam. Our work was acknowledged as invaluable to the II Field Force command. When we were assigned to Cu Chi, our mission was to find and destroy the bad guys where they dwelled and return with less injured and friendly KIAs than our enemy. In Cu Chi, Company F enemy confirmed kills had grown into the hundreds, not counting the kills brought on by helicopter gunships, artillery fire, or B-52 strikes. We felt we had accomplished our mission and a job well done. But now it was time to leave this horrible place.

Unceremoniously, we took to the skies and headed back to our somewhat congenial base camp in Bien Hoa. All I could think about was how good it would feel to sleep in a real bunk with clean sheets and pillowcases instead of on a cot or an air mattress. We learned to appreciate the small things.

By this time I had been in-country long enough to put in for R & R (rest and relaxation). Thad Givins and I went to the CQ to apply for leave to Bangkok, Thailand. I couldn't think of a better person to share that experience with than my buddy Thad.

Between the mortar attacks back in the company area and the ugly fights among the troops, life in the rear was still an adventure. Like every other company in Vietnam, we had our share of good times and bad. Some of the good times happened in the evenings after chow when the potheads rendezvoused to the berm to smoke marijuana. Some of my best recollections of Vietnam came after the sun went down back in the company area. The sunset soiree usually started with music from Armed Forces Radio. Conversations ranged from trash-talking GIs absorbed in discussions about the girls back home to the cars they owned back in the

World and sometimes even to boasting about their football prowess. These gatherings would inevitably lead to us telling stories about hairy Lurp missions.

Surprisingly, the soldiers never talked about themselves when telling these campfire war stories. Instead they would talk about other Lurps in the company, or the Lurps that had already rotated from Company F. The tales of their friends and comrades' bravery made for lasting impressions. These stories were the fuel that added to my itch to be just like them.

When a Lurp achieved legendary status in Vietnam, the respect and admiration of his contemporaries would speak volumes for him. There were many chilling and fascinating missions shared on the berm at night. The captivating stories were chronicled in riveting detail, as only Lurps can tell them. Most of the stories were easy to palate, because they were generally true. Late into the night they would hold court talking endlessly about the special soldiers who made everyday fighting in Southeast Asia a little bit more exciting. The conversations usually featured the hard-core, smart fighters who went beyond the call of duty to get the job done. Lurps like George D. Alexander (Big Al), Jerry Brock, and Michael D. Frazier (Brazzaville). As team leaders these guys radiated confidence out in the field.

I had the privilege of talking to our company commander, Col. William C. Maus, a year before he passed away on April 23, 1998. Colonel Maus was the first commander for Company F 51st LRP (Abn.) Infantry. All of the Company F Lurps who had not served directly under his command were made to know that Colonel Maus was the reason Company F was the best Lurp unit in Vietnam.

During my thirty-minute conversation with the colonel, the only soldier he mentioned was one staff sergeant, George D. Alexander. Colonel Maus acknowledged "Big Al" as the best soldier he had ever commanded, and how proud he was to have Big Al serve in the company as well as the other soldiers of Company F.

After that chat with Colonel Maus, it didn't take me long

to telephone George Alexander and reacquaint myself. Thirty long years had passed before I was able to get in touch with the one person that I have always admired and respected. It was an honor for me to inform him of all the great words Colonel Maus had spoken about him. "Big Al" was a highly decorated black soldier who completed his military career as a command sergeant major. I was extremely proud when Colonel Maus made the distinction. Out of all the other soldiers he could have mentioned, ironically, he chose my hero, "Big Al," Staff Sergeant George D. Alexander. You can see and hear interviews by George Alexander on the "Silent Heroes: LRRPs" documentary that airs on the History Channel.

In the civilian world, little is known about LRRP units and their outstanding soldiers that served in Vietnam, which was my motivation to produce the "Silent Heroes" documentary.

I would be remiss if I didn't mention this. . . . The Long Range Patrol were the soldiers who pulled the high-risk missions that others who sat on their butts at the neighborhood bars lied about after the war. Yeah, I have a bone to pick, because I've heard the stories. It's easy for these prevaricators to pass themselves off as heroes after the war. They claimed to be Lurps after returning home. But where were these so-called heroes while the fight was going on?

One out of seven soldiers in Vietnam was a fighter, the rest were there to support the grunts and the soldiers who were doing the fighting. Most of the military personnel in Vietnam functioned as administrators, cooks, truck drivers, supply troops, military police, intelligence, doctors, and maintenance engineers. Any personnel who didn't fight, fly, live, or work in the jungles of Vietnam were called "REMF," an acronym for "rear echelon motherfuckers." Don't get me wrong, they, too, were much needed; without them, we could not effectively do our job of fighting the war. But after the war was over, some of those same REMF soldiers claimed to be too distraught to talk about the war because of the anxiety it caused. That's fine and dandy. I'm sure a lot of soldiers had valid reasons for feeling that way, but most of those soldiers never saw the enemy and most never fired a weapon in combat. As close as some of these guys ever came to seeing any action was during a food fight in the mess hall. For those who did see action and those who are combat vets, well, these statements obviously do not apply to them.

It has been difficult for me to sit back and listen to the bullshit lies the PX heroes were laying down long after the war was over. From my personal experience, I know that most of the crap I've heard since returning from Vietnam is just that, "crap!"

Another variety of story that continued to surface after the war was spun by some ex–Vietnam vets who never saw action, but claimed that their jobs were too "top secret" to talk about. To that I say, "Bullshit!" Oh sure, I'm familiar with the issues of sensitive materials, but the people I'm talking about were not privileged to sensitive information. The "information acts" of 1985 allowed members of the CIA, Special Forces (Green Berets), LRRP/LRP/Rangers, SOG, Marine Force Recon, and the Navy SEALS to write books and talk openly about what happened in Vietnam, including the assassinations of high-level enemy officials. These books divulge facts about operations inside Cambodia and Laos and also operations on the northern side of the DMZ. The well-thought-out lies from some of these guys simply raised issues with me. There . . . I said it! And, if you are offended by my vents, then you must be one of those guys I'm talking about.

For a long time Vietnam had become a taboo subject. In an incident I had immediately following the war, an instructor in one of my college courses suggested I not talk about the Vietnam War while in group discussions. "No one wants to hear about Vietnam," he stipulated. For years I completely shut down and quit talking about the Vietnam War altogether. I am glad times have changed. I have long wanted to talk about what happened over there. I find myself gratuitously purging my story in this book; it has become a source of therapy. It also gives me a chance to tell a different side of the Vietnam War: the war the LRRPs fought and also the "black experience" as a soldier in the war.

CHAPTER EIGHT

R & R in Bangkok, Thailand

Two weeks after the company moved back to Bien Hoa, Thad and I got orders for R & R to Bangkok, Thailand. The much-needed leave came a lot quicker than we had expected.

From the time Givins and I arrived in Vietnam, we were in competition to buy and collect the best looking tailor-made suits from the shops in downtown Bien Hoa. We picked patterns from *Playboy* magazine and took them to the tailor shops to be copied. By the time we got word to pack for R & R, we were both armed with the latest in apparel and ready to party like it was June 6 of 1969. (That was the date we were both set to DEROS back to the World.)

This time, my all too familiar jeep ride to Tan Son Nhut Airport was a joyous trip for a change. I remember thinking how long it had been since I last smiled. The anticipation of seven days of absolutely no war was exhilarating. We were booked in the same seating section on the airplane. I had the seat next to the window off the left wing. The flight time to Thailand was approximately one hour.

After I'd had a few nods, the pilot alerted the passengers and crew to extinguish all smoking and buckle up for the approach into Bangkok International Airport. When we broke through the clouds, I looked out the window expecting to see a thriving metropolis. Instead, I thought we were flying back into Vietnam with its mountains, rice paddies, and jungles. It was Vietnam reincarnate. Then the jetliner made a final bank to the left, and off the port window I saw the beautiful and breathtaking city of Bangkok. The majestic high-rise buildings and the large exotic hotel came into view just as the plane neared the runway. My smiling jaw muscles that hadn't been used in a while started to ache again. Thad and I were both from a big city, and instinct told us that we were in for the time of our lives.

Bangkok was the epitome of two worlds colliding between the old and the new. Modernistic construction was visible throughout the city. But the backdrop of Bangkok was divided by the old, rural underprivileged society, which was only a few blocks away.

Outside the airport was a parking area with a gathering of privately owned early model cars serving as taxicabs lined up for business.

"Hey, GI! You want numba one cab?" I turned to Thad and jokingly asked, "Are you sure we are in Thailand?" The cabdriver grabbed our bags and threw them in the trunk of his small Toyota sedan.

"I best cabbie in whole city of Bangkok! You see! You want beautiful girls? I get you beautiful girls. You want pot? I get you best pot. I show you best bars and very clean hotels, you like, you see!" The cabdriver seemed to be about thirty-five years old and was very distinguished looking. He seemed to know exactly what we wanted. I was sure he had been around the block more than a few times.

We headed downtown to the outdoor marketplace and a popular park where tourists went to photograph historic statues and other landmarks.

As we stood on the busy curbside, I was drawn to the sweet aroma of barbecued meat cooking on a street vendor's cart. The proprietor, an aging old man with no teeth, was cooking small strips of meat on bamboo skewers. The uncooked meat looked appetizing and smelled very fresh.

"How much?" I asked.

"One dollar each," the old vendor gummed out.

I bought three for me and three for Givins. We both agreed, "This stuff is excellent!" Out of the corner of my eye I saw the taxicab driver snickering as he watched us have our way with the tasty, tender delicacy. Without missing a chewing beat, I turned to him and said, "Mmmm, this is good, what is it?"

He smiled and in his broken English asked . . . "You like very much?"

"Yeah, what is this stuff?"

"Monkey!" He chuckled.

"This is monkey?" Thad and I replied in unison.

"We'll have more!" we said. I immediately shelled out ten more dollars for the both of us. I guess the cabbie thought we would be disgusted after finding out the meat was primate. He didn't know we were Lurps. It would have taken a helluva lot more than monkey meat to repulse us. Besides, the meat was very tasty!

Thad and I had heard a lot about the nightspots in Bangkok from lucky soldiers who ventured there before us. Thailand was unquestionably my first and only choice for R & R. Of course, there were other options I could have selected: Japan, Australia, Hong Kong, Hawaii, and Singapore. But after hearing so many great stories about the fascinating city of Bangkok, this was a once in a lifetime adventure and I had to sample it myself. Going to Thailand was a significant part of the whole Vietnam experience, and I didn't want to miss that part. Especially a club called the Soul Sister's Bar.

The Soul Sister's Bar was an establishment known around Vietnam as "the house of horizontal and vertical pleasures." The restaurant/nightclub was located in the downtown district of Bangkok and was said to be by many soldiers, black and white, a "jewel" of the Orient. It was conveniently set within walking distance of the best hotels.

The scuttlebutt was, Soul Sister's Bar was owned by two black ex–air force cooks who put together an internationally popular restaurant that served real down-home soul food. Although everyone was welcome, the restaurant and club catered primarily to black GIs going to Thailand to take their R & R. It was also rumored that Soul Sister's attracted

the most beautiful girls in all of Thailand. I definitely
wanted to confirm those reports for myself.

Thad and I checked into the Siam Hotel, a swank, comfortable high-rise with about fourteen floors of accommodations. We took two suites next door to each other. When we
looked outside on our balconies, to my delight we could see
a luxurious, shimmering swimming pool that graced the
courtyard. I am one of those people who love to swim, and
with a pool like that, I was in heaven!

Thad and I both wanted to reserve our strength for the
long night ahead. We decided to go to our rooms to get
some rest. The plan was to meet in the lobby at 7:30 for dinner at the Soul Sister's Bar.

Around 5:00 that evening I started taking a shower that
lasted approximately an hour. I was trying to to scrub the
grit and grime of Vietnam from my body. After the shower,
I lay down to get some sleep, but instead I just lay there staring at the hypnotic ceiling fan over the bed. Sleep hell! I
couldn't close my eyes I was so excited!

Neither one of of us could wait until 7:30. At a quarter
till seven I spotted Givins in the lobby loading film in his
Polaroid camera. Thad was decked out in a three-piece gray
silk/mohair suit. And, no surprise, I too was dressed in a
double-breasted green/gray pinstriped suit. I was also armed
with my 35mm Pen EE camera, standard equipment out in
the boonies. As every good Lurp should be, we were ready
for anything.

We left the hotel and walked to the restaurant, both
sporting a hefty "airborne" appetite. At the door of the
restaurant we were greeted by pretty waitresses who spoke
English well enough to make us feel welcome.

Before we settled into the booth for dinner, I made a
quick run to the restroom. While I was standing over the urinal looking straight ahead at the wall in front of me, mind-
ing my own business, someone walked up behind me and
grabbed my "Johnson" and began shaking it down. My first
thought was, some asshole is playing a really sick joke!

The first words out of my mouth were, "Hey! Hey! Hey!

What the hell . . . !" I spun around ready to tear into someone's ass when I encountered two very pretty Thai girls.
They both jumped back a couple feet after I turned to face
them. They were giggling, hopefully at the anger and shock
on my face. After I took a second to recoup from the startling encounter, I happened to look around the room. I discovered I was in a unisex restroom. The women didn't have
a problem using the same facility in front of the male patrons. I turned back to the urinal to finish my business. I
zipped up and nonchalantly worked my way to the water
faucet to wash my hands. Then I was able to officially meet
the two cuties. Appropriately so, especially after they had
become so attached . . . initially.

I hurried back to the table and shared my exciting restroom interlude with Thad. We both got up from the table
and went back to the restroom to take another look. Need
less to say, it was empty except for a couple of GIs.

"Okay mudderfucker, where's the women?" Thad asked.
What could I say, I threw my hands up.

I remember mentioning to Thad as we worked our way
through the crush of gorgeous women in the restaurant,
"Oh man, this is going to be a fun vacation!" I have to admit, I was very excited about what had happened in the restroom, and during the evening I probably made about two or
three more pit stops throughout after that quaint little incident.

We finally sat down to have dinner. The menu read like a
welcome letter from home. Fried chicken, mustard and col-
lard greens (neither of the greens I would ever eat before
that night), cole slaw, roast beef, mashed potatoes with
gravy, macaroni and cheese, and a big slice of sweet potato
pie. I guess "comfort food" is an understatement. After
months of eating nothing but C rations, Lurp rations, and
army mess, this was a soul food festival.

The talking stopped once we started eating. We could
hear only the pulsating dance music through the walls from
the night club side of the restaurant. Our anticipation grew. I
could hardly wait to get to the other side to engage in the

lively soiree that was taking place. And from our vantage point, it sounded like one helluva party going on. We hurried through dessert and generated a few satisfying belches. It was time to hit the club!

When we walked into the relatively large discotheque, I was totally taken aback by the roomful of women, beautiful women everywhere! Not that I expected anything more, but the Soul Sister's Bar did not have one "real" soul sister in the whole damn place. But who cared? We were going to have a ball!

There was a handful of GIs interspersed throughout the room. But in general the club was filled with every type of beautiful and different looking Asian woman one could wish for.

The chic club was well decorated. It came complete with mirror balls, disco lights, and an assortment of the latest soul and R&B tunes. It was a real party! As usual, Thad and I were already engaged in another friendly competition. This time, for a woman. We both scanned the dance floor to find the prettiest girl in the room to claim for ourselves.

I'm not sure if it was club policy or simply routine, but when a certain song was played, all the men left the dance floor to sit and watch the girls dance with each other. As we watched the girls dance to a couple of upbeat songs, I happened to glimpse one girl on the dance floor who was especially attractive. She was staring back at me from across the dance floor. Every time I looked away and glanced back in her direction, I'd find her eyes following me, as if she were mentally beckoning me to choose her.

When the music stopped, the men picked the girl or girls of their choice to take to back to their hotel. I pointed to the one who kept eyeing me. When she came to the table, we made arrangements to spend the evening together. I remember her well. The girl I chose was named Mia. She was nineteen years old. She had silky jet-black hair that shined. Her hair was cut into a "pageboy" hairstyle. Mia had long shapely legs and was dressed in a very short miniskirt. She was unusually tall for a Thai woman. Mia stood above the others girls on the dance floor with her five-foot-seven-inch slender frame.

After Thad made his selection, the four of us squeezed inside the same booth for drinks and chitchat. Without speaking a word, Thad and I compared our two selections, and as far as I can determine I won that competition.

Mia's English was excellent. We surely didn't have a problem communicating.

"Why did you pick me?" she cooed. "You could have picked any one of those girls."

"Because you are the prettiest girl in the whole damn place!" I explained.

And because she was so beautiful, you just knew she was very popular. Mia and her friends in the club were working girls, and it was mandatory for them to carry a government approved health card to confirm they weren't infected with venereal disease. At the table, Mia proudly displayed her card and charged me twelve dollars per night for her services. Most of the Thai girls who worked in the bars and bordellos were financially destitute and sexually exploited by the Thai government. To survive, they had to go to work at a young age to support their families. Personally, I had always been against paying for sex and there had never been a time in my life where I actually had to shell out money. But I would have gladly paid more if she'd asked.

It was the fantasy of most of those girls to attach themselves to vulnerable and lonely GIs who visited Thailand looking for a good time. Some of those soldiers left Thailand thinking they were in love. I knew of such a soldier. He stayed in touch with one of the girls through letters. He wanted Thad and me to deliver a letter to his girlfriend when we arrived. Finding her was easy, because she worked in a bathhouse during the day and showed up at the Soul Sister's Bar at night.

Maybe that soldier did fall in love after having sex for

the first time in his life, but these were working girls who continued selling sex for money to any GI after their euphoric R & R was over. The U.S. military frowned profusely on that type of situation. Myself and others actually tried to discourage our fellow Lurps from making such a mistake. When we returned from R & R we even went so far as to approach the whole thing as a joke, telling him that both Thad and I paid to have sex with his girl while we were in Bangkok. Nothing we said or did helped. The more we tried to talk him out of it, the more he was convinced he was in love. Eventually he was bamboozled into taking the girl back to the States to get married after his tour in Vietnam was over.

Around 3:00 A.M. the party started winding down. A line of customers was beginning to file out the door. It was time to make our move back to the hotel.

While we had been inside the club, a light tropical rain had dampened the streets of Bangkok. As soon as we walked outside and sniffed the night air, simultaneously Thad and I both thought of "Vietnam." The intrusive smell of Vietnam at night sent chills up and down my spine! The distinct scent of humid air after rainfall at night was all too familiar. The staunch reminders of the war continued to haunt us even in Thailand.

We all took an early morning walk by Lumhini Park, which is the largest and most popular park in Bangkok, named after the Buddha's birthplace in Nepal. The park was still brimming with visitors and a few lovers necking into the wee hours of the morning.

When we reached our hotel, we split up and went to our rooms. The fun started as soon as Mia and I got behind closed doors. It didn't take long to get her into the mood. I began to perform a playful striptease before leaping into the air and landing on the bed next to her. The grappling and fooling around was just a prelude of things to come. Mia was gentle as she halfheartedly fought me off. Her soft touches were punctuated with passionate kisses all over my body. The delicate scent of perfume aroused my desire. It had been a long time since I had held a woman in my arms. It was time to have wild, unbridled "protected" sex! I say "protected," because before we left the company to go on R & R, First Sergeant Butts reached in his desk drawer and gave us a fistful of condoms. In his gruff customary style he admonished, "Here, take these! And don't come back here with a drippin' pecker!"

The next morning Mia quietly tried to slip out of the room at daybreak, obviously thinking that I was still asleep. It was difficult for me to sleep soundly. But I could tell Mia had a good time by the way she pressed a long hard kiss against my lips before leaving.

Around 10:00 A.M. I was awakened again by the maid service trying to get into the room. I could hear Givins stirring in the room next door. I knocked on the wall. "Hey Givins, are you up?!"

"Yeah! Are you alone?" he shouted through the walls.

"Yeah," I responded, "let's go eat breakfast and then see the world!" It didn't take much convincing to get a favorable reaction. I could hear Thad on the other side of the wall whooping and howling.

Our cabdriver was already waiting for us in the lobby. I was beginning to like this guy. He wasn't trying to make a career out of charging us a lot money and he didn't appear to be trying to stiff us for a big payday. He seemed more interested in watching us have a good time in his country.

We could have paid to go on one of those boring tour groups, but we decided to stay on our own and have an experienced cabbie show us all the distinguished and fun sites "off the beaten path." We considered ourselves lucky because our cabdriver gave attention to showing us the spots that made Bangkok, "Bangkok."

We started on our excursion by heading downtown to purchase a few gifts and souvenirs. The backstreets had a potpourri of eclectic outdoor and indoor shops. While venturing down one of the little side streets, I wandered into a shop where I found a beautiful tiger-skin rug. I was almost tempted to buy it. But even more than thirty years ago, I was aware of the sensitive nature of the endangered species issues. The skin was rare and expensive, costing about three hundred dollars. It was very attractive and I knew someone would buy it. But I had to pass on it. Today I'm glad I wasn't the one who bought it.

The cabdriver suggested we hire a sampan to tour the crowded sites along the water canals of the Chao Phraya (River). The small boats were powered by single or double outboard motors that whisked customers up and down the busy waterways with relative ease. The long, narrow dugout boats came equipped with overhead canopies to shield patrons from the sweltering sun. The small craft ferried us into places that were otherwise inaccessible by land. A large segment of the Thai population used the water taxi service to get to and from their homes, which were located among the dozens of interconnecting canals surrounding the outskirts of the city. We were able to visit well-known and traditional places such as the "floating marketplace," Wat Phra Kaew, and the Grand Palace, also called the Temple of the Emerald Buddha, which is completely carved from nephrite (a type of jade).

I was totally taken aback by the conditions of the people living on the waterways. I watched young children diving off the decks of their homes into the murky, polluted waters. I couldn't help but be intrigued by how they were able to live and survive in the makeshift city on stilts, constructed of tin and plywood, completely surrounded by water. It was like a photograph right out of *National Geographic* magazine.

After watching an honest to goodness snake charmer coax live cobras from a basket, it was time to return to the hotel and again get ready for dinner at the Soul Sister's Bar. I had a feeling that Mia would be there waiting for me. And how could I not be excited about that? Good food, wild sex in a fantasy city; I couldn't have been happier unless I was back home and out of the war.

Our evening started with another great meal at the restaurant. Thad and I were quickly becoming preferred customers. We also found out, even in Thailand, the girls in the bars gossiped. Our names had passed through the lips of our dates once too often. We had become the focus of conversations among the waitresses. We were starting to get the "special treatment" from the other girls in the bar, who were now making blatant passes at us. Oh yeah . . . We had definitely come to the right place for our rest and recuperation! Now I see why GIs went AWOL once they got a whiff of Bangkok.

Mia and her friend, who was now Thad's date for the last two nights, both showed up carrying their overnight travel bags.

"What the hell are you doing, moving in?" Thad asked jokingly. It was no joke. They were planning to spend the entire vacation with us. "Did we look that easy?" I whispered to Givins.

I just couldn't say no to Mia, even though I was planning to change girls in the next day or so. I had a feeling my plans would either break her heart or really piss her off.

After we finished another great dinner, we all went over to the club side for drinks and dancing. Once we arrived, the girls already had a booth reserved and waiting for us. Mia and her friend were acting kind of strange; we could tell that they were up to something.

"Guess what?" Mia said with a cute, giddy smile that I'll always remember.

"What?" I curiously asked, making direct eye contact.

"You don't have to pay any more money to keep me! I will stay with you until you leave." I was flattered, but somehow I knew there was more to it than what she was letting on.

"Are you sure, because I don't mind paying," I protested.

"No! No! You pay nothing, cause I stay with you whole time!" she insisted. "You big strong man, very handsome man, I like you very much." She wrapped both her hands around my biceps and leaned her head on my shoulder.

Thad was sitting across from me on the other side of the booth. It was obvious he was listening in on the conversation. Thad spit out his drink and burst into a bellowing laugh after identifying the "oh, shit" expression on my face. I was only too happy to amuse him at my expense.

As the night and the party raged on, I danced up a good sweat. I had knocked back a few double rum and cokes to get a nice buzz going.

After absorbing the fun-filled evening, we headed back to the hotel to continue the party in our suites. We ordered room service. The hotel bellhop showed up later with more beverages and snacks.

About an hour later the night started to peter out. Thad and his date went to their suite. Mia and I lay across the bed and talked about our homes and families. We made plans to visit the area where Mia lived and maybe meet her folks the following day.

Mia seemed more interested in knowing about my "girl-friends" back home. I just happened to have several pictures in my wallet of the "girls" I had been writing. When I showed Mia the photographs, she could not believe the pictures were of beautiful American black women. In her own defying words she said, "These not American girls, these Thai girls! Chuck [the white soldier] told me the colored girls in America look like Sapphire" (of *Amos 'n' Andy* television fame). She was serious and very misinformed. Someone had helped her reach the false conclusion that American black women were unattractive. It wasn't her fault; someone before me had painted a misleading picture of black women. Without her knowing, Mia had received her first lesson in "American Racial Prejudices," class #101.

To think that the proliferation of American racial discrimination was able to spread to the far corners of the globe angered and saddened me. I had heard plenty of that kind of talk while in Vietnam, but to actually know that type of racist rhetoric was traveling to all the countries where U.S. soldiers were stationed was absolutely reprehensible.

Maybe I was too naive. I guess I just didn't want to believe that the racial bullshit really was being perpetuated. . . . Well, that was my shortsightedness.

Our chat lasted into the early morning. Mia continued to grill me about the girls back home with a great deal of contempt. The evening turned ugly when she began to learn more about my past. I could feel her jealousy.

During our long talk I began to find out more about her. I discovered she was very bright and had dreams of going to school to become a model. She certainly had the looks and the figure to fulfill her dreams.

Finally the conversation became more relaxed, she started to ease up, and we began to joke around and play with each other again. We started to take up where we had left off the night before, engaging in unbashful sex. During the moments of passion, I could tell Mia was becoming infatuated, or she was putting on a damn good act. In Thailand, I only had room in my heart for lust, not love. I didn't understand it at the time, but it was that type of conditioning that gave me the edge I needed to survive fighting in Vietnam.

The following morning at breakfast, Mia told me that I was having nightmares. She claimed that I was fighting the war in my sleep. I guess I must have frightened her, because when I awakened she was curled up and sleeping in an armchair she had positioned at the foot of the bed. I did remember having strange dreams that night, but I never realized I was animated and acting out my dreams in my sleep.

That afternoon Mia and I took off with the cabdriver and headed to the outskirts of town where her parents lived. They resided in a remote part of Bangkok outside the city limits. The area was best described as a "serious slum." The familiar Third World scent of decaying feces in open sewers and the primitive living conditions the common people of Thailand endured, reeked of Vietnam.

Being poor in Thailand rivaled everything I had ever seen

in the United States. The condition of the roads leading to her house were deplorable. They were in such bad shape the taxicab could not have possibly driven through the muddy street without getting stuck. Just like the shacks on the Chao Phraya River, these houses were made of tin and plywood.

Mia asked me to walk with her to her parents' home, but I opted not to do so. I remained in the car and let her square away her business. She wanted me to meet her parents. I had no reason to meet her folks. What for? We certainly weren't going to see each other after I had left Thailand. I can just see the meeting now.

"Hi Mom and Dad, I want you to meet my 'john,' Ed!'"? I think not!

When we returned to the hotel, Mia and her girlfriend went shopping for more clothes. Thad and I spent the day swimming in the pool.

Personally, I am a water fanatic. Growing up, most of my summer days were spent in the public pools. Over the course of time, I had become a very good swimmer. But the very first time I ever went swimming was at a friend's neighborhood backyard pool, I almost drowned. After getting pushed into the deep end of the pool and going down for the third time, I was pulled out by the juvenile perpetrator who had pushed me into the water in the first place. That was my first brush with death and the first time my life flashed before my eyes. It was on that day, at the tender age of twelve, I decided to learn how to swim. My revenge was learning to swim the very same day I almost drowned.

My buddy George Wallace, Jr. was my partner in crime at the public pools. Whenever we saw someone who couldn't swim, we always made sure we introduced ourselves by dunking them under the water. Okay, it wasn't very nice, but we were kids, what do you want?

Thad was struggling with his breaststroke in the deep end of the pool and couldn't defend himself in water over his head. He was at my mercy and in my element! I witnessed for the first time one of Thad's few vulnerable sides. After I dunked him a few times, Thad abandoned any idea of getting back in the deep end of the water whenever I was nearby. Damn, that was fun!

There were a few attractive women lying poolside. I began entertaining them by diving from the second and third-story hotel balconies into ten feet of water. The hotel management got wind of my shenanigans and threatened to throw me out of the pool for my reckless behavior. It didn't matter, I had already had my fun by mugging and chasing Thad out of the deep water!

That evening, and for the third night in a row, we met the girls for dinner at Soul Sister's Bar. I'd mentioned to Thad that it was time to branch out and experience more than just one place to dine. Of course, he couldn't help but agree, but no other solutions were ever offered.

After dinner, all five of us crowded into the same taxicab and rode around the city of Bangkok sightseeing at night. Most great cities posses a beautiful picturesque skyline, and Bangkok was was right up there with the best of them. At dusk the city of Bangkok actually took on a different flavor. In the warmth of the summerlike nights, Bangkok became vibrant, intoxicating, and romantic. The street noise, the smells and sights, were unforgettable. Bangkok was a jewel that glistened with a majestic flair. One can easily fall in love with the city and all of its charms.

It had been a long, exhausting day. I was feeling the effects of the constant on-the-go activities. I wanted to go back to the hotel to get some sleep. Mia had different plans, she wanted to go back to the hotel for more wild sex. We calmly debated the issue, and her compelling argument made more sense than mine. Mia claimed, "It will be long time before you come back to Thailand to make love again." Well, Mia outright won that argument. And who knew how long it would be before I would be able to touch or hold another woman. When Mia and I got back to the hotel, we started at the door. I'd remembered those words Mia said about not having sex for a long time after leaving Bangkok. With that in mind, I made sure we sampled every sexual position known to man. The sex was so intense, I built up a reservoir of sweat in the small of my back that began to cascade down on her with each body movement. I wanted to make sure Mia would always remember me and that night for the rest of her life.

The following morning Mia left early to go to her day job. I was never exactly sure what she did, that part of her life we never really discussed and it didn't really matter. I was almost certain I would never see her again. I let her leave without telling her good-bye. We'd planned not to go back to the bar that night. Bangkok was full of great-looking women and basically we were there to check out our options. We had heard talk of another club similar to the Soul Sister's Bar, and we wanted to see what that place was about.

I couldn't help thinking that our five days of R & R was almost over. The seven days off from the war went by much too quickly. We had one more full day of freedom left in Thailand. The anxiety attacks began to crop up when I had to start packing and preparing mentally to go back to Vietnam.

I spent the entire day lounging around the pool, sleeping, and ordering drinks from pool service. I was glad I took my R & R with Thad. He was one of the only people I could talk to about anything—politics, girls, sports, the war. There was no limit to the subjects of our conversations. I believed we had a special friendship. We were almost like brothers. I remember telling him while sitting around the pool how well we complemented each other's ability out in the boonies of Vietnam.

I guess perhaps I was looking to fill the void left by the death of my cousin. But our R & R together only reaffirmed that Thad was a great buddy and a gracious friend. We got the chance to know each better after spending those days of R & R time together.

We had planned to have a really big blowout in the final

twenty-four hours in Bangkok, with steam baths, massages, and elegant restaurants downtown. And to top it off, we would find a bar with different women and get "shitface drunk." Well, at least that was our plan. But the money was running a little short, totaling about one hundred dollars between the both of us.

As it turned out, we walked to a local outdoor bar to take in the sights and just relaxed. But always in the back of our minds we knew the final vacation day in Thailand would soon be over. It was a melancholy and sobering thought.

Around 11:30 P.M., I was in bed fighting off a big mosquito that had worked its way into my room. The little bastard was biting me while I was trying to sleep.

There was a loud knock on my door. It wasn't Thad, because he would have been yelling from down the hall as he approached my room. I thought someone may have gotten the wrong room number and hoped they would leave. I tried to ignore the knocks by putting my pillow over my head and pretending I wasn't there. Then the knocks got louder and more emphatic.

"Ed! I know you are in there, open the door, please!"

It was Mia. When I finally got up to open the door, I could see she was visibly upset.

"What happened?" she asked in a demanding tone. "You no come to bar! You don't like me anymore?"

"Of course I like you!" I said. "We just decided to go to another bar."

"You leave soon, why you not tell me where you go? I want to make love, don't you want to make love to me?" She pushed closer to me, pressing her breast against my body.

"Mia, I am here on R & R, I didn't come here to get married or anything. And before you get any ideas, I can't take you back to America."

"I don't want to go to America," she retorted. "I just want to be with you, here, right now!"

"Well, I'm kinda tired, and I want to get some rest. I gotta go back to Vietnam after tomorrow."

"Okay, we no do nothing, just let me stay with you to-night!" she pleaded.

"I don't think that's a good idea . . ."

"No! Please, don't send me away!" She started crying. But I had to remain firm. Even though her pleas were tearing me apart inside, I wasn't going to give in. I suppose I was trying to prove to myself that I could be hard and hold fast in the face of her sobbing. I knew this was going to happen. I'd seen it coming after the first night. I couldn't talk her into leaving, so I had to push her out the door. That was the only way I could get her to leave. She still wouldn't go after being forced out. She began beating on the door and calling my name. . . .

"Ed! Ed! Please open the door!"

For ten minutes straight her crying and knocking went on. For a moment the knocking and crying stopped. I'd thought she had left. I didn't hear any noise. When I pressed my ear against the door, I could hear her sitting on the floor next to my door weeping. Then the pounding on the door started again.

"Please let me in! I want to be with you!"

I couldn't take it anymore. Just when I decided to give in, I opened the door and she was gone. Deep down, I felt ashamed. I had a sadness that turned into emptiness. I liked Mia, but I was a soldier in a war, and she was a prostitute who serviced the soldiers of that war. What the hell kind of relationship was that?

The next morning around 10:00, someone was pounding on my door. When I swung the door open, it was Thad standing there with a big grin on his face. "Oh Eddie, oh Eddie, pleassse let me in!" Thad stood there laughing until he saw that I wasn't amused, then his attitude changed slightly to serious.

"Okay, killer! What the hell happened last night?" he said, holding back a chuckle.

"I guess you heard?" I asked.

"Hell, I'm right next door! How could I not hear?"

I tried to dance around his questions, mostly because I was embarrassed and not feeling very good about myself. What happened that night was nothing I should be proud of. Thad could always tell when my emotions were close to the surface. He tried to console me in a way the Neanderthals did millions of years ago. . . .

"Hey man, don't take this shit serious, she's a fuckin' hooker!" he said, scolding me.

"Yeah, I know. I just feel bad about the way I treated her last night. You saw how she was. She was a really nice, sweet person. I liked her. I felt sorry for how she had to live."

"See, I told you," Thad continued to admonish, "we should have had a different girl every night like we had planned, then we wouldn't have to deal with this kind of shit. But you kept going back because she had great tits."

"Yeah, yeah, yeah! Okay, Givins, you're right! We didn't do what we said we were going to do, so what the hell! And you are as much to blame as I am! Well . . ." I continued, "she did have great tits, didn't she?" We gave each other a fist pound. I started to feel better about things, thanks to Thad and his profound insights.

"Anyway, the hell with this!" I said, snapping back to normal. "Let's go have some breakfast, get a steam bath, and get laid one more time before we blow this place."

I swear, sometimes I believe women scared me as much as the war did. Just like my situation with Wanda, Thad was there to snap me out of my moments of weakness. Again his friendship proved invaluable.

After breakfast we met up with our cabdriver, who had practically taken up residence inside the lobby of the hotel. We asked him to find a clean place to get a steam bath and massage.

"You no worry, I take care of you," he said, reassuring us that he was still on the job. He drove us to some funky part of town that absolutely resembled a main street in Vietnam. He pulled into a parking lot between two buildings.

"Maybe you no understand, we want steam bath!" I said

extra loud and in my best Thai dialect. He winked his eye and nodded his head up and down.

"You like! You like! You see!" Again his assurance comforted us. We followed him through the double doors of a two-story building. Much to our surprise, he had delivered us to a hideaway, a Turkish-owned and run bathhouse that was truly immaculate. Mosaic ceramic tiles covered the floors. The entryway revealed two long narrow pools that were designated hot and cold. Rows of large marble columns were located throughout the building. Behind the double glass doors that reached from floor to ceiling was a sixty-foot-long steam room. The Turks really take their bathhouses seriously.

We were instructed by the hostess to take a twenty-minute steam bath. We encountered eight older Thai businessmen who walked in draped in towels. They stretched out and relaxed on the wooden slabs covering the marble seating area. A few of the Thai men were able to speak pretty good English. They told us how they routinely came in for a steam and massage, almost every day. One old gentleman claimed the therapy helped them to focus and perform better at their jobs. All I knew was, the steam room helped clear my sinuses and made me feel more hygienic.

The upstairs area was delegated to the massage parlor. Waiting for customers to show up were several very pretty and young Thai girls wearing skimpy, practically see-through cotton-type garments. They sprung into action as soon as Thad and I arrived. They worked their magic on us with a soothing finger massage. Weighing no more than ninety pounds, the petite girls had us lie down on our stomachs on top of padded workbenches.

They generously soaped up our entire bodies, then climbed on top of us and began scrubbing against us with the material on their bodies. When their clothing became wet, it turned translucent, leaving nothing to the imagination. After the erotic body scrub, they poured a pail of warm water over us for a complete rinse. Then the girls stepped up on the bench and positioned themselves gently on our backs and walked up and down our spines, cracking every vertebra back into place using toes and heels. It had to be the most erotic massage I had ever seen performed. After the massage was completed, I became dizzy and lightheaded from the rejuvenating aftereffects. The experience was almost spiritual. Before we left the bathhouse, I tipped the girls generously for making me feel like a brand-new person.

The massage helped us work up quite an appetite. Our next stop was a restaurant for our final dinner in Thailand. I was sure our cabdriver had a special place for that, too. Not far from the bathhouse was a small mom and pop restaurant loaded with GIs and their Thai female companions. The restaurant had a long line leading to the outside and a long waiting list to boot. After waiting a half hour to eat, I could see why the place was so popular. The food was excellent!

Our cash was starting to run low, and we had to save enough money to get back home. We paid for our hotel stay in advance, and that took pressure off of us. We wanted to make sure our taxicab driver got a hefty tip for doing such a great job of taking care of us. We were left with enough money to go out for a final romp on the town. But I had way too much fun the entire time we were in Thailand. I was more than content to go back to my room and just watch television. It wasn't exactly HBO, but at least we were able to get Armed Forces Network television in our hotel rooms.

The next morning at 8:00 A.M. we were headed to the airport for our 9:00 A.M. departure for Vietnam. Before leaving Thailand, we made our cabdriver very happy by giving him the remainder of our money. The tip came to more than fifty dollars, twice the amount he had charged. It was worth every penny for the great memories and the wonderful time we had on our R & R to Bangkok, Thailand.

Before visiting Bangkok, I'd had no idea the city was so rich in tradition. It was unquestionably a very extraordinary place to visit. This R & R thing to Thailand was quite a concept and I wanted to remember it forever.

CHAPTER NINE

Such Was War

It was a Sunday afternoon when we arrived back at the company area. No sooner had we returned from R & R than we had a warning order waiting for another mission. I unpacked my travel clothes and packed them to ship home along with other small gifts and souvenirs I had acquired during my trip.

Before leaving for R & R, it was standard procedure and a safety precaution to strip the explosives from our rucksacks and return them to the ammo bunker. Now I had the renewed task of putting my gear back in order. I waited until the last minute to start packing for my next combat mission. I spent about an hour finding and replacing all the weapons and armament I had removed.

Around the ninth of December, back in the States, the Christmas season was officially under way. Several boxes of goodies sent from family and friends were beginning to arrive. My mother and my sisters packed and shipped a small white artificial Christmas tree for me and the guys in my hootch. The tree came with lights, bulbs, the whole nine yards. They also baked and shipped a whole yellow cake with chocolate icing, my favorite. The cake was a little roughed up from being shipped, but we really appreciated the thoughtfulness.

The cans of Vienna sausages sent from my family became a favorite among the troops, perhaps because they were free. My aunt Eloise got word that we wanted more. Out of the soft place in her heart for the guys in the war, she sent two cases of forty-eight cans for Christmas. The gifts

176

were a nice touch for the holiday season, especially since we were all homesick.

There were reports that the Paris peace talks were declaring a cease fire for the Christmas season. It was also rumored that the company would be on a one-week stand-down, from the twenty-first of December through the twenty-seventh day of the month.

The Soul Patrol was designated Team 2-5 for the upcoming mission. The new AO was changed from AO Scout to AO Ace, which was basically just a different area on the map. In a sense it was almost refreshing to get back out into the boonies. Sometimes being out in the field helped me clear my head. It also made the time go by faster. I knew, whenever I returned from a mission, I could always mark off another five or six days from my DEROS calendar. There were times when I actually enjoyed being out in the boonies, that is, if we weren't in any trouble. The peace and quiet, especially at night under the stars, was sometimes very tranquil. The underlying fear and danger of a mission was always present, but sleeping under the stars always made me feel closer to nature and closer to God.

The early morning briefing revealed the "next big test" in this reality "thing" called life and death. My return to the field after R & R was an awesome and spiritual experience.

I remember feeling differently about the war after I had returned from R & R. I didn't feel quite as aggressive toward the enemy. There had been some kind of transformation that I wasn't able to explain.

On this mission the team members were Brock, Reid, Gates, Mann, and myself. Our flight out to the AO was the same as always, intense with heart-pounding apprehension. We were on the ground less than an hour when we realized we had been spotted and were being followed. The enemy made the mistake of giving away their position by slamming shut the bolts of their weapons as they prepared to launch an attack. We identified two VC wearing black PJs. They carried an RPG launcher with about ten rockets between the two of them. They each carried an AK-47 and wore complete web gear full of AK-47 ammo. Gates was on the point. He sighted approximately three or four more enemy running along the wood line on the others side of the LZ. It was obvious we had another group following us. We had two choices, either lure them into our ambush or hide from them. More than likely, the enemy troops on the other side of the LZ were running in the tree line to recruit a larger party. This was real. We were back in Indian country . . . big time!

After having our position compromised, Brock put in a call to TOC for an extraction, which was quickly denied. We were told unless we were in contact, "Charlie Mike" (continue mission) and keep moving toward our objective. Brock put TOC and the choppers on alert. We stopped and set up a defensive perimeter to prepare to initiate an ambush. Our original mission was to infiltrate into a well-covered site on a canal. We were given the green light to make contact on any enemy sampan moving through the remote area. In other words, they wanted to add more numbers to the company body count. Such was war! It was the reason we were in Vietnam in the first place. At this point of my tour, the war seemed so senseless.

We hid in the bush off a main trail and set up for an ambush. As we waited for Charlie to walk into our gun sights, we began to hear numerous signal shots about two hundred meters away. Brock called in, alerting TOC that we were still being stalked. From the company TOC, the company commander got on the radio and ordered us to get to the original ambush site located at the mouth of the river. Only then would the Cobra gunships get airborne and fly out for our support. Brock angrily held the radio handset away from his ear and dropped it to the ground. Then he motioned for us to pick up and move out again.

At 1605 hours we crossed a trail that had been recently used by an oxcart. The cart had been moving from east to west, apparently loaded down with heavy equipment. My gut feeling told me we were very close to something bad, but what and where? I didn't always listen to that little voice in my head, but for some reason this was one of those times when I did listen. We took every step with caution, making sure we wouldn't walk into an ambush. Before we knew it we were right in the middle of an abandoned company-size base camp. Most of the time we couldn't tell whether we were in an uninhabited base camp, because they were always well hidden. The giveaway was the number of camouflaged bunkers concealed around the area. We kept hearing voices on our flanks and to our rear. We didn't panic, we kept moving forward, silently, and with extreme caution. Because Charlie was still hot on our trail, he kept firing harassing signal shots. Each shot sounded closer. They were definitely closing in on us.

TOC contacted an F-4 Phantom jet flying a mission over the area. How those jet pilots in the air, moving at supersonic speeds, were able to see and hit moving targets on the ground was simply beyond me. But they did. We monitored the radio transmission from the Phantom jet and TOC on our PRC-25. The pilot reported covering our tracks as we crossed an open field to get to our objective. The pilot also advised TOC that we were being followed by about seven Victor Charlies who were in hot pursuit about a hundred meters behind us. The Phantom jet made his gun run, firing rockets and .50-caliber miniguns. The cartridges from the .50-caliber miniguns fell back to the earth with such force, they actually toppled large trees and tore off heavy branches. Most of the falling debris was in the direct path of our movement. Some of the cartridges from the jet came very close to our position. Had one of us been hit directly by the ejected cartridges, we wouldn't have had a chance of surviving the impact. Immediately a red flag went up.

"Let's get the hell out of here!" Brock asserted. We took off running an evasive path that led the team far away from the air-to-ground attack.

We came to rest under a tree that overhung the ground. Brock put in a call to "Aloft," who was also flying in the area. We signaled the plane with a mirror. Aloft pinpointed our position and plotted on the map the area where the enemy had fortified and bivouacked a base camp. We were hoping to get a reaction force out there to back us up. No such luck! The team was told to abort the plans of moving to the ambush site on the canal and make use of the remaining daylight to recon the area where the base camp was located. That was real bad news! There was far too much activity in the area to go back and chance walking into the homes of the bad guys. It was only a matter of time before they caught up with us anyway. Brock explained to TOC that their plan would be a bad move, and he was not going to put the team at risk. We took off moving in the direction of the canal, every step slow and planned with caution. We knew Charlie was still on our asses. The assistant team leader, Norman Reid, had the daunting task of watching and covering our "six" (rear security).

It was in the best interest of the team to get to the canal and set up an NDP. Maybe it was an effort to save their ammo, but rather than firing signals shots, Charlie began banging together two bamboo sticks to harass us and let us know they were not going away. The piercing sounds were just as effective and intrusive as firing signal shots. The pinging sound can be heard a long way away. We knew we couldn't outrun them, and certainly by moving hastily we ran the risk of running into an ambush. Brock decided to halt the team and set up a night defensive position about a klick short of our planned ambush site. We assisted each other in putting out our claymore mines. We formed a tight 360-degree star-shaped perimeter. We were close enough to touch each other and keep everyone on alert. I set up the machine gun in the direction I was watching.

To our advantage, the cover and concealment was very thick. That type of terrain always seemed to give us confidence to better do our job. It made a big difference when the team was able to hide in the triple canopy foliage.

When night fell, Charlie continued to look for us. Around 2215 hours we could see and hear them moving all around us. About ten or more got on line and began to search the cracks and crevices by shining flashlights into the bushes. We lay flat on the ground, hidden from view. I pulled about six hand grenades from my ammo pouch and made them ready. I lay motionless, clutching the command detonator to my claymore. I always made a habit to hide my claymore and the wire leading to it extra carefully. The claymores were placed about fifteen to twenty feet away from our perimeter, completely out of view. It was SOP to plant the claymores in front of a large tree or anthill, anything to absorb the backblast. We each had our little tricks on how we would set up our claymores. I always pulled the pin on a trip flare and stuck it underneath my claymore bag. If Charlie did tamper with it, the flare would go off and I would detonate the claymore with my handy dandy, pocket-sized command detonator.

A claymore mine blast can blow four men in half if they are caught directly in the line of fire. Fortunately, Charlie's search led him five feet beyond our perimeter and claymores. The only excuse we would have to open fire would be if one of us were spotted or if the claymores were detected. Otherwise we followed the strict recon rules of observation.

One thing that always scared the hell out of me was getting into a running gun battle in the middle of the pitch-black jungle and having to fight our way to the LZ. That's exactly what we were looking at if Charlie had discovered us. But good fortune prevailed, we were never found. Charlie walked right past our position. It was no secret that they knew we were out there, but to our advantage, they didn't know exactly where. It became a life-and-death game of cat and mouse. Concealing our positions seemed to be one of the benefits we had over Charlie; we were able to hide better than him. Besides, when Lurps could, they made a point of hiding in the most impossible places where no one would ever think to look.

Brock called in artillery support after Charlie went by. He plotted the rounds to drop about a hundred feet all around our position. The artillery would keep Charlie at bay, and it would keep them guessing. The HE (high-explosive) artillery rounds would also make a statement, saying, "Don't fuck with us!"

At 2255 hours we heard large mortar rounds leaving their tubes at 180 degrees and about two hundred meters away. Minutes later we heard another set of mortar rounds being fired at 045 degrees, about the same distance away as the first set of rounds. We had no idea where they were going.

About midnight the movement around our perimeter finally subsided. We still remained on full alert the entire night. No one would get any sleep. We watched the flickering flashlights move farther away into the dense jungle. Charlie knew Lurps didn't attack at night unless they were forced into a fight. Night fighting was our only weakness and sometimes it was exploited.

Those who have been there know that what I am about to say is true. It has probably happened to every Lurp at least once on a mission. I pulled off my mosquito head net to take a drink of water. I took a deep breath and inadvertently inhaled a mosquito. The little bastard flew into my mouth and lodged itself in my throat (another reason to hate mosquitoes). I tried everything from drinking water to muffling and gagging a hacking cough into my boonie hat. I didn't want to be the "one" to give away the team's position. I quietly went into my pill kit and took a couple of codeine tabs for the cough and a couple of Dexedrine tablets to stay alert. The combination of drugs was commonly referred to as a Lurp cocktail. It was my first time ever taking codeine. A few minutes later the cough and tickle in my throat was completely gone. If a codeine tab was able to stop that kind of cough, then it was powerful enough to eradicate any type of cough.

I had heard a lot about these cocktails and was always curious about the effects. I guess I really wanted to see what all the hoopla was about. Some claimed to have taken the pill combination just before a firefight. The dextro tab acted as the high-octane rocket fuel to get you into orbit and the codeine tab would smooth out the ride once you got there.

Well, there was no battle to be fought. I was left twiddling my thumbs and counting stars the remainder of the night. It wasn't a bad trip, I just wish I'd had something to do after taking the cocktail other than reflecting on the war.

Lurps had a genuine need for the pill kits. The kits were designed for all combat situations. Everything from staying awake and alert to malaria attacks. For example, I once sat up one night and watched one of my good buddies shake and shiver all night long from malaria fever. My heart went out to him, but there was nothing I could do. Henry Bonvillian didn't know I had been watching him suffer with the dreadful affliction. I saw him going into his pill kit, taking pill after pill, and by the next morning he was okay.

But when you really didn't have a need to take the pills, gratuitous consumption of these drugs definitely became one of the things "not" to do.

It wasn't enough for Lurp teams to be self-contained and self-sufficient in combat. We also had to have a diverse knowledge of medicine just in case we were wounded or had to tend a wounded comrade while operating on our own for long periods of time. Individually we packed enough drugs in our pill kits to survive for weeks at a time. An individual pill kit held about one hundred assorted drugs including two morphine syringes, about twenty dextro tabs, twenty codeine tabs, twenty malaria pills, a handful of Darvons, and about ten large antishit pills.

The antishit pills would plug us up for five days, making it almost impossible to have bowel movements. There were several reasons to prevent Lurps from "going" out in the field. First of all, we didn't want to get caught with our pants down. Second, human feces can tell a complete story. Certainly our science wasn't as complex as today's forensic pathologist experts who can tell if the subject uses Visa or Mastercard by examining his crap. Our methods were a little more crude. Without going into graphic detail, we were able to gather information from the scent and sight of the droppings. We could tell approximately how long ago the enemy had been in the area, which represented how close or how far away the enemy might be. Whenever we saw small holes poked in the feces, we knew to beware of punji sticks. Charlie fashioned sharp bamboo skewers and laced the tips with human waste. He would then camouflage the sticks in the ground at an upright angle. Anyone perforated by a punji stick was instantly poisoned. The punji stick booby traps were another one of Charlie's nasty tricks to simply put GIs out of commission.

When we were not concerned with serious wounds, we were always involved with some other kind of medical affliction. Sometimes a minor case of "jungle rot" needed attention. After spending a lengthy time in the jungle, a rampant skin infection would grow on soldiers, causing inflammatory lesions. Jungle rot was a green algae or molding fungus in appearance.

It was very important to have at least one member in a team carrying a complete medical pack/pill kit. During the company downtimes, the Lurp teams attended mandatory medical training classes for advanced lifesaving techniques. The training was much more than basic medic training. We received instruction equal to that of a paramedic. This training program kept the team members proficient in treating traumatic wounds and injuries. Subsequently, having months of medical training forced into my head, I felt confident enough to handle everything from a sucking chest wound to a minor snakebite, and anything in between.

I personally carried a pilot's survival kit that was loaded with everything from assorted fine surgical tools to a piano wire weapon designed to dismember the enemy's head from his body. The survival kit was sealed in a watertight hard plastic container. It was formfitted to the upper leg and carried in an OD green Gore-Tex pouch. The kit was slung low and worn like a gun holster, wrapping around one's waist and extending down to the thigh and secured by Velcro fasteners. I always packed and carried it in my rucksack. I never had the occasion to perform field surgery, but if it were needed, I would have been able to handle the job.

When the sun came up the following morning, I was happy to be alive. We had another unforgettable night in the jungles of Vietnam. We figured there were good reasons the enemy was so adamant about finding and eliminating us from this area. Besides the fact of becoming a "first-class hero" for exterminating a Lurp team, we believed they were trying to protect a valuable refuge. If Charlie was trying to hide an important sanctuary, he was successful because we could not find anything.

After the morning sitrep (situation report), we took turns eating breakfast and standing guard before moving out toward the designated ambush site.

Around 0730 hours, just before we started out of our perimeter, the bamboo or wood-on-wood signaling devices began, as if they were watching us. I'm sure it was nothing more than pure coincidence, because if they had seen us, we would have had a big fight on our hands.

Brock whispered in the ear of Ellis Gates, who was standing next to him, "We're getting close to something big, watch for anything unusual. Pass it down."

There was no surprise regarding the message. All the signs of danger were all around us, and as usual we exercised special vigilance.

The team moved out with particular care. We came upon a trail that was well hidden on the side of a hill in the thick jungle foliage. Brock went ahead of Gates, taking the point. We began to follow the trail with apprehension. We came upon a wooden sign nailed to a tree. Brock got on the radio to TOC and read the sign. TOC relayed back the following information; "The sign means, warning to all," advising those who can read the language to beware of mines and booby traps. We had never followed a trail before, not that I can remember, but Brock apparently got orders to find out what Charlie was hiding in the area. I spotted and pointed to an American-made plastic canteen bottle. We were trained not to touch or move anything suspicious looking. After further inspection, without touching it, I could see that the canteen was booby-trapped with a trip wire connected to a GI fragmentation hand grenade. Brock got back on the radio with TOC and reported the findings. We went to one knee and waited for him to complete his report. While on a knee, we happened to look up and saw a stream of smoke coming from a seven-foot-high tree trunk standing upright in the ground. The tree trunk was made to look as if it were just another tree. It was five or six inches in diameter, hollowed out, with black soot lining the insides. It was being used as a smokestack or exhaust conduit for an underground factory. We'd found what we were looking for! We weren't sure what they were making underground, but we were pretty confident it wasn't "world peace."

We finally made it to the ambush site. We were able to melt into the background. Miles and miles of thick vegetation lined the connecting rivers. We positioned ourselves at the mouth of the two canals connecting into the main river, and we waited. And we waited some more. After waiting for a couple days, we were convinced Charlie had put the word out that a Lurp team was lurking in the area. Traffic on the river completely stopped. After a couple of days, we humped back to the area of the factory and planted an emergency UHF radio in the ground. This type of radio emitted signals to air force bombers to permit surgical strikes on specific targets.

We were extracted on December 17 due to the completion of the mission. An air strike was dropped in the factory area only hours after the Lurp teams were pulled out.

It was true what they said about the pressure you feel after your first six months in Vietnam. The first six months you sort of feel invincible. It's hard to explain, but I never believed that I was going to "get it" during that time. When I actually saw my time wind down to five months, I started to become more cautious and less reckless than usual. Although I had always felt that my recklessness is what gave me the "edge" to some degree. But now I was beginning to lose what the old soldiers called my "piss and vinegar."

Seven or eight months into my tour, I started suffering what was diagnosed and treated by army doctors as migraine headaches. I was beginning to feel the stress of war more than at anytime before. Everyone said it would happen, but until you actually get there, you don't believe it will happen to you.

On December 21, Team 2-6 got warning orders for a mission that would last through December 27. A mission on Christmas Day . . . that was the last thing we wanted to hear. What happened to the cease-fire proclaimed in Paris? I guess it didn't matter, we were in a war and we would have to spend our Christmas in the boonies.

Unfortunately, we weren't the only team with warning orders. Teams 1-3 and 1-4 were going out on the same day. The Lurp teams were pissed; there was plenty of moaning and groaning coming from the guys being inserted into the field.

On December 23 at 1300 hours, Team 2-6 was on the chopper headed out to AO Miller. The team consisted of Brock, Gates, Reid, Givins, Mackey, and myself. It was a clean insertion, we were always grateful for that. We stopped for a moment to listen to the jungle just before marking a route.

We moved inside the tree line just off the LZ and found fresh boot tracks. That meant NVA soldiers. It was certainly a big difference fighting the two factions. The Viet Cong would normally hit and run, but North Vietnamese Army soldiers took the fighting very personally, as they were in the battle for the long haul. We also began finding well-hidden bunker and tunnel entrances. All the signs pointed to the fact that we were close to or inside a base camp. We pulled back deeper into the jungle and found a fairly secure RON. We weren't out there looking for a fight, just a desirable place to hide for a few days.

The weather turned cold. It started to rain off and on into

the evening and then all that night. It was a fairly quiet mission. The only thing that caused great concern was a dog barking throughout the night. We didn't hear any signal shots, which in a sense was unusual. I came to the conclusion that the Viet Cong were probably in the town enjoying the holidays with their families, and the NVA soldiers were tucked away in their base camps. So why the hell were we put out there to look for them?

The night passed without incident. The next morning after the usual routine of calling in the morning sitreps and eating chow, it was time to move out to find a better hiding place. It was still raining hard. With no chance of drying out, we were all soaking wet and dreadfully miserable. As we moved to our next location, we came upon fifteen pipes sticking out of the ground. They were approximately two feet long and three to four inches in diameter. They were urinals, the only things missing were the sanitary cakes. We were inside a working base camp with concrete bunkers and all! Obviously the base camp had been abandoned, but still, it was no place to be if we were trying to hide from the enemy. We found a 750-pound bomb that had been disassembled, with the explosives taken out. After Brock made the report to TOC, we humped across an open field to get to another LZ about three hundred meters away.

I couldn't help thinking about all the troops back at the company compound eating Christmas dinner, drinking, and having a merry ol' time. In my mind's eye I was seeing the troops in the mess hall drinking large mugs of exotic beer, swaying back and forth in unison, singing Christmas carols. It wasn't fair! All the teams in the company should have been put on stand-down status. I'm sure everyone else in Team 2-6 was thinking the same thing, because the "unmentionable" came up . . .

"Let's fake a contact so we can get the hell out of here." I can't remember who actually said those words, but faking contact was something none of us had ever done or considered doing before that time. And we would never go through with it unless everyone in the team collectively agreed.

Just as we were planning our escape from the boonies on Christmas Eve, a sniper took a shot at us. It wasn't an AK-47, it sounded like an SKS rifle shot. The round went through my rucksack and hit my fat rat (a water bladder used for storing water). It was just the break we needed. We spotted a puff of smoke on the other side of the LZ about a hundred meters away. We opened fire on that area with all weapons. Almost relieved, Brock got on the horn and yelled, "Contact! Contact! Team 2-6 in contact!"

The fairly nonchalant firefight raged on for about twenty minutes before we realized our ammo was starting to get low. We had thrown almost half of our firepower in the direction of that single shot. We wanted to make sure TOC could continuously hear the firefight going out over the radio. Then we started receiving enemy fire from all sides. Charlie had completely surrounded us and was beginning to close in on our position. By the time the Playboy Cobra gunships arrived on the scene, we were in a full-scale battle. With miniguns and rocket fire blazing, the gunships began scattering Charlie all over the place. We could hear the chopper pilots saying over the radio, "Will you look at these son of a bitches! They are like ants! They're everywhere!"

That wasn't good news for us on the ground. We were caught out in the open trying to fight our way to the LZ pickup point. The command and control ship circling the battle zone gave us an azimuth, and the Playboy Cobras of the 334th Aerial Assault Squadron blazed a trail of fire so we could get to the slick that would be flying in for our extraction.

"Grab your shit! Let's go!" Brock ordered. No time wasted, we picked up and ran for our lives behind the firepower of the Cobra gunships' mighty attack. The rain had let up to a drizzle and the footing was slippery. I could hear only my breathing and my heart pounding as I followed the person in front of me. The smell of rocket fire and automatic weapons choked the air as we ran about 150 meters through the wake of the onslaught. When the extraction helicopter flew in to the LZ, we were being chased and shot at in an open field by a group of enemy soldiers wearing camouflaged fatigues and web gear. The helicopter landed and waited for us. The door gunner on the chopper opened fire.

Charlie dropped to the ground and continued fighting from the prone position. We ran and dived aboard the slick. As the helicopter lifted into the sky, we could see about fifty enemy soldiers dotting the landscape. I was sitting in the door firing my M-60 machine gun when an enemy soldier popped up and began firing on the helicopter as it took off. I let go an eighty-round burst of tracers that walked up from the ground to his right leg and pelted him in the chest three or four times. Small puffs of smoke were visible coming from his body before the bullets knocked him to the ground.

"I got your ass!" I sneered with contempt and anger. I became a different person after being shot at. It scared the hell out of me and I turned that fear into concentrated meanness. The hair on the back of my neck stood on end. I became full of wrath.

It was always a successful mission when there were no U.S. casualties. When we got back to the company area, we headed straight for the briefing room. I sat through as much talk as I could take before getting excused from the remainder of the debriefing due to a severe migraine. Sometimes after a mission I had to take two powerful painkillers prescribed by doctors. The medicine put me to sleep, but when I awoke I had blurred vision in my right eye and the right side of my face was numb. But after a day or so I was okay.

We heard rumors from the guys in Headquarters Platoon, boasting that the assault helicopters had a field day on Charlie after we were extracted. The assault helicopters had racked up about twenty-five kills. Merry Christmas!

Christmas Day, the cooks decorated the mess hall with a lively festive look. They waited for those teams who were coming in from the boonies to have a nice Christmas dinner with all the trimmings. Although there wasn't any caroling and exotic beer drinking, I was still happy to celebrate my Christmas in Vietnam with my teammates. It was the only Christmas we had.

CHAPTER TEN

Rangers... No Stranger to Danger!

In January, the new year brought about major changes, starting with the 1969 Tet holiday. "Tet" is the lunar new year and the largest of the Vietnamese celebrations. The holiday falls between the last ten days of January and the middle part of February. It has always been a festival indicating the communion of man and nature. For three days the Vietnamese take extra care not to show anger or be rude to their fellow men. Tet is an occasion for the people to share a common ideal of peace, concord, and mutual love. Evidently that theory didn't apply to wartime situations.

The 1969 Tet season roared in like a lion and limped out like a lamb. We were on constant alert and advised not to take the situation lightly. Although the North Vietnamese diplomatic team had agreed to a cease-fire at the Paris peace talks, the Allied bombing of North Vietnam continued and the communists made another attempt to regain the territory in spite of the truce.

Company F Lurps were put on tactical alert and exempted from going into the field. If and when we were required to do so, we would be positioned at strategic points on the berm to protect the company compound.

Company F 51st had minefields surrounding the berm side of the company area. The minefields extended out about the size of two football fields. There was also barbed wire and concertina wire protecting the entire area. We also had a surveillance tower overlooking the back side of the compound and didn't really concern ourselves with the enemy trying to overrun us from that side.

Yet, clearly there was a war going on outside the perimeter of the company area. At night the assault helicopters were constantly up in the air streaming red tracers and rocket fire. The tracers from the Cobra gunships checkered the night sky just outside the perimeter for three consecutive nights. Fortunately, the Allied forces once again successfully turned back the communist aggression. In the interim, U.S. forces racked up a very large enemy body count.

Tet a year earlier had been a much different story. It was enough to make your hair stand on end. In 1968 the holiday was the occasion for a massive enemy offensive. U.S. forces intercepted enemy radio traffic pointing to an all-out attack on Saigon. The North Vietnamese Army deployed eighty-four thousand troops and launched coordinated assaults across the whole country. The Tet offensive brought the war in Vietnam from the countrysides into the cities. The primary objective was to take over Saigon and other neighboring cities such as Bien Hoa, Tay Ninh, Long Binh, Cu Chi, and the northern city of Hue, which was the most strategic and intricate part of their ambitious offensive plan. No one really expected the Viet Cong to break the traditional Tet new year truce. As a precaution, U.S. forces did ask the South Vietnam government to call off the truce and cancel army leaves. But for political reasons, the request was ultimately denied.

During the first few days of Tet, the Viet Cong's and the North's hard-core soldiers almost prevailed in their attempt to capture the region. After days of fighting, U.S. and Allied forces drove the enemy into a retreat. Eventually the sites surrounding Saigon, the Tan Son Nhut Airport, and the radio and television broadcast stations were taken back from the enemy forces that briefly held them, and again they were under the protection of Allied forces and out of the control of the communists. Regrettably, order was restored at the cost of many American and civilian lives. I wasn't there for the 1968 Tet offensive, but the stories I heard about Company F Lurps and assault helicopter squadrons going toe to toe with the enemy in downtown Bien Hoa were still on everyone's mind, especially those who had fought there a year earlier.

I can remember going on only two missions in the month of January, and both were with "heavy" teams. A heavy team usually consisted of ten or twelve men. Rather than dodging an enemy encounter, heavy missions were designed to initiate contact. Making contact with a heavy force was meant to undermine the enemy's confidence and disrupt their supply movements.

When I finally got the chance to go out on a heavy, which was seldom, I was chomping at the bit to make contact. However, making contact didn't always happen. Either Charlie completely avoided the Lurp teams large in number or we ran into a bit of bad luck in not finding the enemy.

In mid-January the number of missions for all the teams in Company F had fallen off tremendously. The count of patrols for some of our Lurp teams arrived at "zero missions." And rumors regarding the company breaking up were beginning to take on a life of their own. As it soon became evident, the murmurs were not just rumors anymore.

Around the end of January, all operations in Company F abruptly ceased. The Soul Patrol team and all other teams in the company were officially dismantled. We were instructed to take inventory of the equipment we held and return everything back to supply except our LBE gear, rucksacks, and weapons. Individually we knew that we would be shipped to different parts of Vietnam, but "where" was still a mystery.

On February 1, 1969, it soon came to light, every LRRP and LRP unit in Vietnam would be deactivated and redesignated as a "Ranger" unit. On the day we were officially assigned to move to our new prospective Ranger unit, it turned out to be one of the saddest moments in my Vietnam experience. I was being shipped off to Tay Ninh, located just north of Cu Chi. The new company was designated Company O (Ranger), 75th Infantry (Airborne). Thad Givins was being shipped to Company P (Ranger) located up north near the DMZ in the Quang Tri area. The O Company group of soldiers was the first to be shipped out of the company area. I and about fifty other "new" Rangers were aboard two deuce-and-a-half (two-and-a-half-ton) trucks waiting to move out to our new location. Most of the guys in the company came out to the waiting trucks to say their good-byes and we wished each other well. It was a melancholy scene leaving all of our colleagues and friends behind. There were many acquaintances I had come to know very well over time.

We had orders not to leave the trucks that we were assigned to. I anxiously waited for Thad to come out so we could say our good-byes. I kept looking and waiting, but he never showed up. I sent someone into the hootches to find him and let him know I was about to leave. Still he wouldn't come out to see me off. One of the Lurps came back to the truck and let on that Thad wouldn't leave his hootch because he was weeping and he didn't want anyone to see him like that. I had never seen Thad display emotions about any situation. He was experiencing what I was feeling. Thad didn't want anyone to see his soft side. It was just as well that we didn't see each other off, as I didn't want to embarrass myself and let them see me shed a tear because we were splitting up.

I never got a chance to say good-bye to my buddy Thad before departing Company F on that unfortunate afternoon. To this day I have not seen him or spoken to him. A friendship is something I have never taken for granted. By nature I am very loyal and a very devoted friend. I genuinely believe Thad Givins was the same exact way, that's why we got along so well. Indeed, we had a kindred spirit. Perchance, wherever Thad is, he will pick up this book and read it. Maybe then we can reconnect our friendship once again.

Although the company breakup had been rumored for a while, the act itself came suddenly and the splitting up of friends essentially caught us off guard.

The Company F 51st LRP compound would be renamed Company D 151st Inf. A group of our Lurps would remain behind at the compound to train a National Guard unit being shipped over from Gary, Indiana, to fight in this crazy war.

For the most part, I believe our little group of Rangers that was selected to go to O Company got the better end of the deal. As far as the best troops were concerned, every man chosen to go to O Company Ranger was a capable soldier able to hold his own in any situation. Our group would have been complete if Thad had been able to make the trip. It was not to be.

Company F 51st Infantry (LRP) had produced a group of stellar soldiers. Answering that call and making up the O Company Rangers roster were soldiers like Sgt. Sandy Boyd, S.Sgt. Dave Deshazo, Steven Miles, Lawton Mackey, Thomas Mattox, S.Sgt. Jerry D. Beck, Jaime T. Hernandez, John R. (Piggy) Millender, Henry Bonvillian, and Sgt. Mike Frazier. These were just a few of the names of Lurps, now turned Rangers, I knew I could always depend on when the going got tough.

With the exception of Capt. Donald A. Peters, a quiet gentleman, there was a lot to be desired when it came to the leadership in O Company Rangers.

Personally, I had no confidence in the high-ranking NCOs representing O Company Rangers. One of them was a total lush, and the other, who posed as the first sergeant, had no compassion for his soldiers. Somehow the name "Keystone Kops" always came to mind when describing our leadership.

It didn't take long to start operations in the new company. Although the name never came up in the briefings, we would be operating back in the Hobo Woods AO.

As Rangers, our missions would change dramatically. Instead of working strictly in five- or six-man teams, sometimes we worked in eight- and nine-man teams. I actually felt safer operating in smaller groups. It was easier to hide small teams because there were fewer people to worry about making noise or mistakes.

The helicopter support ships didn't have the same relationship we had enjoyed with the "Playboy" AH-1 (Cobra) elements of the 334th Aerial gunships and the 17th Assault Helicopter Company.

I remember, it was around this time in my tour that I began to feel estranged from the war, our leadership, our missions, and the new Ranger company in general.

In O Company Ranger, I was always bumping heads with the company executive officer, 1st Lt. James S. Presswood. That situation had never happened before while I was in the military. I had always been able to get along well with the officers and top NCOs.

First Lieutenant Presswood was a tall, athletically built, blond Southerner who wore thick-rimmed glasses. I remember him as a person who was always trying to get a tan, but would end up looking like a red lobster instead. Lieutenant Presswood was never comfortable accepting the fact that I could beat him in most of the common sports that we played in the company area, such as basketball, football, softball, and sometimes even pitching horseshoes.

I was never able to figure out Presswood. Certainly, I always made sure to give him the respect his rank required, but I quickly lost all respect for him as a person for the way he treated the black soldiers.

Presswood was proud to be from the state of Tennessee. He often wore his University of Tennessee sweatshirt. Time and again the strained relationship between First Lieutenant Presswood and me continued. He'd smirk with a shit-eating grin, referring to me as "boy." I'd explained to the lieutenant on many occasions that I was a soldier, not a "boy." It was hard for me to maintain military courtesy with Lieutenant Presswood.

The shit from the latrines had to be burned at least once

a week. Lieutenant Presswood repeatedly picked Mackey, Millender, Mattox, and myself . . . all black soldiers, for the shit-burning detail. It quickly became obvious to all of us that this was now a racial issue. The final straw came one day after we had returned from an exhausting mission. Lieutenant Presswood ordered us to burn shit, right after we had completed the detail the week before. While we carried out the duty, we began complaining about the unfair treatment that had now become obvious.

"You know what, man? This is bullshit!" Millender angrily said, and we all agreed.

"Why do they have to keep doing this kind of shit to us? They have motherfuckers in there who haven't burned shit since they got here! That fuckin' Presswood waited for us to come back from a mission so we could burn shit! That's it! I ain't doin' it anymore!"

Something had to be done. Because I had been in-country the longest, I was the one elected to talk to Presswood. I knew Presswood had it in for me and it was time to have it out. I also knew I was in the right, so I relished the challenge.

After we completed the detail, I went to Presswood's hootch to confront him.

"Sir, we've been noticing that you never give the shit-burning detail to any of the white soldiers and, frankly, sir, until this situation is dealt with fairly, we are not going to take your racial bias and we are not going to burn any more shit!"

Presswood shifted a little uncomfortably. "Are you threatening me, soldier?" he asked.

"Yes sir, I am! I'm within my rights and you know it!"

"You are now bordering on insubordination, soldier! You are dismissed, Sergeant Emanuel!"

But I had said my piece. I walked out of the confrontation smiling, almost laughing, and thinking to myself . . . I had it out with Lieutenant Presswood and I had won!

But then I recalled, he had referred to me as Sergeant Emanuel. I wasn't a sergeant and I never really wanted the rank. Receiving an E-5 rank would automatically put me in position to be a team leader and I really didn't want that kind pressure or responsibility.

Soon after that incident, Lieutenant Presswood made the teams rotate the shit-burning detail. That's the way it was supposed to be done in the first place. It was about a month later before we pulled another shit-burning detail. We just wanted to be treated fairly and equally, nothing more and nothing less.

A few weeks went by, and Lieutenant Presswood selected himself to go to the Special Forces Recondo School in Nha Trang, Vietnam. He would be gone approximately one month. Wow! A whole month's hiatus without Presswood! How would we ever survive?

Well, it was no use getting excited about not having him around for a while, because a couple of weeks later Presswood showed up back at the company area with his rifle in one hand and his duffel bag slung over his shoulder, looking sad and dejected. He walked by barely speaking and unable to look me in the eyes. I noticed he didn't have the Recondo patch on his fatigue shirt. The word soon got out that Presswood had flunked out of Recondo School. I actually felt bad for him. I knew the school was tough, but I couldn't believe anyone with his physical ability and intellect could not make it through Recondo School. I figured the lieutenant hadn't taken the training seriously. It was likely he had gone to Recondo School with a cranial rectal inversion (his head up his ass).

It wasn't that I disliked Lieutenant Presswood. I only wished he hadn't had a problem with the black soldiers. As a matter of fact, I had hoped he would represent our new company well at Recondo School and remove my fears about the substandard leadership in our new Ranger assignment.

How would Presswood be able to face the troops, knowing he was the leader of a company who couldn't make the cut at Recondo School? Well, it wasn't long before that question was answered.

In the month of March, spring comes early in Vietnam. The hot, dry season wouldn't be far away. I had already been on about three or four missions in the new Ranger company. We got a warning order for another mission. S.Sgt. Dave Deshazo, Thomas Mattox, Les Ervin, and myself, all combat veterans, were picked to go on a special mission. But this mission would be different from any other I had experienced while serving in Vietnam. For the first time as a Lurp or Ranger, an officer would be leading the patrol. But not just any officer. Are you ready for this? Yep, that's right, you guessed it . . . First Lieutenant Presswood! He would be taking over Staff Sergeant Deshazo's job as team leader. Dave Deshazo, who had just been promoted to staff sergeant, would now become the assistant team leader. Anyone in his right mind knew those roles should have been reversed. Deshazo was a very qualified and capable team leader. The guys all respected and trusted him. As far as we were concerned, Presswood was still a cherry. He had never gone on a mission before.

During the morning briefing, with Captain Peters and First Sergeant Bergeron looking on, Lieutenant Presswood was full of himself, letting us know emphatically that he was the team leader on this mission. After pointing out the area of recon, our artillery support, and escape and evasion routes, he announced with a brief pause in his delivery. "Gentlemen, I want to make one thing perfectly clear, under no circumstance will you fire, I repeat, you will not initiate contact until I do so first!"

We all looked at each other incredulously. Who is he trying to kid? This was a war and not a game. Obviously Presswood had not thought the mission through or he would not have said that. There were people out there waiting to kill us, and here he was telling us to wait for him to fire first! If we were going out for a simple ambush mission, it would be a different story. But to wait for him to give orders to fire, even if we were engaged, was absurd. With him in command, the mission was a recipe for disaster.

The next day around noon we were inserted into the AO.

Seconds after we hit the ground the helicopter flew off and disappeared. It was always an empty feeling when the helicopters couldn't be seen or heard anymore. Especially this time. I had a distinct feeling of déjà vu. The ghastly mission we had experienced in the Hobo Woods came back to mind. The terrain conditions were comparable, the long roads and trails looked very familiar.

We moved about seven hundred meters, staying close to a long row of hedges lining a trail that extended as far as the eye could see. Within the hedge was ample coverage to hide the team. Not hiding immediately after getting off the helicopter was "mistake number one." The second mistake was moving on a trail, the very thing we were trained not to do.

After about a half hour of humping . . . call it fate   but for some reason, we decided to move off the trail to cross into the hedge line for a rest and to take a water break. When we crossed into the bushes, we discovered another trail running parallel to the hedges on the other side. Although the trail was broken and fragmented and not as defined, it was still a trail. We sat down and removed our heavy rucksacks. Approximately sixty seconds later we heard a radio playing Vietnamese music, then we heard talking and laughter. As the sounds moved closer to our position, we had enough time to prepare ourselves for the perfect ambush. Two VCs meandered into our sights. They were laughing and joking. Their AK-47s were slung across their shoulders, the radio playing loudly. We were all relying on Lieutenant Presswood to give the signal to fire the first round. I looked over to see why he hadn't fired yet, and Presswood was on the ground curled into a ball, hugging his weapon close to his body. Staff Sergeant Deshazo, who was positioned next to Presswood, calmly and softly suggested into his ear . . .

"Fire sir," he whispered . . . "Fire sir" . . . he whispered again . . . "Fuckin' fire, sir!" he vehemently said with anger.

By this time Charlie was right in front of us getting ready to pass our position. Deshazo stood up and aimed his M-16 rifle at the enemy and squeezed the trigger . . . *Click!* His weapon misfired! He pulled the bolt back and rechambered another round and fired off a double burst on full automatic. That was my cue to spring into action. I hopped up from the ground and leaped across the hedges onto the trail and caught the two soldiers sprinting away side by side. I fired my weapon from the hip, unleashing a burst of about a hundred rounds with the M-60 machine gun. While in a dead run, one of the enemy soldiers went down under the heavy automatic firepower. He hit the ground hard without breaking his fall. The other soldier helped him up and pulled him into the bushes. Then they both vanished into the foliage.

"Get your ass down before you get your fuckin' head blown off!" Deshazo yelled at me. But I knew that as long as I kept firing the M-60, Charlie would have to keep his head down. That was one of the beauties and the advantage of having the "big gun" on a mission.

When my first belt of ammo ran out, I leaped back through the hedges to reload another continuous belt of 750 rounds of M-60 ammo, which I had linked together in a claymore bag. I looked around and found Presswood still lying on the ground in the fetal position, still clutching his M-16 rifle. I reloaded my weapon and began firing through the trees and bushes at no particular target.

This might be the first time I have ever told this particular part of this story. Maybe because I really didn't understand exactly what had happened, and maybe it was hard for me to believe what I am about to say.

As I stood in a crouch, firing off belts of ammo from the M-60 machine gun and moving around trying to find a better position, the ground beneath my feet began to move. Whatever I was standing on was slowly crawling forward, like I was riding on the back of a huge tortoise or something. I saw a long hump of an impression under the thick layers of dried out, dead vegetation. But during the heated moments of battle, I thought nothing about the large object moving underneath my feet.

After the firing ceased, we moved down the hedge line to

make a sweep of the area where we believed the VCs had disappeared. We began to follow a trail of blood leading into the bushes. We came upon a "spider hole" with a camouflaged entrance to an underground tunnel. The entryway was splattered with blood.

"I knew I hit that son of a bitch!" I thought to myself.

Dave Deshazo blew the hole by dropping a couple of hand grenades down the opening. We couldn't find Charlie, so we moved out from the tree line area toward the trail. That's when we started receiving fire from the direction we had just reconned. I dropped to the ground and began to return fire. Although it came much too late and seemingly out of context, Lieutenant Presswood finally came to life and started to direct fire.

I was lying in the prone position firing into the tree line when Thomas Mattox plunged to the ground next to me and began firing his weapon about twelve inches from my right ear. In that instant the pain was so intense I thought I had been hit in the head with a bullet. Instinctively, I rolled away from the muzzle of his weapon and checked my head for blood. Fortunately there was none, but afterward I couldn't hear a thing except for the high-pitched ringing in both my ears.

During the firefight the helicopters seemed to appear out of nowhere. We threw red smoke grenades in the direction of the enemy fire and the Cobra gunships made their gun runs. The recovery slick swooped out of the sky and touched down on the hard-packed dirt. We sprinted from our circle of security and jumped aboard the chopper. As we flew out of the area, I thought about another missed opportunity. We could have easily secured one or two prisoners, or at the very least two enemy KIAs. But, Lieutenant Presswood froze. His inexperience exposed his inability to function as a team leader and as a Ranger. Not to mention, from that time forward he totally lost the trust of the soldiers under his command.

In the debriefing Presswood acted as though nothing had

happened. He was jovial and joked around, praising the team for a job well done. But we knew the truth. We saw how he'd responded to the type of situation that had become routine for us.

After the debriefing was over, Captain Peters pulled me aside. I thought I was going to get my ass chewed for being too aggressive with the M-60 machine gun during the firefight.

"Don't worry about packing to go back out with the team tomorrow," Captain Peters said with a smile. "You'll be going to Recondo School. Get your gear ready, you leave tomorrow morning." I was absolutely delighted. I was on cloud nine. And I was certainly ready for the challenge. More important, I didn't have to complete that lame-ass mission with Lieutenant Presswood in charge.

Going to Recondo School was a privilege. For me, it meant I would be able to train with the most elite U.S. and Allied forces serving in Vietnam, the best of the best! Recondo School was said to be the "Harvard" of military combat schools. It also meant that Captain Peters had confidence in my ability as a leader. Although it was nice to be thought of that way, I did not want to become a team leader.

The next morning I went to the chopper pad and watched the team of Rangers head out to the same AO from which we had just been extracted. Thank God for S.Sgt. David Deshazo, because he was still on the team. If he weren't out there with those guys, I would have worried knowing Lieutenant Presswood was out there alone with the team.

I later heard that the team completed the remainder of the mission without further incident.

Now, getting back to that thing that moved under my feet . . . it surely wasn't the ground. I spent years trying to figure out what I was standing on that day. I finally came to the conclusion, it wasn't a tortoise, because they are not indigenous to Vietnam.

Realizing that years and years of vegetation and foliage falling to the ground and dying off made for a thick carpet of dead plants, underneath this thick, dead vegetation perhaps lived one of the largest snakes never recorded. If it was a snake, it had to be at least three feet in diameter.

To this day I still don't know why I didn't fire on it. Maybe because I was so caught up in the moment of the firefight and, whatever it was, it really didn't pose a threat.

CHAPTER ELEVEN

Recondo School

Around 0930 hours I left my hootch carrying a few necessary items like my M-16 rifle, web gear, and a duffel bag with cammies, extra socks, underwear, and a change of civilian clothes. I was taken to the nearest helipad by jeep. Once I arrived at the chopper pad, I was flown to Bien Hoa Airport to a waiting C-130 cargo plane.

Hopping on an aircraft and flying around Vietnam was no mystery to me. I had done it enough times to feel like an old pro. But for eight months, this was the flight I had been waiting to take. I was going to a school that would enhance my skills as a warrior. I guess deep inside, I wanted to prove to myself that I belonged within the ranks of the elite soldiers. Not that I had any real doubts, but Recondo School was a chance to prove that I could train and prevail among the best soldiers the U.S. military and the Allied world had to offer.

Months before, when I first applied for Recondo School, attending the school became almost an obsession. Acceptance into Recondo School was hard to come by. They admitted only sixty students per class and approved only seasoned veterans of many missions. I had made a promise to myself; if I were ever admitted into Recondo School, I would not squander this unique opportunity. I had complete confidence that I would graduate the rigorous school.

Everyone who had gone before me told me how intense the training program was, and I certainly believed them. It was for that reason I needed the opportunity to challenge

myself and win the Recondo "V." It was just the encouragement I needed to complete my experience in Vietnam.

During the loud and bumpy flight, the large Hercules
transport plane trembled as it flew through the turbulent air.
I moved from the netted seats and lay on the steel floor.
Both were equally uncomfortable. As I leaned against my
rucksack, I thought about the embarrassment of flunking out
of the school. The notion of failing sent chills down my
spine. There was no way in hell I would go back to my unit
a failure. Washing out was totally unacceptable. Even
though the Recondo School dropout rate was extremely
high, the word "defeat" did not exist in my vocabulary. At
the time I had no way of realizing that was exactly the right
attitude! I was precisely the type of student Recondo School
was looking for.

The Recondo patch was well sought after among Vietnam's elite warriors. The colors on the patch were a light
olive drab background and a bold, black letter "V," which
stands for valor and Vietnam. The color combination meant
"capable of operating day or night." An arrowhead with the
tip pointed downward symbolized air-to-ground methods of
infiltration behind the lines and into enemy territory. The arrowhead also represented survival and scouting skills per-
fected by the American Indians. The word RECONDO was
embroidered in black letters across the top of the arrowhead.
The word is taken from the terms reconnaissance, commando, and the World War I heroes known as Doughboys.
In Vietnam the coveted Recondo insignia was truly a badge
of honor for those who attended and graduated the school.
Among the Vietnam enlisted and noncommissioned recon
soldiers, it was certainly more prestigious than the Army
Ranger School tab.

Woefully, there was only one momentous obstacle standing in the way of potential graduates of the school, and that
was finishing the school . . . alive! That within itself was a
formidable task at best. Recondo School was the only
school of its kind where we got a chance to meet and challenge the enemy in a live-fire training exercise . . . a real

combat situation. It was the first time in the history of the U.S. military that a school was designed to provide this type of training. And, for all intents and purposes, it's probably the last time it will ever happen.

After about an hour's flight, the large aircraft banked and flew into Nha Trang Airport. After a few minutes the engines shut down and the cargo door lowered to the ground exposing a warm, pleasant Saturday afternoon in the city of Nha Trang, Vietnam.

The sun was shining brightly with a few high clouds. As I disembarked the plane and walked toward the terminal, the all too familiar scent of concentrated jet fuel permeated the air. An intermittent gust of wind blew the sweet smell of saltwater off the ocean as it whipped across my nose. I always became excited when I smelled the ocean, it made me feel closer to home.

Nha Trang is located on the South China Sea just above Cam Ranh Bay. The entire coastline was beautiful and impressive, a perfect candidate for a vacation spot seen in an upscale travel magazine : . . if it weren't for the war, of course.

I slung my gear over one shoulder and headed for the downtown district, which turned out to be a hotbed of activity. Pedicabs, motorcycles, and small compact cars were jamming traffic. Street vendors lined the streets selling everything from fast foods to American black market goods. It was strange to see the civilian population outnumbering military personnel.

I stopped three U.S. "Airborne" Force Recon Marines who were sporting their jump wings on their chests along with their newly earned Recondo patches. Obviously they had just graduated from the school and were out celebrating. In an abbreviated conversation, they revealed that they would be shipping back to their units Sunday afternoon. I asked about the best places to stay while visiting downtown Nha Trang. By the looks of them, they were taking their drinking campaign a bit too seriously for so early in the day.

The intoxicated Marines' slurred speech barely made any sense at all. Resembling a team of comedians, they all pointed in different directions showing me the way to the hotels. I was told that Hotel Nha Trang would be the best place to get a room.

Throughout the city, signs were posted in almost every establishment stating "No public drunkenness, no weapons allowed on the streets of downtown Nha Trang and a late night curfew will be enforced by the Military Police."

When I arrived at the hotel in the middle of the day, the lobby and bar were crowded with servicemen from every branch of the military, including the Special Operations Groups of our Allies.

After I'd checked in, I put away my web gear and M-16 rifle. I took my .357 Magnum, put it in its holster, and stuck it in the waistband of my pants at the small of my back. The pistol was well disguised by my baggy fatigue shirt.

In Vietnam we were instructed by our superiors in Company F 51st LRP, "You are in a combat zone. You never know what you might come up against in this environment. Always carry some type of weapon for your protection." I took that advice seriously.

I settled into my room and then decided to go for a walk down the main strip just outside the hotel. I wanted to make a quick recon of the area. This also became part of my routine for my personal safety. The main street in the downtown area was lined with French-style buildings and outdoor restaurants.

The women in Nha Trang were much more attractive than the women in other places I had visited in Vietnam. The few women that I thought were attractive looked to be a combination of French, Vietnamese, and black, but at the same time they had a genuine American flavor to their look and fashion.

American music was a major part of the Nha Trang ambience. The popular Otis Redding song "Sitting on the Dock of the Bay," and a plethora of Beatles songs could be heard streaming from the jukeboxes inside the businesses along the strip. Every other building on the street was either a bar, a nightclub, or a brothel.

"Yep, I do believe I'm going to like this place!" I said aloud. The city of Nha Trang reminded me of the Old West, a city of sin and lust, spawned by a lot of bad men. I was told to watch out for the Vietnamese street gang called the Cowboys. If you weren't careful, they were known to rob you at gunpoint. I dared the little shits!

Later in the day I was hungry enough to eat a water buffalo. Although in Vietnam that was nothing to joke about. After my quick recon, I did an about-face and went back to the hotel's restaurant for lunch. I ordered a thick steak, plenty of french fries, and several bottles of Coca-Cola. When the meal reached my table, the steak was lean and tender, still smoking hot off the grill. That lunch happened to be one of those meals you always remember. It was so good, I ordered another. And if those steaks were water buffalo, then kudos to the chef.

After stuffing myself, I left the restaurant and turned in the direction of the loudest "soul" music coming from a nearby bar. I walked into a funky little bar on the strip that reeked of old cigarette smoke and stale beer. Inside the dimly lit bar the jukebox was blaring the song "I Heard It through the Grapevine" by Marvin Gaye. Several nude dancers were onstage alternating duties as though they were a tag team.

Personally, I can't dance, but I couldn't hold back my chuckles while watching the female dancers onstage, who looked more like they were swatting at a swarm of angry bees rather than making a soulful dance step. Hell, I hadn't seen gawky moves like that since watching that singer Mick Jagger trying to dance. I guess dancing onstage totally naked in front of a bunch of wild and rowdy GIs whistling and yelling "Hey, baby, come sit on this hunk of love!" would throw anyone off the beat.

I started drinking rum and coke. Then, I wanted to see how much alcohol I could consume before falling into the abyss of stupidity. After joining in on the whooping and howling with the rest of the numbskulls in the club, I decided to "go for it" and really live dangerously. I began ordering and drinking that ghastly Vietnamese beer, "33" Export Ba Muoi Ba. It always tasted like it had just been scooped from someone's dirty bathtub and coerced into a contaminated bottle for public consumption. It was an acquired taste to be sure.

I watched a tall, lean, square-jawed Green Beret sergeant enter and walk toward the bar. The sergeant sported a pilot's handlebar mustache that partially covered the smile on his face. He weaved his way through the crowded club and placed a multibreed mutt on the countertop of the bar. The Special Forces NCO (noncommissioned officer) had both sleeves of his fatigue jacket rolled up to the third stripe on his chevron. I couldn't tell whether his stripes indicated an E-5 or E-9. But I was able to tell right away that he was up to no good. A group of soldiers, including other Green Beanies, gathered around the dog and his owner. The sergeant poured beer and whiskey into a small bowl and began feeding it to the dog on the counter. When the dog was good and drunk, a menacing grin came over the SF sergeant. He began to masturbate the horny little pooch to the applause and amazement of the audience. It seemed that everyone from the bartender to the barmaids, who eventually walked away in disgust, knew the little sideshow was going to take place.

When my consumption included a final glass of rum and coke, the room started to spin. It was time to leave! I had already violated two of the posted ordinances . . . I was working on the third, "no public drunkenness." I stumbled out the door and aimed myself toward my hotel. I don't know how I got there, but I was able to get to my room. I flopped onto the bed and slipped into an intoxicated sleep. The bed began to spin. I have no idea how that could have happened. . . . Yeah right! Hanging over a smelly toilet bowl seemed like familiar territory, and I was at it again.

Let it be known, I have never considered myself an alcoholic, nor did I really enjoy the taste of alcohol, but when I did drink, it was to get drunk. And Vietnam seemed to be the perfect place to get that job done.

Around midnight I was startled from a semiconscious sleep by shots being fired on the floor above. I heard a woman screaming, followed by lots of footsteps running through the halls. I rolled out of bed onto the floor and crawled to the crack of light filtering in underneath the door. I was conscious enough to wedge a chair tightly against the doorknob. Then I crawled back to bed and secured my Colt .357 Magnum pistol and passed out again. Even in my drunken stupor I was aware of my surroundings. I could still hear the ruckus upstairs continuing on for over forty-five minutes, or so it felt.

The next morning around 1030 hours, I lay in bed struggling to open my eyes. A knock on the door from the cleaning person jolted me to sit straight up in bed. That's when I realized I had one of those professional hangovers. The garden variety type you get after indulging way beyond your capacity. This was one of those real good smoldering headaches, with dry heaves accompanied by dry mouth. The kind of cotton mouth that tasted like the entire Russian army had just marched over your tongue with dirty socks. And if I've said it once, I've said it a thousand times, "I'll never do that again!" Some people will never learn.

I was glad to be checking out of that hotel. I had never seen flying cockroaches before. I suppose the attacks from the little green lizards on the walls would make any insect fly.

As I handed the checkout clerk my room key and several piasters (Vietnamese money), I asked, "What was all the commotion about last night?" But the clerk didn't seem very anxious to talk about it at all.

"You go now!" he responded. "Hotel very busy today!"

Like I really cared what had happened . . . I was only making idle conversation, anything to get my mind off the awful headache I was suffering.

I lumbered out of the hotel onto the street and flagged

down a pedicab. I had the driver shuttle me to the Recondo training facility about a mile away.

At 1200 hours on Sunday I checked into the Recondo School. I had heard that the Special Forces Mess Association laid a good table and I didn't want to miss the noon chow. Guess what they were serving that day? Yep . . . that's right, steak!

Upon my arrival at the school, I was assigned to a bunk and given a team number. I was enrolled in class RS-17-69. Throughout the day the trainees began to filter into the compound in small groups. After I had returned from chow, my headache was almost gone. I had a full belly of great food and earlier I had taken a couple of Darvon capsules to get rid of the pain.

I noticed that all the bunks that had been rolled up before were now turned down, with someone's duffel bag and gear on them.

After more troops arrived at the school, I started to hear startling reports about a battalion of NVA soldiers with Russian-made tanks attacking the Special Forces camp up in the Central Highlands the night before. The rumors were still unconfirmed, that was until the entire Recondo School was issued ammo and put on standby. We were told to be ready to respond as a reaction force if the situation in the Highlands worsened.

It was "get nervous time" for everyone. Most of the arriving trainees were pretty jumpy about being shipped out to the embattled SF camp. Quite frankly, I wasn't particularly happy about going up into the Highlands for the fight. Nor was I mentally prepared to go up against a battalion of tanks and a division of hard-core North Vietnamese regulars. All I wanted to do was pull my three weeks at the school, earn my "V," and go back to my unit. But of course, if we were called upon to mobilize as a reaction force, I would do my part without so much as a squeak or squawk. Besides, it wouldn't have helped had I made a fuss. We were consistently reminded by the army, "Don't sweat the small shit, gentlemen! It ain't nothing but something to do." That was the classic military proverb used to motivate the troops. Sometimes those words of wisdom helped a great deal in getting us through the day.

I'd heard from a reliable source that even though the Special Forces group suffered heavy casualties during the raging battle, they still kicked the shit out of the enemy and racked up a hefty body count that would escalate into the hundreds. Those bodies were found the next morning on the battlefield. Who knew how many other wounded enemy were carried off the battlefield to die.

Monday morning at 0750 hours the new Recondo troops were assembled in the main classroom. The large classroom was a well-constructed building made of plywood with a tin roof and a concrete floor. Down the center of the aisle was an inset, or countersunk, trench, if you will. Rows of desks were placed on both sides of the aisle on a two-foot-high concrete platform.

The classroom is where we spent the majority of our study time. It soon became clear that Recondo School was half academics and half field training.

The new class of Recondo students sat at their desks anxiously awaiting the opening ceremony. Like most army training programs, Recondo School would commence with the history of the school and an introduction of the top Recondo cadre.

At 0800 sharp someone yelled, "Ten-hut!" We snapped to our feet. A young-looking major strutted across the stage wearing his Green Beret. He stopped in front of a podium painted in the Vietnam-style tiger stripes and bearing a large Recondo emblem. Directly behind him was a dark curtain that also exhibited a large Recondo patch, and to the right of that sign was a sizable Special Forces emblem.

"Take seats, gentlemen," the Major said in a rather cool and by-the-way manner. A row of empty chairs had already been placed behind him waiting to be filled. He removed his beret and stuffed it into the cargo pocket of his fatigue pants and began walking back and forth across the stage, never taking his eyes away from us.

"Welcome to Recondo School! I am Major Bob Lunday, assistant commandant of the MACV 5th Special Forces Group Airborne Recondo School. It is considered an honor and privilege to be chosen to attend this training program. I want to congratulate each and every one of you for, first of all, volunteering to attend this program and, second, for being selected by your company commanders to come here. By directions of the USARV [United States Army Republic of Vietnam] commander, no person is accepted for training at this installation except for volunteers. I ask you to look around at your classmates. You are all special soldiers. You were all chosen by your individual units to receive an elite and unique training course, which has been recognized as the pride of the United States Army." As all eyes followed the SF major back and forth across the stage, we leaned on his every word.

"General William C. Westmoreland, the commander of MACV [Military Assistance Command, Vietnam] and a longtime advocate of the Recondo School, realized the need to produce a recon commando training program. It was also the foresight of General Westmoreland, who said, 'A Recondo must be skilled, smart, tough, confident, and courageous.' I'm sure most of you fit that description or you wouldn't be here. The MACV Recondo School is designed to give you supreme confidence in your survival skills, which are literally unmatched on the battlefield. You will gain more combat knowledge in this three-week training program than most field commanders will learn in an entire year of duty in Vietnam.

"The Long Range Reconnaissance Patrol units were fostered here in Vietnam. Our Long Range Reconnaissance Patrol training was developed by Project Delta, B-52. In September 1965, Detachment B-52 of the 5th Special Forces Group Airborne began a unit training program on long range reconnaissance patrol techniques. Thus, in September of

1966, General Westmoreland ordered the Recondo School program opened and extended its function to all U.S. and Allied Special Operations units needing long range patrol capabilities.

"Today we have in attendance personnel from the U.S. Marine Force Recon, the U.S. Navy, U.S. Air Force, Royal Thai Army, members from the Australian army SAS, and ROK [Republic of Korea], and, of course, LRRPs or designated Rangers. The MACV Recondo School has been long considered the finishing school for LRRP, LRP, and now the Ranger units in Vietnam. Our mission here is to train students in proper combat intelligence-gathering and patrolling techniques, which are aptly taught by our distinguished U.S. Army 5th Special Forces cadre.

"If you make it through this course, just know, you are the select group of men in the free world to wear this prestigious Recondo patch." He pointed to the large Recondo emblem behind him.

"Training in this school could lead to combat situations, which sometimes result in casualties. We call it 'getting baptized under fire.' I personally ask you to refrain from getting wounded or killed while attending this school. It is not permitted due to the hardships on your families back home. It also makes for more paperwork for my instructors, who prefer spending their leisure time drinking beers in the NCO club."

The major tried to ease our tension. As he continued his speech, he made us realize that we were in a very special program, more than I had ever imagined. I felt proud to be there. The Recondo program would last twenty days, which amounted to a 260-hour block of instruction.

The one-hour ceremony concluded with the introduction of the school's six officers and most of the forty-eight NCOs. Major Lunday was a good motivational speaker. He had me ready to run hundreds of miles and do hundreds of push-ups. And eventually I would.

On Tuesday at 0400 hours, in the darkest hour, we fell out to the sound of blaring music followed by a chorus of harassing yells. We assembled at the center of the compound.

For me, this training was what I had long waited for; my Recondo School education had begun. It was a very regimented physical training program that went strictly by the book. The first forty-five minutes consisted of jumping jacks, chin-ups, push-ups, squat thrusts, and other rigorous exercises. The entire time we were being pushed and prodded by the SF cadre.

Just when I felt my body couldn't stand another exercise, we were introduced to the infamous and grueling five-mile run along the beach and the outskirts of Nha Trang. During the running segments of the training we were weighted down in full combat gear. Because we were training in a combat zone, we ran the course with loaded weapons, full web gear, hand grenades, canteens filled with water, and twelve magazine clips with ammo. Inside our rucksacks we each carried a forty-pound sandbag. If the sandbag was tampered with, meaning, if one lightened his load, that trainee would be embarrassed in front of the company and immediately dismissed from the program.

It was standard operating procedure to do everything as a team. If a person was not able to make the run, another team member would have to fall out and help his teammate complete the course. There were no exceptions.

After I finished close to the front of the pack on the first day, I was confident I could get through the run. One Thai soldier was out in front by at least three full minutes, and some tall lanky soldier from the 101st Airborne LRRPs stayed about a minute behind him. I remember seeing them after they had reached the turnaround point. They passed by us going the opposite direction. I began to target them as my competition. When it came to running and training, I knew I was as tough as anyone. I was ready to take on any and all comers. After having gone through so many army training programs, I was able to develop the attitude, "If someone else was able to make it through the training, I knew damn well, so could I."

After the brutal first-day run, we assembled behind our gear in the center of the compound. Only after everyone was accounted for were we able to move out in teams to eat morning chow. The cadre took special care to make sure the trainees were well fed. The food served at the school was impressive. It tasted more like Stateside restaurant food.

While we were in training, the individual teams were instructed to eat together, study together, and train together. Every class module, including eating in the mess hall, was timed out to a strict schedule. And don't even think about showing up late to a training class, it was one of those infractions that was absolutely not permitted and could get you excused from the program.

Right from the start, all the training classes were back to back. They kept us busier than a one-eyed cat watching three mouse holes.

During the first few days we had a CBS News crew come to the school and film the troop training out in the field and in the classrooms. The cameraman made a slow pan shot across our row of desks. When the camera came to me, the operator pushed in to a close-up, focusing on me jotting notes in my book. The field producer told us to write home and tell our families to look for the story on the evening news. In 1969, most remote news stories were shot on film. The average Vietnam story timeline in those days took about seven to ten days. Nowadays they bounce stories off the birds (satellites) and news around the world becomes instantaneous. Who knew?

I didn't get a chance to write home and tell anyone about the filming. But a few weeks later, after I had finished Recondo training, my mother wrote me after seeing me and the story on the evening news.

One of the first and most arduous Recondo classes was "map reading." It was without a doubt the toughest of the academic courses. The map reading course was the main reason most students washed out of the school. Back in Company F, I had made sure to learn how to read maps and a compass just in case I had to take over a team or in case I had to go on an E & E (escape and evasion) course. It was strictly a matter of survival.

We started the class by learning how to make map "overlays." The instructor told us to name the "point of origin" on the overlays anything we wanted. The point of origin simply meant, the point of insertion. In my infamous wisdom, I named my point of origin "Fuck It." At the time I wrote those scholarly words on my onionskin paper, it summed up how I felt about my situation in Vietnam . . . "Fuck it!" For me, "Fuck it" actually meant I was going for broke, or anything goes. It was just an expression I would use when I wanted to go to my "bad ass" place or the "mean" place inside me.

Evidently, that attitude didn't sit well with the instructor who came by to view my work.

"What the hell is this?" he questioned in an angry tone.

"It's my point of origin, Sergeant."

"Are you trying to make fun of me, soldier?"

"No, Sergeant! You said we could name the point of origin anything we wanted." I had no idea he would take the name so personally.

"What's your name, soldier?" he questioned, as he eyed the name tag on my fatigue shirt. "Emanuel! Okay, Emanuel! My 'fuck it' boy. I'll remember that name." I knew I was in trouble, and the only way out of that predicament would be to do a good job on the assignment. I expeditiously changed the point of origin to Compton and made sure I did an excellent job on the assignment. When the instructor came back around, he looked at my work and let out a satisfied but hard-nosed grunt, indicating, Your work is good, but you are still on my "shit list."

Later that day the Recondo cadre hit us with a surprise "read and recognition" class. The instructor stood in front of the class, loosely talking about the different sounds that weapons made out in the field. All of a sudden a couple of thirty-round clips coming from AK-47s were fired at full burst just outside the classroom. Thinking the compound was under attack, I reacted to the AK firing by diving onto the concrete floor, low-crawling down into the sunken aisle separating the rows of desks, and heading for the exit. I looked back to see how many were behind me, and that's when I realized the entire class was watching and laughing at me. I was choked with embarrassment! Then the instructor said in an admonishing tone, "While all of you are sitting there laughing at him, the rest of you are dead! This is the only soldier in the whole damn class who made the right decision to survive!" By this time I was on my feet. "What's your name, soldier?" he asked.

"Spec Four Emanuel, Sergeant!" I responded with much relief.

"Now, Spec Four Emanuel here recognized the sound of an AK-47 and understood that we are still in a war zone and reacted properly." The instructor turned to me. "Well done, son!" Then he turned back to the class and continued to scold.

"This demonstration was an exercise to see how you would all react to a surprise attack on the compound. Our main objective here at Recondo School is teaching you how to survive. All of you except for Spec Four Emanuel failed the test. Every one of you should have been in the aisle right behind him." Personally, I was very relieved to know I was noted for doing something right, especially after that "Fuck It" debacle.

The next class was basic first aid. It would be one of many medical courses we received in the Recondo training program. The memorable exercise that stands out in almost everyone's mind after attending this class is the four-inch-long needle we had to stick into each other's arms to demonstrate administering serum albumin. Serum albumin serves as a blood expander that replaces lost blood. It was given to severely wounded or injured soldiers. One of your own team members was designated to practice on your person by inserting a hideously long, thick, and painfully dull needle into the vein in your arm. And, turnabout being fair play, you got a chance to do the exact same thing to your teammate.

The worst part of the exercise was watching someone with hardly any experience perforating your skin and missing the important artery that supplies the blood. I always worried about getting an air bubble into my bloodstream, or in someone else's bloodstream for that matter, which sometimes can result in death.

Later that day the training moved to an outside class just a few feet from the indoor classroom. An ominous looking fifty-foot rappelling tower loomed over the yard. The tower was surrounded by a beachlike sandpit. The tower came complete with a rope ladder. When you climbed up the rope ladder, every time you took one step up, it felt as though you were sinking down another three steps. As part of the training we were made to carry our weapon and full web gear along with a forty-pound sandbag in our rucksacks up the rope ladder. The extra weight was a special little treat to create a more challenging climb up the ladder, and also to simulate the amount of weight carried on a mission.

Besides a good tight grip, one of the only things that could save your ass going up the exhausting climb and also keep you from falling off the ladder was a trusty D-ring. As part of our mandatory equipment, a D-ring was attached to the upper part of the web gear harness. At a moment of desperate weakness, we could attach the D-ring onto the rope ladder for security. It was not a good idea to have such a moment in this school.

When we reached the top of the fifty-foot platform, it was time to rappel down. With all the yelling and harassment going on, it wasn't the most pleasant of experiences.

On my first try off the tower, I did an adequate job. And after the rappel, all trainees were ordered to report to the instructor's station located on the ground in front of the tower. Trainees were required to lock their heels and shout out their name and number to the instructor for a critique of their rappelling efforts.

With my heels tightly locked, I reported in at staunch attention. . . .

"Spec Four Emanuel, Sergeant!" I shouted.

"Emanuel, Emanuel . . . What did you do wrong, Emanuel?" The instructor began to thumb through the pages in his notebook, trying to remember why he would know that name.

"Coming down, I might have gripped the rope too tightly with my left hand, Sergeant!" Then, I think the sergeant recognized my voice.

"Oh yeah, Emanuel! You're my 'fuck it' boy! Where are you from, Emanuel?

"Los Angeles, California, Sergeant!" I shouted.

"Do you know who Charlie Pride is, Emanuel?"

"Who, Sergeant?" I questioned. "I am not sure who you are talking about. . . ."

"Charlie Pride, boy, my favorite country singer!"

"No, Sergeant, I've never heard of Charlie Pride before, Sergeant!" I affirmed, still at attention.

"Drop down and give me fifty push-ups for not knowing my favorite country/western singer, Emanuel!" the sergeant demanded. I dropped into the soft, deep sandpit and knocked off fifty push-ups. And after a brief pause, still in the front leaning rest position, I proceeded to give him twenty-five more push-ups just to show the sergeant that his punishment wasn't shit! At the time I entered Recondo School, I happened to be in the best physical condition of my life and I was ready for his harassment.

The sergeant leaned down toward me and began shouting in my ear.

"Are you trying to be a smart-ass again, Emanuel? I know you don't like me, and you're trying to piss me off, ain't you?"

"No, Sergeant! I have never heard of Charlie Pride before, Sergeant!" I said, appealing my case.

"On your feet, soldier! I guarantee you'll learn all about my favorite country/western singer, Charlie Pride, before you leave here. You hear me, Emanuel!?!"

"Yes, Sergeant!" I barked and snapped to my feet at attention.

"Git your ass back up that ladder and give me another jump! And this time, no mistakes!"

Most of the trainees had to rappel only once off the tower. It was very taxing to do it twice. As I started up the ladder, everyone was watching. My arms were shaking with exhaustion. I wanted to use the D-ring and take a breather, but I refused to give the sergeant the satisfaction of knowing I had weakened from the extra push-ups. When I reached the top of the tower, my energy was spent. It would have been nice to get a quick rest before rappelling off. That didn't happen! While I was still pissed off and trembling with exhaustion, I set to go off the tower. I took a deep breath to settle my nerves, and my descent down the tower was flawless. I reported back to the instructor's table. The sergeant was sitting at the table waiting for me to report in.

"Who is Charlie Pride, Emanuel?" the sergeant challenged.

"Charlie Pride is your favorite country/western singer, Sergeant!" I said, sounding off.

"That's right, boy! Now, git your ass out of here before I make you listen to my Merle Haggard albums!" At that point the dialogue was starting to become a big joke to the other troops and SF cadre. I was one of the two black soldiers enrolled in the school, but it was my innate defiance that began to gain attention.

I never liked Charlie Pride or his music after that day. At nineteen years of age I absolutely did not enjoy country/western music. And because of my taste in music, I was getting flak from an old redneck sergeant. Judging from his Southern accent, he was from the Ozark Mountains or somewhere else in the deep dark South.

Oh sure, we all experienced a sergeant in the military that made life hell. But I truly believed by the spirit of our interactions, he was giving me both barrels of racism. Personally, I don't think I had experienced real racism in such a genuine form until I joined the military. As a kid growing up in Compton, California, I wasn't really able to grasp the true meaning of racial prejudice. In the army you are exposed to all types of people and their sordid ideas about race, however backward they might be.

The old sergeant was trying to crawl under my skin with some of his remarks. The whole time, I took everything he said in stride. After a while, when I refused to break under his pressure, I believed the old sergeant started to take a liking to me. At every opportunity he made a point to seek me out to tell me lame jokes about California, the queers and steers, the longhair hippies, hippie music, and his favorite subject, the Black Panther movement in Oakland, California. His amusing little comments never bothered me. I was only focused on getting my Recondo "V" and going back to my unit, alive!

In a respectful way I rebutted the old sergeant, telling him he had been in the military too long and that he was completely out of touch with reality and the real world, or something to that effect. Believe me, no matter what I told him, I could never find the right words.

One of the most frightening experiences I ever faced while serving in the military was rappelling from a helicopter. That's exactly what we had to do that same day following the tower training. After lunch, with a full load of gear strapped to our backs and no real safety net to speak of, we were 120 feet up in the air, suspended out over the skids of the helicopter with just a rope for security.

After watching the expert-SF cadre demonstrate the right way to descend down the lines, one of the rappelling ropes snapped and the SF sergeant fell to the ground, breaking his collarbone. Now, there's a ringing endorsement for leaping out of a helicopter tethered only to nylon ropes. The SF instructors were amazingly good at their jobs, but not always perfect.

When my turn came, my knees were knocking and my heart pounded furiously. In so many words, I was scared to death. The SF instructor who served as the bellyman onboard the chopper threatened to flunk me out of the school if I didn't release off his chopper skids. With that in mind I pushed off, holding a death grip with my left hand that was supposed to be my guide hand to steer me down. Under the circumstances, I was holding the line too tight, again. When I finally reached the ground, my gloves were smoking like kindling. I burned my fingers on my left hand, only to realize that to become proficient at this maneuver I would need more practice. And unfortunately, we had to rappel down twice that day. But on the second try, it all clicked. I made a smooth and efficient descent. I couldn't have been happier when that part of the training was over. We returned to the classroom that evening; the long arduous day turned into a late-night study session. We sat through another brain-twisting map reading class. In Recondo School, I was one note-takin' fool. I took more notes in my two weeks in Recondo School classes than I had taken in my entire three years of high school. I was almost possessed. I had never been so determined to pass a training course.

Around 2200 hours we were able to retire. At this school, they made sure you remembered the true meaning of "sleep deprivation." When I reached my hootch, I collapsed on my bunk and passed out from exhaustion. No sooner had I closed my eyes and drifted off into a semiconscious sleep than the PA system started to blare loud music. The constant harassment coming from the public address system had our attention early in the morning. It was another day, and another day to do forty-five minutes or an hour of continuous PT and then run six miles before the sun came up.

In the early mornings, the streets of Nha Trang were quiet. Again, we made the run through the course of Nha Trang, downtown and beyond. The unison footsteps of seventy pairs of jungle boots could be heard from a distance, shuffling and pounding the pavement and the dirt road in the wee hours of the mornings.

I remember hearing laborious breathing from nearby runners trying to catch a second wind. The distance had been increased by another mile from the day before. By the third day we would run seven miles a day, every day.

On this morning I tried to run with the Royal Thai Special Forces soldier who had been blowing past everybody. Around the company area his name became synonymous with most running conversations. "Am-Nuay!" He was all legs, lungs, and heart. The harder I tried to stay within his reach, the farther the gap became. After a couple of miles struggling to stay in the front of the pack, I watched helplessly as Sgt. Ron Reynolds, a tall, lanky soldier from the 101st LRRPs, trotted past me like a large thoroughbred horse. Reynolds took off, attempting to reel in Am-Nuay. They were both good strong runners, and I was simply outclassed with no chance in the world of catching them. Am-Nuay came in first on that morning, as he did every morning after that. For me, I had achieved a personal best that day, finishing among the first ten.

That morning, after finishing the exhausting long run, we were in the chow line when I heard more conversation regarding the attack on the Special Forces camp in the Highlands. Only after the threat of being shipped out had totally subsided were we told by one of the Recondo cadre that we were just a radio transmission and a signature away from being shipped to the Highlands to relieve the Special Forces advisers in combat. We were also informed that the situation up there was much worse than what we had actually been told.

There was no such thing as a day off the first two weeks of the school. We operated almost twenty-four hours a day, every day. The intensity in the classrooms had become equivalent to a wartime environment.

We never knew what was coming next. One day after lunch, we stood at attention in the hot afternoon sun. The entire class was loaded down with full weapons and gear. Then we double-timed two to three miles to the beach. I had heard about this day. Our classroom was being held on the ocean front. We had to continue our individual qualifying to stay in the school. This class exercise would be the one-mile

swim. The swim consisted of a half mile to a floating platform off the beach and a half mile back to shore. If you
weren't able to complete the swim, you were disqualified
from the school.

The instructor teaching the class was the cantankerous
old sergeant who made a career out of making my life a living hell. In his instructions, he pointed out to the class, "If
you can't swim or you can't make the distance, raise your
hand now! Because if you get your sorry ass out in the middle of that ocean and drown, I'll personally kill you. Now,
this is your last chance to step forward and speak up." No
one moved.

"We have provided each of you with a life preserver just
in case you get out there and get too tired to finish. When
you feel you can't go on or you start to go under, I want you
to put this nozzle in your mouth and blow into it, and that
will inflate the life vest." I raised my hand and the instructor
acknowledged me.

"Hey look, my 'fuck it' boy has a question! What is it,
'fuck it' boy? Oh, by the way, I hear you soul brothers can't
swim, is that true?"

The instructor continued to ride my ass like I was a government mule, and I continued to ignore his comments.

"How would we be able to blow into the life vest while
we are drowning?" I asked.

"Well, that's a damn good question, Emanuel. And, the
answer is . . . don't put yourself in a situation where you
have to use it." Personally, I wasn't worried. I knew I could
make the swim.

It was an overcast day. The water was rough and choppy.
I lined up next to a Force Recon Marine. The command was
given, "Go!" We entered the water in pairs. I dived through
a medium-size wave and started my journey with the breaststroke until I began to tire. Then I settled into a smooth and
easy frog kick. By the time I reached the floating raft, I realized that the raft and the half mile distance was a lot farther
away than I had anticipated. I never saw the Marine I had
started with. I wasn't sure if he had finished the swim or not.

When it came to the swim exercise, the washout rate at Recondo School was about 30 percent. Maybe the Marine fell victim to that statistic. The SF instructor on the floating raft kept yelling encouraging commands, "Good job, soldier! You got it, just don't quit! Keep moving! When you make the turn, don't touch the platform!"

I decided to show off my aquatic prowess by disappearing underneath his platform and coming up about twenty feet away from the raft in the direction of the shore. While skimming underneath the water, I thought to myself, This ought to put to rest those bullshit comments about "brothers can't swim." I realized that I had been motivated by a negative stereotype that drove me to do better. While others were struggling to make the swim, I was having fun.

When I reached shore, I reported in to my favorite harassing instructor, and true to form, he didn't disappoint me.

"Boy, how in the hell did you get back here so fast, Emanuel, did you cheat, boy?"

"No, Sergeant, it was black power!" I responded jokingly without thinking first.

"That's not black power, this is black power," he said, pointing to my M-16 rifle. "And, for being a smart-ass again, I want you to hold your weapon over your head with both hands and duckwalk up and down my beach until I get tired. Now!" he shouted, with fury in his voice and in his eyes. When I got into position, the sergeant stood behind me and yelled, "I want you to say loud enough so everyone can hear you, I am a duck, quack, quack!" I guess the sergeant was having a really bad day and he was more than ready to take it out on me. But, of course, I had to put a different spin on the harassment situation. I put in a few extra words of my own. . . .

"Black power! Black Power! I'm a duck, quack, quack!" I really wanted the sergeant to get the message that he could not intimidate me. I watched the old sergeant fume as I waddled up and down the sandy beach yelling, "Black power, black power! Quack! Quack!"

I also noticed other SF cadre laughing at my defiance,

which inevitably spurred me on. Finally the exhaustion factor set in. It took another cadre instructor to walk over and pull me away from the punishment. It was time to participate in another class exercise. If it had not been for the eight-man infiltration raft training, I would still be duckwalking up and down that beach.

For me, all the water exercises in the South China Sea were fun. It was a pure adrenaline rush. It was also an area where I did some of my best work. The eight-man rubber raft infiltration exercises taught us how to sneak a team into enemy territory without making excessive noise, enabling the team to launch a successful attack. We learned as a team how to flip the rubber rafts over and hide underneath, then upright them again. I enjoyed the "water" part of the training.

Back in the classroom, one of the most intriguing and noteworthy tests I can recall taking at the MACV Recondo School was a survival aptitude test, which included logical questions on how to survive on the "moon," of all places. Had I been on the moon, I would have survived.

The second week of training was a four-day field exercise held on Hon Tre Island, a small island just off the coast of the Vietnam mainland. Helicopters lined up at the helipad and began transporting the troops in the groups of their team.

We flew out over the water, the choppers breaking through the low cloud cover and morning mist. The land mass sat out in the middle of the ocean like a perfect little island paradise. Visible from above were the triple canopy jungles, but in other areas the island was practically barren of trees or any vegetation.

The various exercises on the island were designed to teach each team member how to use the PRC-25 radio when calling in field artillery and also to learn the correct procedures while utilizing forward air control (FAC) for air strikes. The all-important advanced map reading courses were another part of these exercises.

"Small-arms weapons" was another segment of the program. It was actually fun familiarizing ourselves with the live firing of a variety of different small-arms assault weapons. Most of the exotic and vintage weapons were from World War II. I got a chance to handle and fire weapons I'd only heard about, like the M-1 carbine rifle, BAR (Browning automatic rifle), the Tommy gun, the Grease gun (a type of machine gun that actually looks like a grease gun tool) the AK-47, and all the other various Chi-Com automatic assault weapons at our disposal for test-firing. The purpose for learning to operate other weapons was primarily to accustom ourselves with all types of fire-power we might encounter in a firefight. If our personal weapon were damaged or if we ran out of ammo, sometimes in a firefight we would be able to access the enemy's firearms. With this training, we would be in a position to know how to use whatever weapons were available to us.

To my advantage, I had already experienced a significant amount of Recondo field training. In Company F 51st LRPs, we were indoctrinated with the Recondo training manual before ever going on a patrol.

During my Recondo training, one particular class really captivated my attention. The class exercises taught us how to incapacitate or dismantle your enemy with lightning speed using "quick kill" techniques. At the time of this training, I kept thinking, this quick kill stuff could really come in handy back on the block. Although this kind of training was not practical in the real world, it was certainly interesting to have that type of knowledge.

In team groups, we walked through live-fire courses with pop-up targets. The instructors were right behind us scoring our every move. Most of the Recondo training was pretty intense, so I tried to find creative ways of making it fun.

Although the island was fairly secure, we still conducted mop-up operations and pulled the same security duties that were normally fulfilled on a regular mission.

A company of CIDG (Civilian Irregular Defense Group) strikers was already on the island when we arrived. They were the Montagnards from the mainland participating in operations in conjunction with the Recondo School students. In spite of the language barriers, we did a pretty good job of communicating with them. It's amazing how food can transcend boundaries and become an international language. We sat around our little C-4 cookout campfires and shared our different cultures. We traded our C rations and Lurp rations for their rice and mutton. I had never tasted or heard of mutton before that day. It is dried-out strips of sheep meat with a sweet and pungent aftertaste, and it chews like beef jerky. I was immediately drawn to the flavor and the texture of this indigenous staple.

The four-day field exercise went by pretty fast. It was time to get back to the compound to prepare for the testing that would determine who would qualify for graduation week.

All the classroom and field exercises we had digested resulted in a series of complicated classroom tests to measure what we had learned. This was the program's way of finding out which trainees would be accepted into the third and final week of Recondo School training. Needless to say, I was extremely nervous. The academic testing consisted of map reading, small-arms weapons, communications, first aid and medical training, radio procedures, enemy interrogations, intelligence-gathering and patrolling techniques, forward air control, and artillery support.

Most of the problem-solving questions I was able to accomplish lickety-split. But when it came to the map reading section, some of the questions and situations I had never encountered before. I took every minute allotted to finish that part of the test, and still I wasn't sure if I had even come close to giving the right answers. When the instructors came by to collect the test papers, they took pity on my tenacity to do well. They could see that I was still trying to wrangle the right answer from my tired brain. The instructors actually gave me a few extra minutes to finish the test. I could tell that most of the SF training staff was pulling for me to do well.

The day following the testing, the school set aside time for the trainees to relax and prepare for the live combat training mission. Of course, we would only be able to go on the mission provided our academic test scores were satisfactory.

That day during the noon chow, the list of potential grads was posted. The trainees gathered around the bulletin board located outside the orderly room in the PT area. I stood apprehensively in the background watching the reactions of those who approached the board to read the list. There were more looks of disappointment than expressions of jubilation.

Finally, I collected enough nerve to walk over to see if my name was among the few who had passed. And it was! I was elated!

I whooped and hollered for a good three or four minutes, probably annoying those who didn't make the grade. But hell, I didn't care, I had just passed the Recondo School exams. Every instructor I came across, I thanked him and shook his hand with ardent gratitude.

Now I was able to go and pack my gear for the upcoming mission with complete confidence. Those troops who had posted low scores could only look forward to packing their belongings and returning to their units. All that hard work and nothing to show for it, except the privilege of attending the school. It was one of those times in my military career when I wasn't in that crowd.

I was told, "Toward the end of the cycle, the Recondo School students will be dropping out like flies." I found myself flourishing because of the extremely hard work I had put into successfully completing the course. I was grateful and proud to be among the good guys.

On the eve of the final training mission, we sat quietly in the small, shadowy room waiting for the Recondo School cadre to start the briefing. After all participants showed up, the usual discussions took place. Questions and answers concerning the LZ, helicopter and artillery support, radio

SOI, and E & E routes were discussed. One particular subject covered was warning the team to carry extra bladders of water because of the high temperature and hilly and mountainous terrain. The extra water would apparently give us more weight to lug into the field. I also learned that I would be teamed up with a group of soldiers I was not familiar with. It was always unpredictable to work with someone you didn't know. Most of the time you didn't know how a person would react under certain combat situations. The two other guys I had been training with, and who were supposed to be on my team, didn't make the final cut.

When all was said and done, our team consisted of a Recondo School instructor, myself and another American soldier, and two Thai Special Forces soldiers who didn't have quite the command of the English language we would have liked. I had to force myself into approaching the training mission as though it were just another patrol, but in reality it wasn't.

The next morning at 0800 hours we were aboard the helicopter flying over the mountain range of the Central Highlands. From two thousand feet up, the choppers started to descend toward what looked to be a very small hole in the jungle floor. As we flew into the small landing zone, we realized the tight squeeze gave the helicopter pilot very little margin for error. The chopper barely had enough room to fit the blades inside the small landing area. We hovered between trees that varied in height from about sixteen to twenty feet. For a split second the helicopter rotor blades clipping tree branches sounded like we were receiving enemy automatic weapons fire.

About an hour before that mission, the U.S. supporting artillery battery was given a fire mission to drop numerous 8-inch rounds on the side of a hill that was designated as our landing zone. The large artillery rounds were supposed to knock down the tall trees and clear out an area large enough to let the helicopter land safely. The only problem was, the artillery rounds didn't knock the trees down at the roots, the trees were splintered and broken off about twelve to sixteen feet above the ground. There was no way for us to know the results or the effects of the artillery fire until we arrived over the LZ.

When an insertion helicopter hovers in one place longer than ten seconds, the situation can becomes very distressing, not to mention dangerous. While anxiously hovering over the debris-infested bomb craters, we took turns jumping out the starboard door and then the port door to keep the helicopter balanced. We were ordered by the pilot to stand on the skids and wait for the chopper to descend to the closest point to the ground before we leaped off. As I stood out on the skid, I could hear the pilot instruct the soldier on the opposite side of the craft to "go." When the soldier leaped from the skid, the craft suddenly lurched and yawed to the left, throwing me up in the air and onto the ground below. I was carrying more than one hundred pounds of equipment and weapons strapped to my person, all of which went tumbling head over heels. I crashed on the ground, landing on my back and sprawling over a log about three feet in diameter. I actually heard my back snap when I landed. The log had been decapitated by artillery fire. As I slid down off the log onto the ground, I was gasping for air. I knew I was hurt, but how badly hurt was unknown at that moment. I wanted to just lie there and assess the damage to my body before moving a muscle. The hard fall rendered me dazed and lethargic. I found myself desperately fighting through a temporary fog in my head. I could still hear the distant echoing yells from the SF instructor telling me to "get on my feet and get a move on it." There are no time-outs in war, and Charlie certainly wasn't going to take pity on me and my ailing back. Wincing from the torturous pain, I struggled to my feet. I limped into the tree line to meet up with the rest of the team.

"Are you all right?" the instructor asked, hoping I would say yes. I was slumped over at the waist and still trying to get air back into my lungs. I bobbed my head up and down, barely able to utter a single word, but I managed to groan out, "I'm okay."

But I was lying. I wasn't okay, I was hurt badly. I started

to lose the feeling in my left leg, and the pain shooting up and down my spine was excruciating. My back felt like it was going to unhinge from my lower body. It wasn't a good way to start the mission, but now it was time to suck it up. I adjusted and tightened the straps to my rucksack and continued the mission.

The more I tried to make this Recondo mission seem like just another assignment, the more the elements proved me wrong. For example, we were constantly climbing mountains and hills. Our maps kept reading, peaks and summits. In my regular AO, where Company F 51st Inf. and Company O Ranger operated, it was rare although not unusual to spend an entire day trying to reach the top of a mountain.

The SF instructor wanted to show us a few tricks concerning map reading. Without the use of a compass or help from Aloft (a bird dog airplane), after reaching the top of a summit we could still find exactly where we were on a map by reading the fingers running along the side of distant hills or mountains located around our position. The survival skills learned in this school were incredible.

As part of our training exercises, at one time or another each member of the team would assume every position in the team from point man to rear security and each position in between. It was mandatory for us to experience them all. I positively dreaded walking point, but there was no getting around it. I knew if we inadvertently walked into an ambush, the point man was one of the main targets, as well as the team leader. When I carried the M-60 machine gun, I always felt secure walking in the fourth-man spot. The M-60 machine gun was not allowed on Recondo School training missions.

The following day it was my turn to walk point. I was beyond nervous. The SF instructor on the mission tried to act as an observer only. I'm sure he sensed that I was very uncomfortable at the point position. The instructor kept a watchful eye on me.

And wouldn't you know it, after breaking through a heavily vegetated area, I spotted two enemy soldiers with weapons who were dressed in green uniforms walking straight toward us approximately fifty meters away. Charlie and I locked eyes for a split second. They were too far away to get an effective first shot on them. After they figured out I was too large to be one of them, they quickly took cover, ducking behind a tree and then disappearing into the jungle. I held up a raised fist and went to one knee with my weapon aimed in the direction of the enemy. The SF instructor moved forward and kneeled down beside me.

"What do we have?" he whispered.

I whispered in his ear and pointed to an area in front of our line of sight. "Two gooks with weapons walking toward us about fifty meters just beyond that clearing."

"Did anyone else see them?" he inquired.

"I don't know. I saw them," I responded, a bit agitated because he seemed not to believe me. Besides, everyone else was in the rear and they wouldn't have had a chance to see them. The instructor moved down the line asking if anyone saw anything. Everyone responded with a "no" by shaking their heads.

"Let me take over point," the instructor said in a huff. That was fine with me. I didn't want to walk point anyway.

We moved out, not altering our path. About an hour later we heard someone following us. Those little bastards were stalking us. We kept moving until it got dark. Just before the sun set and the jungle turned completely dark, we moved down into a ravine to set up our RON. The ravine was down the side of a cliff that was situated at a 45-degree angle. We had to tie ourselves to trees to keep from sliding down the hill. The way we were strapped into the trees certainly didn't help the pain in my back, but hang in there I did. In our case, that term was used literally. We weren't able to fortify our position with claymore mines, but I believe we were in the safest place to RON.

The jungle turned pitch black. Around 2000 hours the silence and darkness were abruptly interrupted with loud flashes of light from exploding hand grenades. The grenades were being rolled down the hill, one by one and ten meters apart. Charlie was toying with us. Another thing, these weren't Chi-Com grenades being rolled down the hill, they were definitely American willy peters (white phosphorous) and fragment grenades.

"Don't anyone move. They are trying to get us to return fire!" the instructor whispered. The enemy's search for us went on for about a half hour or so. The closest they ever came to actually hitting our position was about thirty meters away. They had no real idea where we were hiding. Either Charlie ran out of ammunition or realized they weren't going to get a response from us, so eventually the assaults stopped.

There was no opportunity to move from our position while it was still dark. We were in quite a fix the way we were situated on the side of the hill. All night long, large chunks of rocks and gravel slipped from underneath our feet and rolled down the hillside into the valley below. There was nothing we could do about it. We simply had to play the cards we were dealt in order to survive.

The next morning after sunrise we expected to see Charlie waiting for us. I'd hoped they had not recruited any more soldiers to come to the fight. We prepared ourselves for any problem that might occur.

We clawed our way out of the abyss and reached the top of the ravine. After reaching stable ground, we made sure we were safe before heading to the next ambush site. It was our good fortune Charlie was nowhere to be found. Had the enemy been waiting for us, they surely would have attacked.

As usual, sleep wasn't an option on the six-man Lurp team. I felt weak and lethargic without rest. Stress was running high among the team members, although the fear of death always seemed to override any exhaustion. The concern of being ambushed dominated our thoughts. We moved with extreme caution, careful not to walk into trouble.

After a few days of mountain climbing, the water supply was getting noticeably low. During the month of March the weather in the Highlands was hot and dry, except for the early mornings when the chill of ground fog was prevalent.

We found a safe place to hide and set up an ambush site. We took turns eating a quick breakfast. After a couple of hours of rest, we slipped on our gear and started to move again. I didn't believe Charlie was tailing us anymore, but now was not the time to take chances. We continued to operate as though we were being followed. The team moved from the high area of the mountain to the valley below, staying close alongside a foot trail. There had been a lot of troop movement on the path. From the boot marks left behind, we surmised they were NVA soldiers. The G-2 information claimed that large groups of NVA soldiers were known to roam through this neck of the woods moving their supplies.

After we set up in a heavily vegetated defensive area, we put out our full complement of claymore mines. The site was about twenty meters off the trail. We settled in for the wait. The ambush site was a welcome break from humping the hills and mountains. Through a bunch of trees in the wooded area we could see and hear rushing water coming down from the high mountain range. The water was estimated to be about fifty meters beyond our position. To get to the water we would have to scale a ten-foot cliff that dropped down to the stream. To the front of our position was a high-speed trail. And to our rear was a fast-flowing babbling brook with huge, almost perfectly round boulders located along the stream. It was actually a very scenic spot to settle into.

In the days following we heard shots fired into the air for signals, but there was no activity along the trail that we were watching. For the remainder of the time we sat like deer hunters hoping and waiting to lure the prey into our trap.

It soon became increasingly obvious to everyone, we were running alarmingly low on water. I had enough to last me the next two days, and so I would ration it accordingly.

The morning of the fourth day into the mission we were completely out of water, although it didn't matter because we were due for extraction around 1500 hours that day. At least that's what we had been led to believe.

Unfortunately, things don't always go according to plan. Early that morning we got the call to stay put for another twenty-four hours. By this time the team was completely exhausted and so was the water supply. Without water, we couldn't make or eat a meal. The only food we carried was dehydrated Lurp rations.

"Why can't we go to the stream and fill up our canteens?" I asked the instructor.

"Because," he replied, "if we got into a firefight down there, we would never make it out alive. The rounds from automatic weapons fire would continue to ricochet off the big boulders until we were all hit, and I am not ready to risk our lives for a drink of water. We'll have to make do until we get extracted."

At the time his explanation made sense, but the longer I sat there listening to the water and then watching it settle into cool, crystal clear wading pools, the more I was ready to say, "Fuck this, they are just going to have to shoot my ass." But because I was a Lurp, it was imperative to remain disciplined at all times, even under the most extreme situations.

All night long we listened to the sounds of the cool water rushing down into the streams. I kept thinking how good it would be to have that cold wet stuff dampen my parched dried lips. It was sheer torture to be so close and not be able to take a swig of probably some of the best water I could drink.

That next morning my skin began to itch all over, as I was starting to dehydrate. I knew I was in trouble when I pinched the skin on my arm and it stayed at a peak. The elasticity was gone from my body. That's a classic sign of dehydration.

Overnight I lay curled into a ball to relieve the pain in my back. My back muscles had stiffened up. When I tried to stand upright, it just didn't happen. I had to remain hunched over like an old man. The pain in the lower region of my back was excruciating. I tried not to let on how badly I was really hurting. If the team had to call in a dustoff (medevac helicopter) for me during a mission, there is no way I would be able to complete the course. And I didn't want to do anything to jeopardize my chances of being there for graduation day. Nothing would stop me from getting my Recondo "V" badge.

We could hardly wait for our midday extraction. No food, no water, and me in a great deal of pain, what else could go wrong? Well, it didn't take long before that question was answered. Just before noon we got another call to sit tight and wait for a first light extraction the following morning.

"Are they shittin' me?" I said to myself, silently contemplating dreadful thoughts. "We are never going to get out of this place." I got the impression they were not going to extract us until we made contact. I looked around and monitored the expressions and reaction on everyone's face after hearing the news. I could almost hear morale drop to the ground. Now we had to sweat out a four-day mission that had basically turned into a six-day torture test. We went two and a half days without food or water. I don't think any one of us was looking for a fight. The fight had been sapped out of us due to thirst, hunger, and lack of sleep. The remaining time in the boonies was nothing more than time spent, because there certainly wasn't any enemy activity going on in our area.

After another night listening to the nearby water rushing out of the mountain springs, the first-light extraction was only a few hours away. Throughout the night, about every thirty minutes or so, I'd pull back the tape that covered my trusty Casio watch and peer at the illuminated dial. I counted every hour to daybreak.

Finally the night passed, but not fast enough. The sun began peeking over the mountain and through the trees. The ground haze started to dissipate.

"Pack it up. The choppers are on the way," the instructor whispered to those individuals who were already awake. The stirring got everyone who was trying to get in that last-minute shut-eye up and ready to move down to the LZ for the early morning rendezvous. As we approached the LZ we could hear the thumping of the choppers in the distance. Soon a team of Cobras was circling the landing zone. We popped purple smoke to mark our position and the extraction slick swooped out of the sky and hovered a few feet over the tall and thick elephant grass. The team was already hiding among the heavy grass on the LZ. The dash to the helicopter was less than a hundred feet. We expeditiously dived aboard the chopper. The craft lifted straight up, making a 180-degree turn in midair. After clearing the trees, the nose of the chopper dipped and took off, gaining maximum speed heading back to the city of Nha Trang. My Recondo School training was finally over.

Besides going back "alive," I had achieved one of my biggest and most important goals as a Lurp in Vietnam. My Recondo badge was a mere ceremony away.

After off-loading the chopper, I immediately headed for the mess hall to get a bucket of ice and canteens full of water. I had boxes of C rations already stashed away in my footlocker for that "just in case meal." I had lost about twelve pounds in seven days. My skin itched unbearably. I couldn't scratch hard or deep enough to satisfy the hanker. I drank as much water as my shrunken stomach could hold. No matter how much water I drank, it was never enough.

After unpacking my combat gear and gobbling down enough food to make the hunger pangs go away, I headed to the showers for one of my classic long, cool showers to wash the grit and grime of Vietnam from my body.

When I emerged from my ritual, I discovered that we had stayed out longer than the other training teams. And because of our extended stay in the field, we had missed a few parties and celebrations.

The next day would be the traditional handing out of the Recondo "V" badge and the barbecue party on the beach. But in the interim, we began hearing reports regarding other missions of the Recondo teams in the field, including the story about the captured NVA officer.

It was 1998, more than a quarter of a century later, while I was interviewing Lurp book authors for my History Channel television documentary "Silent Heroes," when I found out that Larry Chambers was the person who bagged the valuable NVA officer during the Recondo School training exercise. Larry Chambers also wrote the book *Recondo*. I was surprised to find out that I was mentioned in that book on page 158. A photo printed with yours truly listed as "unidentified" is also in his book.

For me, graduation day was a proud day indeed. At 0930 hours the teams gathered in the main classroom. All the top brass showed up for the ceremony. The school commandant handed out the traditional Special Forces dagger to the top student. Only this time, there would be a tie for the dagger. Our class would have two winners. The best soldiers and the ones with the highest academic test scores would receive the honors. In class RS-17-69, Sgt. Ronald Burns Reynolds, from the 101st Airborne Lurps and L Company Rangers, and Am-Nuay from the Royal Thai Army (Special Forces) were the recipients of the prestigious dagger award, presented to them by Col. Harold A. Aaron, the school's commander.

We were each handed a team photo and an authentic Recondo patch to wear on our fatigue shirts. It wasn't a fancy presentation, but it was very meaningful to me. I couldn't help walking away from the ceremony thinking, "If I had worked harder, I could have received that ceremonial dagger."

Later that day just before lunch, we were shipped to the beach by deuce-and-a-half truck for a day of fun, food, and and all the beer we could drink. The rubber rafts were there for water sports.

As I made my way to the barrels for a can of beer, I heard my name being called, "Emanuel! Emanuel! Come here, boy!"

I turned to see who was calling me. It was the old E-7 sergeant who had made it a point to give me a hard time.

"You can't fuck with me now, Sarge! I'm out of here to-morrow," I said, initiating the first volley.

"At ease, soldier, this is a mission of peace. It's my job to weed out the weak. I didn't think you belonged here and I tried to break you. But I'll be damned if you didn't turn out to be one of the toughest bastards I ever had the pleasure to train."

The old sergeant stuck out his hand and we shook. He squeezed my hand and looked me straight in the eyes and said, "Keep your head down, son. Don't go gittin' yourself killed over here." The way he said it sent chills up my spine. His firm handshake impressed upon me that he was sincere. After all the antics I had gone through with him, I was almost ready to punch his lights out. Now I was fighting to hold back a tear.

"Damn, Sarge . . . thanks," I said, choking back the crackle in my voice. I was totally taken aback. It was a true revelation for him to come forward and say something like that. He reached in the tub and pulled out two cans of beer and handed me one.

"Here, now go and have some fun, you deserve it." With apologies and regret, I honestly don't remember his name, nor can I visualize exactly what he really looked like. All I know is he was an older E-7 nearing retirement age. He was a cigarette smoker and a drinker and obviously from the South. Maybe a photograph would help. But after thirty years, I can't find my own Recondo team photo. The beach party would be the last time to be among these brave young soldiers with whom I had the privilege to spend the most exciting three weeks of my Vietnam experience.

The following morning we were packed and out of the school by noon. Besides myself, Spec Four Hillard was one of the only black soldiers training at Recondo School. We decided to team up and brave the always challenging wilds of the downtown districts of Nha Trang.

Our first stop was a little bar along the strip. When we walked into the establishment, it was filled with a group of all white soldiers from the 1st Cavalry Division. Besides

Hillard and myself, I didn't see one "brother" in the entire place.

It was clear that the soldiers had had more than their share to drink. They were all singing in unison, "I want to go home." They all wore black drill instructor–type hats, like the one Robert Duvall wore in *Apocalypse Now*.

I walked up to the bar and ordered two mugs of beer. Sitting at the bar was a blue-eyed, bloodshot, glassy-eyed drunken soldier who nonchalantly turned to me and said, "Hi, Nigger!"

I was stunned for an instant; because of all the ambient noise, I wasn't really sure of what I thought he'd said.

I asked, "What did you say?"

"I said, 'Hi, *Nigger*'!" he repeated, this time with emphasis. Then he apathetically turned away from me and continued singing. Spec Four Hillard immediately sensed the danger in what was about to happen.

"Don't say anything," Hillard said, tugging at my arm. My heart was pounding furiously! I stood at the bar boiling like a volcano ready to blow. When the mugs of beer arrived, the inner urge was just too great. I swung the mug of beer and hit that son of a bitch in the face as hard as I could! A stream of blood gushed from his nose. It was not a very wise move on my part. Before I knew it, the mother of all fights had broken out in the little bar. The only problem was, the place was filled with nothing but them against the two of us. I was punched, kicked, and stomped. Although it was futile, I never stopped fighting and trying to dish out an offense of my own.

After absorbing a number of punishing blows, a team of them picked us up one by one and threw us out the front door onto the dusty dirt road.

Battered and beaten, I felt pain from my head to my toes. I had bruised ribs on the right side of my body from hard-toe jungle boots being repeatedly planted in my side. I limped away wiping blood from my face. We made our way down the street in a hurry. I took satisfaction in knowing that the soldier who had so freely called me "Nigger" would indelibly remember me by the scar left on his face.

Two jeeps loaded with military police rushed by, headed toward the bar. Hillard and I ducked into a small shop, trying to blend into the crowd. We slipped into the back alleys, but never far away from the main street bars and shops. The backstreets of Nha Trang came complete with standing water and foul-smelling garbage.

Once we realized we were out of immediate danger, we broke into a sidesplitting laugh. Albeit a painful and nervous laugh, but a laugh nevertheless. I think I was more grateful that we hadn't actually been killed in the brief melee.

We found a cheap, obscure hotel room for an overnight stay. The floor-level hotel room had two beds. We each paid for a single night. I had an uneasy tension building inside me because of the hotel's location. I couldn't help being on guard, hoping the place wasn't a setup. We were two Lurps just out of Recondo School in a back alley hotel in the city of Nha Trang. We were prime targets and easy pickings. Charlie could have easily burst into the room and taken us out, and no one would be the wiser.

After taking a shower, I administered first aid to myself, then we had a couple of hours' rest. After the quick nod, we took off and found a little French/Vietnamese restaurant off the beaten path and had dinner. We were the only GIs in the restaurant, making it difficult to enjoy the meal. It was always unsettling to be constantly reminded that we were in a combat zone. We had the MPs after us, the group wearing the black hats still pissed off at us, the Viet Cong, NVA soldiers, and the "Cowboy" street gang always looking to make examples of stray GIs. It made perfect sense to hide out until daybreak.

After returning to our room, I lay on my bed and watched the ceiling fan rotate to the beat of country music emanating from a jukebox next door. The music from the bar twanged its way through the walls until we couldn't stand any more.

"Wait here, I'll be right back!" Hillard said, springing off his bed and pulling money from his wallet.

"Where are you going?" I asked.

"I'm gonna pick us up a couple of prostitutes and some beer and bring the party back here!"

"Here, take my .357 just in case you run into trouble."

I handed Hillard my pistol with the belt wrapped around the holster. After he'd left, I unpacked my M-16 rifle from my duffel bag and assembled it. I chambered the first round with the safety on and leaned the weapon next to the head of my bed.

After more than an hour passed, Hillard hadn't showed up yet. I figured he was either testing the merchandise or in trouble. In the badlands of Nha Trang, you just never knew what was going to happen. I was beginning to wish I had gone with him.

Just when I had decided to go out to look for Hillard, he showed up banging at the door. I could hear beer bottles clanking and giggles from a couple of girls on the other side of the door. Apparently, Hillard had accomplished his mission. I was able to breathe a sigh of relief. When I unlocked the door, I was greeted by two cheerful, fun-filled girls who were ready to party. I immediately gravitated to the attractive, caramel-skinned Vietnamese girl who had a great body. She had soft, smooth skin and gentle angelic features. She was uncommonly pretty for a Vietnamese girl.

In Vietnam, it seemed that the American soldiers were always looking for Asian women who looked Anglo. A commonly used description was, "She looks like a round-eye." The more American they looked, the better. This one looked exactly like an American woman.

"Uh, the other one is yours, Bro. This one is mine," Hillard sheepishly explained. The other girl he'd brought for me wasn't bad. She was pretty in an ugly sort of way. But I wanted the one he had picked for himself.

It turned out that the girl picked for me was a total and complete dud. The sex between us was lame. That nasty, unmistakable contempt toward American GIs began to surface.

During the middle of the night, I watched Hillard's girl get out of bed without any clothes on. Her body was near perfect. She had beautiful breasts and a small round butt like a real soul sister. For the moment I was in love!

"Damn!" I thought to myself. "I should have gone with him to help fetch the party." It was just like me to not be satisfied with what I had. But, trust me, had you seen her, you would understand why I felt as I did.

The girls left before daybreak. If they had been spies for Charlie, well, they now knew where we were. I couldn't wait to get out of there.

Around 1030 hours Hillard and I said our good-byes and headed our separate ways. I caught a ride on a truck convoy rolling south toward Bear Cat, at the base down south. It would take a least a day and a half to get back to Tay Ninh.

With confidence . . . my head held high, I had a Recondo patch riveted to my chest and heart. I was feeling good about myself. I had accomplished a goal that only a handful of men or soldiers will ever know or understand. I had a right to be proud, I was a Lurp, Ranger, and now a Recondo School graduate!

CHAPTER TWELVE

Getting Short

I caught a deuce-and-a-half truck departing with a large convoy headed south. I slung my weapon over my shoulder and threw my duffel bag aboard the truck. In a loud and painful groan, I winced as I got aboard. There were two other GIs already on board making up the passenger list. Right away I noticed the 1st Cav patch on their sleeves. Immediately I got a feeling and wondered if either one of them had been part of the barroom brawl we had encountered the day before.

"Damn, Bro! What the hell happened to you?" A big grin came to the face of one of the passengers as he almost reached to help me aboard. I snarled and grunted, then gave him one of those "Don't fuck with me" looks. He totally ignored my warning signs and continued to engage me in conversation.

"You a Lurp?" Not waiting for a response, he continued, "What's that like?" My body was hurting all over and I really didn't much feel like talking to anyone. I was starting to settle into the pain from being launched from the helicopter in training and then getting kicked and beaten by guys wearing the same patch he wore on his sleeve. I tried my best to ignore him but he wouldn't have it. He persisted with questions about Rangers and Lurp units. I could tell he was an infantry soldier from the muddy hand grenades on his web gear. Finally I gave in to his pestering and reluctantly fielded his questions with short answers.

The ride south was especially warm underneath the canvas canopy covering the truck bed. When the soldier's conversation reached a low, I was able to reflect on the inspiration that I had only ninety something days left in-country. I had become short while I was in Recondo School and didn't have time to think about it, mainly because we were always so busy. I had become what was commonly referred to as a "double digit midget!" The thought of getting out of Vietnam and going home conjured up a whole lot of inner excitement. Even with my aches and pains, it held a certain satisfaction just to know I was now "short."

We traveled Highway 1, a two-lane asphalt road that ran north and south. The truck convoy extended out about a mile. The trip south was a long, hard, bumpy ride. I watched the line of trucks kick up rooster tails from the fine red Vietnam dirt. At times the trucks behind us seemed to disappear under the clouds of red dust.

If Charlie wanted to disrupt our supply lines, these truck convoys were always easy targets for mortar attacks, ambushes, and land mines. Just in case something like that did happen, I was told, the ideal position for the ride was near the rear-middle of the pack, and you can believe, that's where I rode.

Around 1600 hours the convoy rolled in to the "Big Red One" base camp near Tay Ninh. I was only a few miles from the O Company Ranger compound, but the "Big Red One" mess hall was open and they were serving chow for the evening. I really didn't need to be back at my company until the next morning.

After dinner I was directed to a barracks for GIs in transit. I was the only Airborne soldier in an all "leg" heavy equipment mechanized base camp. The brief experience gave me a chance to see how other soldiers in the army lived and functioned in this war.

One of the good things about being in a Lurp or Ranger unit was that everyone who was there volunteered to be there. I could tell right away, these guys didn't want to be in this leg outfit. There was no discipline, the environment appeared hostile, and the soldiers didn't have that fighting intensity I was used to being around.

I unrolled the mattress to an empty bunk and stretched out. Apparently I had dozed off without trying, because I was awakened from the effortless sleep by a disturbance outside the hootch. The high-pitched tone of a black man's voice trying to make a point was unmistakable. I was able to make out a small part of their angry conversation. . . . Somebody stole some money from somebody's wallet. Then a big thud hit the wall from the outside right near my bunk. A fight was on! I jumped out of my bunk and walked outside to see what was happening. Pressed against the waist-high rows of OD green sandbags was a small-framed, skinny black soldier and a large, husky white soldier. They were grappling with each other like two madmen. They noticed me at the same time and for some odd reason, after I'd showed up, they both stopped fighting. They slowly untangled, then separated.

In the meantime a group of black and white soldiers had gathered and paired into two groups. I took a quick assessment of the head count, five on each side; that was just about even. When the small, skinny black soldier saw he had his support group in place, he went back into his tirade. I decided this was not my fight. I tried to slip away unnoticed. I made it inside the hootch and lay on my bunk. Then the fight started up again. I'd hoped the two combatants would fight it out among themselves and leave others out of it. That was just before the fight worked itself inside the hootch directly in front of my bunk. This time the bigmouthed brother talked himself into a real good ass-whippin'!

"Hey man, git this big motherfucka off me!" he pleaded, as they waltzed by my bunk punching and grabbing each other. His appeal fell upon deaf ears. I had no intention of going anywhere near their little problem unless the number of participants on one side became lopsided.

After "homeboy" realized he was on his own and no one was going to intervene, the brave comments diminished. Ten minutes later the fight ended and all was quiet. The two warring parties seemed to settle their differences. I was finally able to get a night's rest.

For every morning I was blessed to wake up, I was another day shorter. But don't get me wrong, being "short" wasn't all it was cracked up to be. It too brought about its own little problems. Like trying too hard to be too safe was the kiss of death. Most infantrymen who were short were prone to making stupid mistakes. The "too careful" phenomenon became an additional red flag we had to worry about during our time in the field.

Around 1100 hours the next morning I hitched a ride on the back of a truck going toward the O Company compound. I had not seen my gang in close to a month. It was fun going back and showing off my new hardware. I guess I was happy to see everyone again . . . Mackey, Millender, Boyd, Miles, Hernandez, Gunther, and the rest of the guys.

It had always been a big deal to come back from Recondo School with the "V" on your chest. While we were in Company F, First Sergeant Butts had always acknowledged the accomplishment. And so did everyone else. The distinction carried a great deal of respect, and after going through the program, I understood why.

The ride to O Company took about thirty minutes. The truck let me off at a cross street. I walked about fifty meters to the company compound.

When I arrived, the small six-building complex seemed almost like a ghost town. All the doors were shut and no one was outside. Most of the time someone would be on the basketball court in the middle of the day.

"That's odd!" I remember saying aloud. I opened the screen door to my hootch, and when I entered, I remember seeing Spec Four Mackey in the room. I don't recall seeing anyone else. He was sitting on his footlocker cleaning his M-16. I dropped my weapon and my gear on my bunk.

"Mackey! What's happening?" I said. I was really happy to see him.

"Hey, Ed, you're back! We've been waiting for you."

"Well, I'm probably a day or so late," I admitted sheepishly.

"You should have been here when we needed you!" he

said, almost scolding me. Mackey had one of those funny looks in his eyes, the kind of look he got when he was upset about something. At first I thought he was putting me on.

"Needed me? Why . . . what happened?" I questioned.

"Nothing . . ." he muttered, gazing away as if to ignore me. It wasn't like Mackey to not look me directly in the eye unless he was lying or joking about something. From his demeanor I knew something was wrong.

"What?!" I asked in a solicitous manner, grasping for some kind of real response.

"Man, I ain't sayin' nothing," he snapped, "'cause the bullshit is just gonna start up again. Go ask Piggy [Millender] if you want to know what happened!"

"Why can't you tell me?" I paused for an answer that never came. I was becoming impatient with his silence.

"Where is Millender? Never mind, I'll find him myself!" I headed to the hootch next door. Millender was in his bunk with the mosquito net drawn shut.

"Hey, Piggy! What's going on?" He poked his head from behind the net.

"Emanuel! Aw, man, you did it!" He pointed to the Recondo patch on my fatigue shirt. "Congratulations, man!"

"Thanks!" We shook hands. "It wasn't easy," I conceded. "Hey, Piggy, what the hell's been going on here?"

"Aw, man! You haven't heard?"

I shook my head "No."

"Yeah, man, we had ourselves a little race riot around here." He pulled his mosquito net completely back from his face and sat up on his bunk.

"What happened?" I asked.

"Aw, man! You know how those motherfuckers are when they start drinking. It always happens, somebody sez the wrong thing and a fight breaks out. Before you know it, a cheap shot is thrown and everybody is fighting."

"Well, who said what?" I asked with frustration.

"Naw, man. It's best that we leave it alone, cause I know how you are, you won't let it go! Besides, it's over, everybody made up. It's like Mackey sez, 'It don't mean nothing! It don't mean a damn thing!'"

"Come on, Piggy! You can't expect me to walk into something like this and then ask me to drop it like nothing happened. This affects me, too! This is bullshit! It's only a few of us here. How can those bastards let something like this happen? When did all this take place?" I persisted.

"A couple of days ago. But everything's cool. We worked everything out. Now we know who our friends are. All I want to do is finish my four months and get the fuck out of this motherfucking place! You know what I mean?"

"Yeah, I do know what you mean."

Millender made a concerted effort to reassure me that the heated ordeal had been defused and put to rest. But in my mind, I had actually let down my friends by not being there when they needed me most. The reality of it was, I didn't know what I could have done, if anything at all. Maybe it was just as well that I wasn't there. Who knows what would have happened?

I was angry that the guys in the company would stoop to the level of fighting each other because of someone's skin color. It wasn't easy to accept the terms of dropping the subject. But whether I liked it or not, I had to respect Millender's decision. I had to promise not to say anything about the incident. I could tell that his answers were sincere, and that "they," whoever "they" were, obviously had come to some kind of an agreement.

With that said, it wasn't easy for any of the young soldiers of the Lurps and Rangers who were caught up in the Vietnam War at such a profound level. We had to go about doing our jobs clandestinely and covertly, completely unknown to the outside world. There was no moral support for us, we didn't exist. Black or white, we all felt the pain and anxiety of fighting a war, some more than others.

Frankly, I was very disappointed and disillusioned by the actions of my company as a whole. I thought we were much more cohesive than that. However, I can't put all the blame in the laps of the soldiers. In my opinion, our leadership didn't do the proper things to ease the tension. Letting racial tensions get out of control in such a small unit was inexcusable. I will always blame the leaders of O Company for a large part of the unit's dysfunction on and off the battlefield.

About an hour later I squared away my gear and began reading the mail that had accumulated on my bunk. Then I reported for duty. Captain Peters and SFC Bergeron were both in the CQ office. This was my chance to proudly display my "V" and let them know I had completed the mission. To say there wasn't a lot of fanfare is an understatement. I knew that Captain Peters expected me to complete the Recondo School course. SFC Bergeron never reacted. For him it was a nonissue. That was okay, too. It was common knowledge that, unlike First Sergeant Butts, SFC Bergeron had a hard time relating to his soldiers. Our platoon sergeant was usually so drunk by this time of day, he probably didn't know who he was. So for the most part, my return from Recondo School was a nonevent.

That evening after chow, a movie was being shown in the company area. That was enough activity to get everyone stirring about and out of their hootches. A few guys were congregating in the CQ office. I was in conversation with someone when Sergeant Lambert walked over to me and said, "You missed it! You'd better be glad you weren't here!" Then he paused after thinking for a second and added, "Or maybe we should be glad you weren't here."

"I think you're right, you'd better be glad I wasn't here." I responded to his comment and stared him down. I was hoping he would go further into the conversation, but instead he abruptly ended the discussion. He seemed to make an effort not to fan the flames from the past event.

As far as I can remember, Lambert's comment was the last I heard regarding that particular incident for the remainder of my time in O Company Ranger.

It was too bad the racial incident happened. But the line had been crossed, and it's hard to go back once that delicate allegiance has been violated. Among a few, the trust factor was completely gone, and the harmonious atmosphere would never be the same again in O Company Ranger.

I made my way out to the tent where the movie was being shown. Minutes later, First Lieutenant Presswood showed up. With his hand extended, he walked toward me with a big smile on his face.

"Congratulations, Emanuel. Airborne!"

"All the way, sir!" I quickly responded.

I made a sharp salute, and he returned the salute directly.

"Thank you, sir!" I said. I was sort of taken aback by his initial response.

"Wasn't that fun? How did you like that rappelling stuff from the helicopter?" The lieutenant beamed almost too playfully.

"Well, sir, to be honest, it scared the shit out of me! And I was glad when that class was over." I remember standing there feeling a bit uncomfortable as he went on about his Recondo School war stories. It was kind of like . . . "Okay, where is all this leading?" I got the feeling the lieutenant wanted to be a good sport about the competition we seemed to possess. His behavior was much like whenever I would beat him in a game of basketball or some other sport; he would become overly gracious.

Out of nowhere the lieutenant hit me with a bombshell.

"I hear you are getting your own team!" he said. "What do you think about that?"

Me hearing news like that was like taking a hard punch to the stomach. I was stunned for a second.

"Well, sir, I'd never given it much thought." I tried to show no emotion.

"Aren't you excited?" he inquired.

"Not really, sir." I took a pause because I knew this was going to be one of those moments when I was going to be brutally honest and probably get myself into trouble. "Sir, being a team leader is a big responsibility. I don't think I'm ready to take a team to the field. Besides, I don't think I would even make a good team leader."

Most soldiers would have jumped at this kind of opportunity. I knew I didn't want the responsibility of that type of leadership.

"Well, that's the way it goes in this man's army, soldier!" Lieutenant Presswood smiled and said sort of angrily, "The company needs more qualified team leaders. That's why you were sent to Recondo School. We thought you'd make a good team leader."

Sure, you can call it a cop-out for not wanting the job. But I don't think it was unreasonable, with my three months left in-country, to simply want to fade into the backdrop of my Vietnam experience and go home alive. I didn't want to seem ungrateful, but I had no ambition whatsoever of becoming a team leader. I was happy and secure being the machine gunner. That spot in the team's formation was my comfort zone and my safe passage home, or so I believed.

"In a few weeks," the lieutenant continued, "you and a couple others are going up in front of the board for sergeant E-5 promotions. I suggest you start preparing for the exam. Get your current events in order. Read and learn the Ranger handbook. Those gentlemen on the board hate long hair and big afro hairdos, so I suggest you start by getting a haircut."

Making sergeant E-5 is what most Lurps looked forward to achieving. Just think, all the privileges of an NCO and, most of all, no shit-burning details. But still, with all the freedom that comes with making sergeant E-5, a deeply entrenched apprehension continued to haunt me. Although I had toned down my aggressiveness in the boonies somewhat, I believed that I was still too reckless. At this stage of my Lurping career, I wanted more notches on my gun, more enemy kills. Having said that, I believed that I was too afraid of making one of those life-ending mistakes. I didn't want to be the cause of or be responsible for a team member's death. The speculation of getting someone's son, brother, or father killed because of my performance terrified me. I was still fragile because of my cousin Ricky's death. My uncertainty forced me to worry about my own sanity. I knew if I made it home alive and in one piece, whatever ill-fated events that happened while in Vietnam would somehow impact how I felt about myself for years to come. I wanted to come back home with a clear and clean conscience.

In midconversation with Lieutenant Presswood, the movie started. They were showing one of my favorites, *The Night They Raided Minsky's*. I had seen it once before while in the military. It was a funny and arousing movie. The lieutenant and I concluded our talk and separated into the flickering dark room to search for seats. Halfway through the movie it became apparent that the film had been butchered. All the best nude scenes had been cut out and were being used for someone's personal pleasure. Everyone in the tent who had seen the film before vocalized his disappointment.

About this time the neighboring artillery company began a fire mission using the big "8-inchers." When the big guns initially discharged, I almost jumped out of my skin. The explosion sent me diving on the ground for cover. It sounded like a big mortar round had exploded very close by. It was embarrassing to be the only fool ducking for cover with everyone sitting and watching. I'd realized that I had become exceedingly jumpy and nervous about the routine sounds that were a part of the Vietnam experience.

But in my defense, I have to say, I had not heard an artillery battery firing so close by in a long time. In Recondo School the artillery bases were miles away.

I couldn't sit through the remainder of the movie. I grabbed a couple cans of beer from the beer tub and went to my hootch to answer my mail.

I had always considered myself a team player. That's the way I had been trained. If I were ordered to take a team to the field, I would follow the orders given, or get busted, or even worse . . . go to jail for insubordination. Not wanting to accept the new position of team leader was not an act of defiance, it was an act of self-preservation, which would prove to hurt me later on in my tour.

Well, I never did get that haircut. And exactly one week later, they had me taking out my first team as a Spec Four team leader.

While I was away at Recondo School, we had an influx of new troops that came into the company, some of whom should not have been in a Ranger company in the first place. A few of the new troops were nonairborne and some had been outcast from their previous companies, so you just knew they had no discipline.

My first mission as a team leader was met with a lot of mixed emotions. I was taking out a five-man team with two cherries who had absolutely no Lurp or Ranger training or experience whatsoever. But on this mission, I realized how valuable and effective my Recondo School training had become. Even in the face of adversity, I felt confident and very much in control. All the procedures and radio communications were correct, everything seemed to come naturally. As far as I was concerned, the mission was run completely by the book. However, very few missions go without some kind of incident.

It was early April; the hot, dry, season was approaching. The Tay Ninh AO was much like the Cu Chi area; a lot of rice paddies, small oases fringed with trees, and limited patches of vegetation freckled the flat landscape. The area was bare of the kind of large trees we looked for to set up our RON. Any area that protected us from incoming rounds was a good spot.

The second day of the mission we were on the move and looking for trouble. Oh sure, we could have gone out and hidden in the bushes the entire time. But our job was to recon the area. The LZ and pickup point was a few klicks to our north, and we had to move in that direction for a couple days to be extracted.

Before our mission we weren't able to get helicopters for

an overflight. I really wanted to see what was out there so I could better plan the mission. Once on the ground, I wanted to find out how close the nearest inhabitants were. We set out to identify underground bunker complexes, which were usually associated with this type of terrain.

We moved across an open pineapple field that had dried out from the hot sun. The team kept spotting human bones embedded in the topsoil. We stopped for a few seconds to sample the small pineapples that grew to the size of a mango. The fruit was very sweet and tasty. Then we proceeded to cross over a dike and stepped down into a trench that ran for about two hundred meters. Inside the trench were more than four hundred bleached out skeleton remains that had been scattered along the three-foot-deep ditch. At one time that entire field had been a killing field, fertilized in human blood. I guess that explains why those little pineapples were so sweet and juicy.

Moving for the better part of the day, we found nothing that would indicate recent enemy activities. With evening fast approaching, we set up an ambush site on a dike that was surrounded with ample coverage. For miles we had a view of all sides of our field of fire. A beautiful clear river ran alongside the dike where we had chosen to RON. That night, after we settled into our secured position, all was going well until one of the new guys on the team decided to light a cigarette in the pitch black of night. I could not believe it, he was actually trying to light up! I had never seen that kind of blatant disregard for the team's safety before. Because we were on a mound sparsely covered with vegetation, even the slightest flint could be seen for miles in that flat terrain. I was on his ass instantaneously! I rushed from my position over to his with my pistol drawn. I shoved the barrel of my revolver deep into his soft doughy belly and forcibly whispered in his ear, "You son of a bitch! If you ever do that again, I swear to God I'll pull this trigger!" Believe me, I'd have no problem firing my .357 Magnum into his fat gut at close range. That stupid son of a bitch was try-

ing to get my team killed. I wrestled the Zippo lighter from
his tightly closed grip. When I got back to my position, I
threw his lighter into the river.

To be honest, when he first tried to light the cigarette, I
thought he was signaling Charlie. He had just given away
our position to enemy eyes for a three-mile radius. I lay back
on my rucksack trembling with anger. I was pissed because
I didn't shoot him. I thought about how Sergeant Frazier
must have felt when he had to admonish me for losing my
nerve on my first mission. But this was much different from
that incident. This asshole didn't care if he sacrificed the
lives of the whole team for a fucking cigarette. From that incident on, every time I got a chance to harass him, I did so.

Today, some thirty years later, I don't have the urge to
shoot him anymore, but I think a good ass kickin' would
still be in order! And I am still just the guy who can do it!

Recently I was filming the "Silent Heroes" documentary
for the History Channel. During an interview, I was told that
this same person did the same thing on another team
leader's patrol. That team leader also threatened the life of
this idiot by pulling a pistol on him. Too bad neither of us
shot his dumb ass.

That soldier was representative of the type of personnel
the company was receiving toward the end of my tour. It became hazardous to go out to the field with some members of
your own team. The guys who served as Lurps in Company
F 51st and those who had to endure the O Company operations, I'm sure they would agree to the above statements.

The next day, because of the open land, I decided to stay
put. It didn't make sense to keep exposing the team any
more than necessary. Besides, our position was the safest
spot around.

At midmorning, around 1030 hours, we took aim on a
one-man sampan making its way down the river. The sampan came close enough for us to be able to look down inside
the dugout canoe. I didn't see any weapons, but I did see
fishing baskets, which led me to believe the old man was
just a fisherman trying to provide for his family. The sampan

and the old man stopped right in front of us. He started to re-trieve fish traps from the river. Although the area was a free-fire zone, in order for me to fire on him, I personally had to observe a weapon, which I didn't.

I was keeping close watch on the fisherman when a team member left our perimeter carrying his M-16 rifle and walked toward the old man and his sampan.

"What the hell is he doing?" I questioned the other team members in a whisper. They all shrugged their shoulders as if to say, "We don't know!" He reached into his pockets and handed the old papa-san a few piasters (Vietnamese money). The fisherman handed him a couple of small fish. When he returned to the perimeter, he never said a word. He acted as though his action was an everyday occurrence out in the boonies.

I never did say anything to him about his half-witted be-havior. Maybe I should have, but he knew better. And maybe I didn't say anything because I blamed myself for what he had done. I tried so hard to remain just one of the fellows, I was never able to put emphasis on me being a team leader. After getting thrust into the position of leader-ship, I never had a chance to show the team I was serious about my job. Assuming leadership of a Lurp or Ranger team in Vietnam was a huge responsibility, and I truly didn't want the job. That negative attitude transferred to the other team members. And before I had an opportunity to change the team's perception of my views, this mission hap-pened. Those Vietnam Lurp and Ranger team leaders who did take on the task and executed their jobs successfully, I commend them. It certainly wasn't that I couldn't handle the job. I guess mentally, I didn't want to handle the job. At the time I believed I was carrying way too much baggage to efficiently carry out my duty as a good team leader.

Considering the novice personnel on my team, "success" was returning from a mission without making contact and getting someone killed. Although we had a few glitches along the way, overall it was a successful mission for a first-time patrol leader.

In O Company, whenever I returned from a mission I would make a direct line to my footlocker to take those awful pills for my headaches. Whenever I took the pills, all I could do afterward was sleep. When I pulled back the mosquito net from my bunk, I noticed several letters sitting in a pile on my bed. One of the correspondence was from "P Company Ranger." It was a letter from Thad Givins. At first I didn't know what to think. My emotions were mixed, I was shocked, then surprised, angry, and happy all at the same time.

Thad's letter started off by apologizing for not seeing me off on the day Company F split up. He confessed, he was saddened because the company was breaking up, and he wanted to keep his dignity as a soldier.

Thad was working with P Company Ranger, which was previously 79th Infantry LRP before turning Ranger. His company was operating out of Phu Bai near the DMZ. I was happy to know he was okay. As I read through his letter, he wrote about a mission he and his team had just completed.

Staff Sergeant Carter was the team leader and Thad was the assistant team leader. They were set up on an ambush patrol when they heard voices coming down a trail. But the voices they heard were of Russian dialect and not Vietnamese. Thad went on to say that a six-man enemy counterrecon team comprised of five North Vietnamese soldiers and one Russian officer, all dressed in tiger-striped camouflage fatigues, was reconning the bush in an ardent effort to find the Ranger team in their AO. Staff Sergeant Carter and his team attacked the enemy force, killing all members. The Ranger team was able to recover and extract the Russian soldier's body for evidence. This was definitive proof that the Soviets were training the North Vietnamese elite army.

After putting away my gear, I sat down to write what turned out to be a five-page letter. I had to abandon the idea of taking those pills for the moment, at least until I had finished writing.

I brought Thad up to date on our situation at O Company and informed him about his close friends like Steven Miles,

Mackey, Boyd, and Millender, who were all doing fine. I knew he would be interested in that information. Barring details of the letter, I guess that communication was the last time I ever heard from Thad Givins, even to this date. From his letter, I understood what he was saying without having to use the words. He was saying, "Take care, buddy, I am releasing myself from worrying about you." In Vietnam, that's how we approached how we felt about each other.

Our new Ranger company kept creating a great deal of stress among the troops. . . . This book is not a "point your finger" type of book, I will not mention any names. Mainly because I don't remember their names. . . . But when you are dealing with nineteen- and twenty-year-old kids carrying state-of-the-art weapons in an environment like Vietnam, where fear is the primary ingredient, mistakes happen . . . Big mistakes.

A few examples . . . I wasn't on the mission, but here's the story as I remember it. A six-man team was inserted on a four-day mission. When night fell, one of the team members decided to stand up to look outside their small perimeter. Someone inside the perimeter panicked after seeing the figure standing within the defensive position and fired a burst on automatic, killing the Ranger. The team was extracted, and the person who fired those fatal shots was one of the new guys who had been shipped into the company. The soldier was quickly removed from the company and never seen or heard from again.

While we are on the subject, let's talk about the time we were on an eight-man patrol. We were ordered to walk through the middle of a village that was under suspicion of harboring VC and NVA troops. I knew all the time that we had been sent into the village to draw fire. The 82d Airborne command was willing to sacrifice an entire Ranger team to find out if there were any bad guys inside the small hamlet. A mechanized company of tanks and APCs (armored personnel carriers) was waiting out of eyesight, about a klick away. They were under orders to roll in and level the place had we been fired upon.

That evening our team secured an NDP (night defensive perimeter). We found an area down in a dried-out rain gully. While we were positioned side by side, someone rolled over on an M-79 grenade launcher, discharging a round that struck Jaime Hernandez in his right side. Jaime, only a foot or so away from the barrel of the weapon, took the impact of that round in true Lurp fashion, absorbing the blow without a whimper. An M-79 grenade round had to travel a certain distance and make about twelve revolutions before it armed itself and exploded. Thank God, Jaime was sitting too close or we all would have been in trouble. I was lying right next to him. Had that HE (high explosive) round exploded, it would have easily taken out half of the eight-man team.

On a different mission, I had to break in a cherry soldier who had lived in New York City prior to his enlistment. The kid had a heavy New York accent, the loud New Yorker attitude, the whole nine yards. He claimed to have joined the army because his true love died in a automobile accident while they were dating. The young soldier alleged that he had stopped believing in God because of the death of his girlfriend. He claimed that the one and only time he called on God's help, it never materialized.

On the first night of the mission, not once, but twice in the middle of the night, he had a nightmare. He started screaming at the top of his lungs, calling out the name of his girlfriend. I had to literally smother his screams by putting my hands and my boonie hat over his mouth. His screams came at a time I believed we were getting enemy movement. I forced him to take a couple dextro tablets to stay awake for the remainder of the night. After the mission was over, I did everything I could to get him thrown out of the company. Maybe he went on one more mission before he was gone. It was evident that the integrity of the elite warriors who were once Lurps had been reduced as Rangers.

In Vietnam, units periodically received what we Vietnam vets called a "shake 'n' brake" NCO or an "instant NCO," meaning he and others like him had gone through an accelerated course in order to become noncommissioned officers. Most grunts who had time and grade in the war had contempt for their ranks and held little respect for their leadership. I don't want to sound like I'm putting down this group of soldiers, because I am not. I know for a fact, scores of brave and good leaders came out of that program.

There was a certain black "shake 'n' bake" staff sergeant with a Ranger tab who came into the company. I was breaking him in to take my place as a team leader. The five-day mission went smoothly, but under "standard operating procedures" the team sprints from the wood line and boards the helicopter on team extractions. And as SOP would have it, we all did the same on this particular mission, everyone except for the Ranger tab instant E-6. We screamed and yelled for him to run and get on board the chopper with the rest of the team. He literally walked from the tree line as though he were taking a stroll through Central Park.

I remember hearing the chopper pilot saying, "What the hell's wrong with this guy? I ought to take off and leave his ass out here!"

As the "instant" staff sergeant meandered toward the helicopter, he responded to us, saying, "Man, I ain't running, it ain't nobody out here!"

We finally got him on board, and the helicopter lifted into the sky heading back to the company area. I was only a Spec Four, but I jumped down his shit. I explained to the staff sergeant, the longer the ship is on the ground, the more dangerous it was for all of us.

After reading him the riot act, he realized his potentially costly mistake. Had that "shake 'n' bake" Ranger staff sergeant received Lurp training, I don't think he would have made such an inexperienced mistake, which could have possibly gotten the entire team and chopper crew killed on his first mission. So . . . as you can see, just surviving O Company was the "real" challenge in the Vietnam War.

On April 6, 1969, I had just returned from the field when I heard the terrible news about one of our teams that made contact and had been shot up pretty badly. S.Sgt. Jerry D. Beck and Sp4. Daren L. Koenig walked into an ambush. It was my understanding that Jerry Beck was killed instantly in a brief encounter with the enemy.

I remember the first time I met S.Sgt. Jerry Beck. It was on the morning after the Company F Lurps went on one of their infamous all-night drinking and fighting rampages. "Jerry Beck" had gotten into a fight with my team leader, "Jerry Brock." I know the two names are similar, don't confuse the two.

After First Sergeant Butts finished chewing us a new asshole in formation that morning, I walked over to Staff Sergeant Beck and informed him that whenever he fought a member of my team, he also had to fight me. S.Sgt. Jerry Beck responded to me in such a way that made me feel bad about what I had just done.

"Hey, man, I don't want to fight you, I want to be your friend," Beck said in a very unassuming timbre. From that moment on we did become friends. I learned more about farming and the cows on his farm than I cared to know. S.Sgt. Jerry Beck was one of those "instant NCOs" or "shake 'n' bakes." I'll say this about S.Sgt. Jerry Beck, he was different from the usual caliber of accelerated NCOs spread throughout Vietnam. Jerry Beck was one of the good team leaders that came from that program.

In war, it was downright hard to adjust to the loss of a friend. I was devastated after learning about Beck and Koenig's demise that day. The entire company took their deaths very painfully. This would be Sp4. Daren L. Koenig's first and only mission. The irony was, Koenig was in commo, he didn't have go out on a mission. But he wanted to earn the notable CIB (Combat Infantry Badge). And the only way to earn a CIB was to participate in a combat situation.

Staff Sergeant Beck and Koenig decided to go on a two-man recon in pursuit of the CIB when they walked into a small enemy ambush. Beck took one round in the middle of his forehead and Koenig took several rounds in the chest and was mortally wounded. He died on the way to the hospital. Sp4. Daren L. Koenig paid the ultimate price for his Combat Infantry Badge.

As fate would have it, in the month of April 1969, O Company Ranger met with more than its share of disastrous results. In that month alone we suffered four of our company's five KIAs. In addition to Beck's and Koenig's deaths in April '69, we also lost Sp4. Michael Kelly on April 8 and S.Sgt. John A. La Polla on April 15.

It wasn't until September 19, 1969, several months after I had left Vietnam, that O Company lost our final Ranger, PFC Charles H. Wright. Each of these brave young soldiers now has his name engraved on a brick placed at the Ranger Memorial at Fort Benning, Georgia. They will never be forgotten. "God Bless Them."

CHAPTER THIRTEEN

Home Is Where the Heart Is

When you are young, time seems to be perpetual. The month of April felt like an eternity. I pulled three missions within twenty-seven days. That month the company got its money's worth out of me as a team leader. The upside, I was getting short!

I had less than forty-five days left in-country when we got warning orders to go on a mission in an AO that was filled with dried rice paddies and dikes and the same old routine, not enough cover. They were truly suicide missions when the teams had to operate in this type of open terrain.

I hiked our six-man team to the nearest small isolated patch of vegetation. The patch of foliage sat out in the open like an oasis in a desert. About three hundred meters due north across from our position was a lightly wooded area with a tree line. I figured, there had to be some kind of action over there. We sat and watched the area for about thirty minutes before crossing the open rice field to get to the wood line. I have to admit, it was out of sheer boredom that I entertained the urge to go on the hunt. I had a need to pick a fight with Charlie. My plan was very unconventional and I was going against the grain of everything I had been taught. But I was hoping to draw Charlie out into the open for a confrontation. So we tried flushing Charlie from his hiding places by blowing up his tunnels, bunkers, pagodas, and any other suspicious sites we could stuff a grenade, C-4, or TNT into. While setting off several explosions, one hand grenade blast found my left leg and a piece of shrapnel tore into the flesh of my calf muscle.

"Aw shit!" I winced and grabbed my leg after feeling the hit. Personally, I didn't think the wound was serious, that was until a pool of blood collected inside my boot. I had been hit twice before by shrapnel and never reported it; usually the hot metal from the hand grenade would fuse the flesh together, preventing a lot of bleeding, but this wound was too deep for that.

I had to call for an unscheduled extraction. Because we were a small recon team, I had hoped the entire team would be pulled out of the field along with myself. Surely the arrival of a helicopter would be enough to stir up Charlie's attention, and the team's position would be compromised. It was SOP (standard operating procedure) to remove a team from the field after it had showed its hand. Instead of an extraction helicopter, a medevac chopper showed up and sat down on the dried-out rice field. Just before I boarded the helicopter, I gave away all of my ammo and grenades to my teammates.

I couldn't help sporting a halfhearted smile before the helicopter lifted off the ground. A thought clung to my mind . . . I had just chalked up at least two weeks out of the field and two weeks of not being shot at. Was I lucky? I don't know . . . I do know that each team member felt like an extension of myself, and I really didn't want to leave my team out in the field. The bond, always present, now was overwhelming. As the helicopter lifted into the sky, I remember the feeling of leaving a piece of "myself" behind in the field.

I was being flown to the army hospital, downtown Saigon. The medics aboard the helicopter had a hard time trying to stop the bleeding. I was starting to feel weak from the loss of blood. The helicopter finally set down in what looked to be a large parking lot. As I walked toward the hospital entrance, from a short distance away I could see doctors and nurses frantically working in a makeshift triage set up in the hospital parking area. Their area was covered with a parachute canopy, screening them from the hot afternoon sun. The team of doctors and nurses raced about, receiving and treating numerous critically injured soldiers as they came off the battlefields. I can still hear the piercing screams from a young soldier who had just stepped on a land mine and lost both legs. His bloodcurdling cries for his mother were gut-wrenching to witness. His yells weakened as he started to choke for air. The surgical staff was doing everything to put him under. As I walked by, watching the poor soldier fighting for his life, I was overcome with a tremendous sense of guilt.

"That should have been me!" I thought to myself. I actually felt ashamed that I wasn't hurt as badly as the wailing soldier who was covered with blood, dirt, and his own mangled body parts. The team of doctors and nurses feverishly rushed about in the little space trying to avoid bumping into each other. On a gurney next to him was another injured soldier who was pretty much covered in blood. From their appearance, they had come in at the same time. The other soldier was unconscious and didn't look to be as disfigured as his buddy. I checked to see if his limbs were still intact; they were.

That scene at the hospital was more than I was ready to take. And yet every day, this is what the war looked like to the American men and women who took care of us at the medical facilities in Vietnam. I truly applaud their courageous contributions.

I was expeditiously moved to a surgery room for treatment. I was put in the hands of a Spec Four medic who seemed to be having fun at his job. He gave me a local anesthetic and began cutting into my leg, looking for pieces of shrapnel. After the medic made a few comments regarding the exposed bone in my leg, he sewed me up. I was then placed in a ward with other GIs who had similar wounds.

After three days in the Saigon hospital, I was informed that I would be shipped to the hospital at Cam Ranh Bay as part of the healing process. Cam Ranh Bay was just a few miles south of the Recondo School in Nha Trang. I had heard about this medical facility, but I never thought I would be a patient there. I was told the hospital was almost like a holiday resort with its location on the beach of the South China Sea.

In a couple of days I was flown to the Cam Ranh Bay facility along with other wounded GIs. It was hard to believe . . . beautiful Cam Ranh Bay, a vacation spot for anyone lucky enough to be stationed there. The days were filled with nothing to do except sleep, and read books inside the air-conditioned hospital library. The other part of the day I spent long hours working out in the hospital gym. My doctor made it mandatory for me to take extensive swims in the turquoise blue beach waters to keep the wound clean. If there was such a thing as an army perk, this was it.

Cam Ranh Bay was probably no different from anywhere else in Vietnam, with the same routine being played out daily. Just like clockwork, every evening after dinner chow and just before the sun went down, the hospital beach was lined with pot-smoking GIs administering their self-medication. It was no secret, everyone from the commanding officer of the hospital to the chaplain knew what was going on. But they dared not bother the soldiers, nor did they ever try to stop them from using. At least not while I was there. For the most part it was the best time of day for the wounded GIs. The much-needed marijuana had a calming effect on the battle-fatigued soldiers. I am not advocating the use of marijuana, but these incidents are what I experienced while I served in Vietnam.

Somehow I always knew there would come a time when I would write about this particular part of my story. All the veterans who ever sat on the beach at Cam Ranh Bay will testify to what I am about to say. . . .

Over the course of time, and several miles off the coast of Vietnam, a chain of islands developed and somehow assumed the shape of Abraham Lincoln. No lie! From the top of his hairline down to his forehead, nose, lips, chin, beard, shoulders, and chest, it is a spitting replica of our sixteenth president lying on his back looking skyward. The resemblance was astounding. Anyone who saw the figure was amazed at the likeness. It was weird, somehow the rock formation gave us a comforting feeling of home.

I spent ten days at the hospital recovering. While I was there I never felt like I was in a war zone. Nor did I see or hear a weapon being fired there. The GIs in attendance at the hospital positively refused to talk about the war, and for good reason.

All good things must come to an end. I hated to leave the "almost" vacation spot of Cam Ranh Bay. I boarded a C-130 along with about eight other GIs. We were whisked back to Saigon, Tan Son Nhut Airport. It didn't take long to arrive back at the O Company Ranger compound. When I reported in to Captain Peters, he was aware that I had less than thirty days left in-country. Captain Peters informed me that I was scheduled to go in front of the E-5 promotion board in a week.

Captain Peters was full of surprises that day; he also told me that I wouldn't have to go back out into the boonies anymore. My duties now would include physical training instructor, and because of my Recondo training, whenever the company had teams in the field, I would be working at a relay station on an artillery firebase located out in the middle of nowhere. I had to remain out there for five days at a time, or for the length of the team's mission.

Captain Peters didn't have to take me out of the field, but I think he was just as interested in seeing me go home alive as I was. Although monitoring teams in the field from a supporting firebase wasn't as bad as going on a mission, it was much more dangerous than I had ever imagined. Still, it was a blessing to get out of the boonies for the remainder of my Vietnam tour.

While I was away at the hospital, Mackey attended Recondo School and graduated. I was very proud of him for achieving that goal. That also put him in contention for an E-5 promotion. Mackey's success at Recondo School helped elevate him to team leader status.

My first assignment at the relay station/firebase was to

monitor Mackey's team out in the field. More than ever, I began to understand why the map reading courses at Recondo School were so important and so demanding. The Recondo School instructors made a fuss to ensure that students understood the concepts of grids and coordinates, because the tiniest mistake could cost someone's life.

On one particular night, I was the only person on duty at the relay station. I was monitoring Mackey's team set up in their RON. Mackey began hearing enemy movement on the other side of a Y-shaped river. He called in a fire mission. I plotted his position on the big map board inside the radio room. Then I had to call and wake up the artillery officer for authorization to commence firing. Permission was granted expeditiously. Had Mackey or I made a mistake reading the coordinates, I could have blown his team to bits with any one of the HE rounds he had requested. I radioed back to Mackey for a fix on the first marker round I fired. I wanted to make sure the ordnance was dropping on the right side of the river. The problem was, Mackey's team was in the "V" part of the Y-shaped river. Not to mention, a team leader trying to read a map and plot his location in the dark had an especially tricky job at best. We made a few adjustments on the first rounds. After receiving Mackey's "okay" on the second marker, with pinpoint accuracy we fired for effect. When the fire mission was completed, the enemy movement had stopped. Mackey remarked, "The shots were right on the money!" We both congratulated each other for a job well done. It was the first time either of us had executed a fire mission since our artillery training at Recondo School.

The next night at around 2100 hours, I was lying on my bunk waiting for my shift to start. I didn't have to be on duty until midnight. The relay station/firebase was located up on a hilltop, away from the rest of the world. There wasn't much to do there except listen to Armed Forces Radio and write letters home. The radio became my music videos. The first time I heard Edwin Star's new song, "Twenty-five Miles From Home," I imagined every scene as the song played. Before the record finished playing, the firebase suddenly came under attack. Charlie hit us with an all-out small weapons assault. Green and red tracers streamed into the compound from four sides, we were surrounded! I grabbed my M-16 and hurried out to the nearest perimeter bunker to join the fight. The artillery soldiers were already in position, laying down heavy machine gun fire into the tree lines that were separated from us by fifty meters of man-made clearing. Then Charlie launched a monstrous mortar attack. They were zeroed in on the middle of the base camp. The mortar rounds rained down relentlessly. At our Lurp or Ranger base camp we'd had our share of mortar attacks, but it was never like this! Inside a bunker, I commandeered an M-60 machine gun that wasn't being used. I began to protect my field of fire with zeal, firing madly at the tracers and muzzle flashes coming from the wood line.

For a full hour the barrage of large mortar rounds whistled in, impacting the compound. All the while I thought about the song I had just heard on Armed Forces Radio, "Twenty-five Miles from Home." I kept thinking about how short I was and how these bastards were not going to stop me from achieving my objective, which was getting out of Vietnam alive and in one piece. The thought of going home made me fight harder; I became meaner and fought with a helluva lot more determination. The hard-fought battle lasted about ninety minutes with a few serious casualties. Finally all was quiet again, except for the intermittent jolts of outgoing artillery rounds. After the fight I had to report for duty monitoring the radio. The TOC had taken a few hits but it wasn't damaged. The radio room was underground and fortified with rows and rows of sandbags. It was a pretty safe environment, unless we were overrun.

The next day Mackey's team was extracted. I was happy to leave the firebase to return to the Ranger company area for a few days' rest. The helicopter that brought in the mail and supplies was the same chopper that flew me back to the helipad near the company area. I was looking forward to marking five more days off my DEROS calendar, which became something of a ritual.

"Hell, I'm getting so short, I can smell Mom's home cooking," was one of my "short" comments I'd make to anyone in the hootch who would listen to my boasting remarks.

I dumped my gear on my bunk and happened to look down and notice a two-week-old copy of *Stars and Stripes* newspaper sitting on someone's footlocker. The headlines recorded . . .

103 AMERICAN GIS KILLED AT CAM RANH BAY HOSPITAL. Exactly three days after I had left the hospital at Cam Ranh Bay, it was overrun by several NVA sapper squads. Late into the night, Charlie infiltrated the hospital from the beaches and from inland. The enemy was able to sneak inside the facility and kill 103 helpless GIs while they slept, and those who did try to get away were shot down. During my entire stay at the hospital, never once did I see a weapon or an armed guard anywhere. The killing spree of unarmed soldiers who were already wounded and who had no means of defending themselves was murder, plain and simple. It was a coordinated attack that was deemed successful by enemy standards. As I continued to read the newspaper, it also stated that several female nurses were killed while hiding in their quarters. I remembered the nurses at the hospital as being jovial and ready to help those who needed help. They regularly had a friendly smile and words of encouragement for the homesick and lonely. I couldn't help shedding a tear for people I had come to know and admired. It was difficult not to be upset after reading something like that, but at the same time I felt blessed, realizing I had been only a few days away from being a victim of that tragic attack.

On May 18, 2001, some thirty-two years after leaving the Vietnam War, I went to a reunion for the 187th Infantry, 506th (Rakkassans) at Fort Campbell, Kentucky, home of the 101st Airborne Screaming Eagles. I was producing and directing a documentary series entitled "Great Battles of the Vietnam War" (Hamburger Hill . . . the documentary). Each year the 3d Brigade holds a memorial service to remember the Battle of Dong Ap Bia—Hill 937 (Hamburger Hill). I had the honor and privilege to meet and interview the brave soldiers who fiercely fought the Dong Ap Bia battle.

I interviewed a plethora of terrific and forthcoming ex-soldiers. In a conversation with George T. Bennett, I learned that George had been a sergeant E-5 squad leader for 3/187 B Company, 101st Airborne Division during the Hamburger Hill battle.

George T. Bennett was wounded the first week of the action. He also revealed that he was at the Cam Ranh Bay hospital recovering from his wounds when the attack on the hospital happened. He told me the story about enemy soldiers running through the hospital barracks shooting wounded American GIs in their bunks. George actually confronted one of the enemy by yelling at him. Charlie stopped and looked at George but did not fire. Considering the battle on Hamburger Hill, George T. Bennett's life was spared once again.

And, for the sake of this book, I thank George for sharing that incredible story with me, as he was able to verify the reports from the *Stars and Stripes* newspaper from thirty-two years ago.

That incident at the hospital only substantiated what I already knew . . . in Vietnam, I was protected by God. I know, to the nonbeliever, these words are easily said, but even then and surely now, I truly believed them.

On the following Tuesday morning, Mackey and I prepared for the E-5 promotion board. I donned my freshly pressed and starched OD fatigues. My dress jungle boots had a high gloss spit-shine and I looked good with my very short afro hairdo. If you are thinking . . . "Why didn't he get his hair cut?" Well, to be honest, I didn't want to. It's just that simple. It's not that I wasn't proud of my new military lineage, but I was going home in a few weeks and didn't want to appear too military in a world that was antimilitary.

Besides, in the military I never let my hair grow more than a half inch. And, during that part of my young life, my hair was a very important part of me and my personality, and the army always wanted to control how long it should be. This was my chance to dictate the length of my hair.

Today, of course, hindsight is always twenty-twenty. I wish I'd changed my negative attitude about making E-5 and conformed to the "army" length for my hair. It certainly would have looked better on my record to make sergeant. It was too bad, but back then I was becoming more and more rebellious and REALLY didn't care about the rank.

When Mackey and I showed up at the promotion board, we were ready for the interrogation. We were both armed with the confidence that comes from finishing Recondo School. That alone gave us an edge.

I was the first to enter the lion's den. Behind a seven-foot-long table, two captains and four high-ranking NCOs sat facing me. I sat in the middle, facing them. I had to turn and look directly into the eyes of each person who asked a question, and answer them directly. The situation was designed to intimidate, but I felt comfortable.

I efficiently fielded each question with quick and concise responses. I knew the answers to all the questions. After the examination was over, I was able to surmise, I did well on the oral exam. I came away from the meeting feeling good about my performance.

About a week later, Captain Peters gave me the preliminary results of the sergeant E-5 board. He explained to me, almost apologizing, that I'd done well in front of the board and they were impressed with my efficiency. But my hair was too long and I looked too rebellious, and that might have an impact on their decision.

"Well, so be it!" I responded very nonchalantly. Hell, I was going home, for crying out loud. Nothing else really mattered. My job here was done. I was sick and tired of the war and just wanted out of Vietnam. I figured I could handle any problem when I didn't have to deal with the daily notion of dying in a firefight. But after they made their decision not to promote me, well, that started to bother me. One of my only regrets was, I didn't put the kind of fight into the E-5 promotion that it deserved.

Tying up the loose ends and preparing to go home was a very exciting time of my tour. I knew I wouldn't be allowed to take my .357 Magnum pistol out of the country without a bunch of red tape. I'd paid $350 for it and sold it for that same amount. For the likes of me, I can't remember who I sold the revolver to, but I remember the guys were itching to get their hands on it. If that pistol could talk, it would tell a story all its own.

On June 5, 1969, I was only one day away from boarding one of those big beautiful birds that sometimes flew over the company area. Whenever we saw a commercial jetliner overhead, everyone stopped in their tracks and looked skyward and dreamed about going home. And now it was my turn to actually fly over Vietnam and go back to the World.

That night my closest friends threw a beer and pot party for my going-away present. It was a chance for us to say our good-byes and lie about how close we would stay in touch once we'd parted company.

During the course of the little evening party, something was said that made me realize my time in Vietnam had been worthwhile. Word for word, I can't remember, but I recall the tone and the spirit of the comments. It was an emotional compliment from my fellow Lurps. Piggy (Millender) and Mackey both remarked, "Damn, Emanuel, you came to Vietnam and kicked ass and now you get to go home. We will always think of you as one of the bad-ass brothers who made it out of here alive."

Coming from those guys, I was honored by their compliments. But at the same time, I admitted to them, I was a lightweight compared to the heroic Lurps I had come to know while serving in Vietnam. I, like them, simply did the job that was asked, and I was blessed to go home alive.

I acknowledged my many friends while experiencing the

Vietnam War, and it was hard leaving them behind. But it was time for me to go . . . "home."

Without embarrassing any of them, I will always have much brotherly love for them. They know who they are . . .

It was June 6, 1969, one year to the date when I arrived in Vietnam. Oh, this was a glorious day indeed!! I was too excited to sleep that night. I got up at first light. The only thing that came to mind, I would soon be able to see and hug my mother, my brother and sisters, my family.

I tried not to make a big production about my leaving. About 0500 hours I threw my remaining belongings inside my duffel bag. Most of my property had been mailed home weeks in advance. I'd said my good-byes the night before. I wanted to exit the company area without making a scene.

At 0700 hours I was driven by jeep to Tan Son Nhut Air Base. As we approached the airport, I watched a commercial jetliner full of homeward bound GIs climb into the sky and vanish beyond the high, puffy clouds. That's when it really hit me. This was real. I was actually going home . . . for good!

"Thank you, Heavenly Father," I prayed in silence. I followed the plane with my eyes until it finally disappeared. Hundreds of thoughts flashed through my mind. The adventures of Vietnam would soon become a memory, and most of all, I was going home alive and in one piece. I had worked hard for this day!

My numerous thoughts always transferred me back to going home. Who should I call first when I get home? Should I surprise everyone by just showing up out of the clear blue? How much has the world changed since I've been away? Then, I worried, what if the plane gets shot down and we crash before I reach the homeland?

"Please God, I prayed, if this plane does crash, just don't let it crash in Vietnam. Anywhere but Vietnam!"

I arrived at the airport four or five hours before my departure. I had to process out of Vietnam the way I processed in. Every time I finished with one line of inspections, another was waiting. Finally I cleared all of the obstacles. The only thing to do now was wait. My flight was scheduled for 1300 hours.

The waiting only gave me more time to think. I kept thinking about what I was going to do when I boarded the plane. I envisioned myself reaching the top of the steps, and right at the threshold of the cabin door, before entering the aircraft, I would turn around and give the whole country of Vietnam the finger! Yeah, that's what I'll do! I'll turn around and say, "Fuck you, Vietnam!" Then, I'll leave this hellhole of a country, never to return!

Of course, at 1300 hours, when it was my turn to board the plane, I entered with class and dignity. I didn't flip off Vietnam with the "bird" like I wanted to do. Maybe I should have, but I didn't.

After the plane was loaded with passengers and the doors were secured, an eerie silence consumed the cabin of the airbus. The big 727 jetliner taxied onto the runway, then it began to roll faster and faster, and when the plane broke ground, a chorus of rejoicing cheers erupted throughout the aircraft. We were on our way back to the World!

For the first time in a long time, I was actually able to relax. I acted like I didn't have a worry in the world. It was absolutely amazing to feel the stress of war being lifted off my shoulders. I certainly remember feeling older and much wiser beyond my years. I promised myself that I would savor each moment of life and live life like there was no tomorrow. Although, that promise seems to be one of my problems today. In my quest to live life to its fullest, sometimes I continue to push the envelope in search of the all-mighty adrenaline rush. I find it hard to say no to the very "life-force" that once kept me alive.

We crossed the International Date Line at 4:00 P.M. Pacific Time and finally landed at San Francisco International Airport. During the flight, I visualized what I was going to do when I disembarked the plane. I thought about kneeling down and kissing the ground of the good ol' U.S. of A. But

when we landed I couldn't go through with it. I was somehow able to restrain my emotions.

Coming home . . . what a moment in time for me. Somehow I can still feel that excitement. When I stepped onto my
home turf, words simply cannot describe the relief I felt.

I had a connecting flight to LAX, which was a bit of a
wait. I didn't get in to the Los Angeles airport until 7:00 P.M.
that same evening. I surprised my family by calling them to
let them know I was in need of a ride home from the airport.
Everyone was so excited, but not as much as myself. My sister Sheryl and her husband showed up at the airport to take
me home. We celebrated briefly at the airport with hugs,
kisses, and crying, but my mission was to see my mother.
When I was able to see Mom again, then everything was all
right. I felt proud to be a soldier showing up at home in my
complete Airborne uniform, with my medals, spit-shined
boots, and my arms outstretched to hug and kiss my mother.

One of the things that concerned me the most about coming home was how I thought the world had dramatically
changed. In reality the world hadn't changed much in one
year, I was the one who had changed. I wasn't the same person who left Compton, California, a year earlier, and come
to find out, I was the last person to know.

The day before I left for Vietnam, I washed a pair of my
underwear for the overseas trip. With all of the anxiety and
tension of leaving home, I forgot to take them with me.
They were left to dry on the shower door in my sister's
bathroom. One year later, when I arrived back at my sister's
house that evening, I went into the bathroom and saw that
same pair of underwear still hanging over the shower door,
the very ones I had left a year ago. My sister Sheryl
wouldn't let anyone touch, much less take down, my underwear until I had returned home from Vietnam. That really
moved me to tears. And so, I did the honor of removing my
underwear, signifying I was home again.

I grabbed my duffel bag and took it into my room. I

looked at my watch to record the exact time I reached home. Talk about your irony . . . Remember that Casio watch I bought my first couple days in Vietnam? Well, that watch stopped at the exact time I arrived home. . . . 8:20 P.M., June 6, 1969, Pacific time. I was never able to revive that watch or make it tick another second from that day forward. For 363 days, that watch and I went through hell together. My Casio watch did the job that was required, and expired when the mission was over.

This thing called "Life" seems to be a series of time, events, and deaths. The "time" between June 6, 1968, to June 6, 1969, was the most extraordinary one year "event" of my young "life."

There are thousands of exciting and compelling chronicles regarding the Vietnam War. This is my story . . .

In Memory of

Company F (Long Range Patrol),
51st Infantry (Airborne)

Sp4. Daniel H. Lindsey	KIA 5 Dec. 67
1st Lt. John H. Lattin	KIA 15 Dec. 67
Sp4. Jan V. Henrickson	KIA 2 Aug. 68
Sp4. Kenneth R. Blair	KIA 12 Aug. 68
PFC Willie Whitfield, Jr.	KIA 12 Aug. 68
Sp4. Raymond M. Enczi	KIA 31 Oct. 68
Sgt. Richard W. Diers	KIA 20 Nov. 68
S.Sgt. Larry L. Cunningham	KIA 3 Dec. 68
Sp4. Leslie D. Rosekrans	KIA 3 Dec. 68
PFC David L. Urban	KIA 3 Dec. 68
Sp4. Freemon Evans	DRHA 4 Dec. 68
PFC Roy A. Aubain	DRHA 4 Jan. 69

Company O (Ranger),
75th Infantry (Airborne)

S.Sgt Jerry D. Beck	KIA 6 Apr. 69
Sp4. Michael Kelley	KIA 8 Apr. 69
Sp4. Daren L. Koenig	KIA 6 Apr. 69
S.Sgt John A. La Polla	KIA 15 Apr. 69
PFC Charles H. Wright	KIA 19 Sept. 69

Company P (Ranger), 75th Infantry (Airborne)

S.Sgt David E. Carter	KIA 10 Aug. 69
Sgt. Rodney K. Mills	KIA 5 May 70

Deceased

Alexander, James F.

Malichi, Bobby

Clemons, Donald L.   3 Sept. 69

Montez, Jose 1970

Crowe, Don A. 1970

Presswood, James S.

Gates, Ellis, Jr.

Rivera, Joseph R   23 Oct. 81

Goodner, Gary E.   21 Sept. 93

Rodriguez, Edward R.   11 June 83

Kane, John P.

Steuernagel, Daniel   11 April 94

Maggart, Thomas H.   22 April 92

Zummo, Joseph J.

Don't miss these tales of heroism and
fierce loyalty from the most decorated
sniper unit in the Vietnam War

---

13 CENT KILLERS
The 5th Marine Snipers in Vietnam

---

by John J. Culbertson

In 1967, a bullet cost thirteen cents, and no one
gave Uncle Sam a bigger bang for his buck than the
5th Marine Regiment Sniper Platoon. Now noted
Vietnam author John Culbertson presents the true
stories of young Americans who fought during the
fiercest combat of the war, from 1967 through the
desperate Tet battle for Hue in early '68.
Harrowing and unforgettable, these accounts pay
tribute to the heroes who made the greatest sacrifice of all—and leave no doubt that among 5th
Marine snipers uncommon valor was truly a common virtue.

Published by Presidio Press
www.presidiopress.com
Available in paperback wherever books are sold

Look for this remarkable memoir of small-unit leadership and the coming of age of a young soldier in Vietnam

PLATOON LEADER

A Memoir of Command in Combat

by James R. McDonough

"Using a lean style and a sense of pacing drawn from the tautest of novels, McDonough has produced a gripping account of his first command. . . . Rather than present a potpourri of combat yarns. . . McDonough has focused a seasoned storyteller's eye on the details, people, and incidents that best communicate a visceral feel of command under fire. . . . For the author's honesty and literary craftsmanship, *Platoon Leader* seems destined to be read for a long time by second lieutenants trying to prepare for the future, veterans trying to remember the past, and civilians trying to understand what the profession of arms is all about." —*Army Times*

Published by Presidio Press
www.presidiopress.com
Available in paperback wherever books are sold

Don't miss this *New York Times*
bestselling classic by Al Santoli

EVERYTHING WE HAD

An Oral History of the Vietnam War by
Thirty-Three American Soldiers Who Fought It

"SIMPLY A MAGNIFICENT ACHIEVEMENT...
If there are to be any heroes in America, then let
us begin with the 33 men and women in this
book, and millions of others like them."
—*The Washington Post BookWorld*

EVERYTHING WE HAD "Can take its place
alongside Philip Caputo's *A Rumor of War*...as one
of the best books about Vietnam."
—*People*

Published by Ballantine Books
Available in paperback wherever books are sold